THE STORIED CITY

THE STORIED CITY

THE QUEST FOR TIMBUKTU

AND THE FANTASTIC MISSION

TO SAVE ITS PAST

///////////

CHARLIE ENGLISH

RIVERHEAD BOOKS

NEW YORK

2017

RIVERHEAD BOOKS
An imprint of Penguin Random House LLC
375 Hudson Street
New York, New York 10014

Library of Congress Cataloging-in-Publication Data

Names: English, Charlie, author.
Title: The storied city : the quest for Timbuktu and the fantastic
mission to save its past / Charlie English.
Description: New York : Riverhead Books, 2017. |
Includes bibliographical references and index.
Identifiers: LCCN 2016039192 | ISBN 9781594634284
Subjects: LCSH: Tombouctou (Mali)—Discovery and exploration. |
Tombouctou (Mali)—Antiquities. | Mali—History—Tuareg Rebellion, 2012—
Destruction and pillage. | Manuscripts, Arabic—Mali—Tombouctou. |
Libraries—Destruction and pillage—Mali—Tombouctou. | Islamic learning and
scholarship—Mali—Tombouctou. | Cultural property—Protection—Mali—Tombouctou.
Classification: LCC DT551.9.T55 E54 2017 | DDC 966.23—dc23
LC record available at https://lccn.loc.gov/2016039192
p.   cm.

Printed in the United States of America
1   3   5   7   9   10   8   6   4   2

BOOK DESIGN AND MAPS BY MEIGHAN CAVANAUGH

Frontispiece: Nineteenth-century drawing of Timbuktu,
based on a description by the French explorer René Caillié

For Lucy

CONTENTS

PART ONE

OCCUPATION

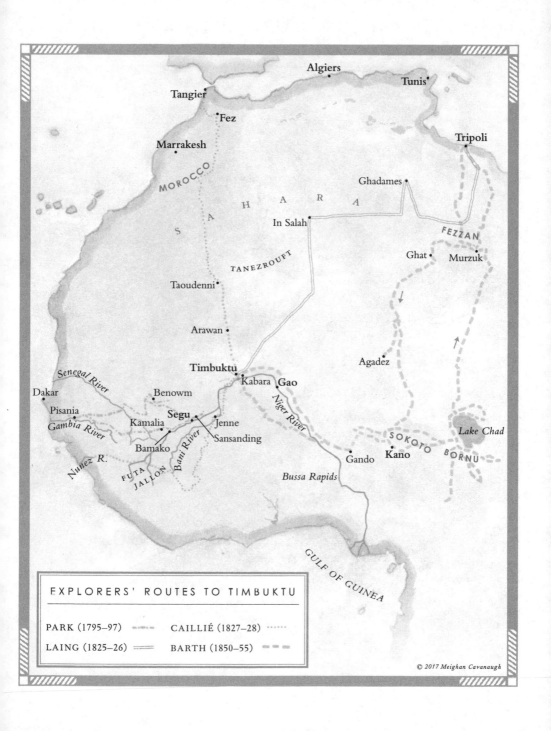

Algiers

Tunis

Tangier

Fez

Tripoli

Marrakesh

MOROCCO

Ghadames

S   A   H   A   R   A

In Salah

FEZZAN

TANEZROUFT

Ghat   Murzuk

Taoudenni

Arawan

Agadez

Timbuktu

Kabara Gao

Senegal River

Benowm

Dakar

Niger River

Pisania

Segu

Kamalia

Jenne

Lake Chad

Gambia River

Sansanding

SOKOTO

Bamako

Bani River

BORNU

Gando   Kano

Nunez R.

FUTA

JALLON

Bussa Rapids

GULF OF GUINEA

EXPLORERS' ROUTES TO TIMBUKTU

PARK (1795–97)   CAILLIÉ (1827–28)

LAING (1825–26)   BARTH (1850–55)

© 2017 Meighan Cavanaugh

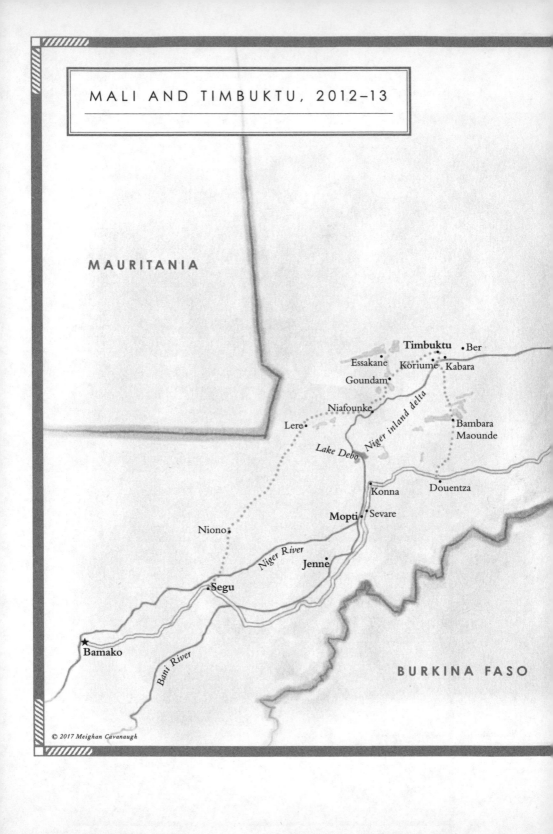

MALI AND TIMBUKTU, 2012–13

MAURITANIA

Timbuktu • Ber
Essakane • Koriume• •Kabara
Goundam•
Niafounke•
Niger inland delta
Lere•
•Bambara
Maounde
Lake Debo
Douentza•
•Konna
Niono• Mopti•• Sevare
Niger River
•Jenné
Segu•
★
Bamako
Bani River

BURKINA FASO

© 2017 Meighan Cavanaugh

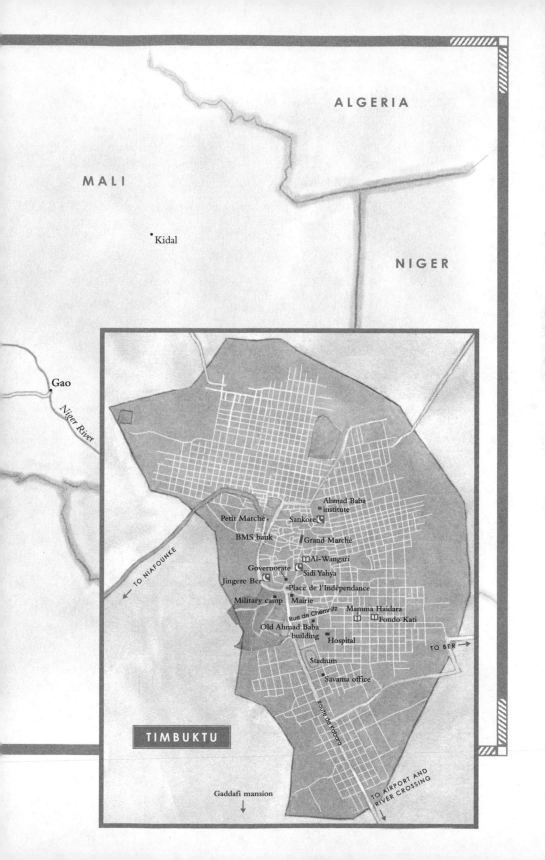

ALGERIA

MALI

• Kidal

NIGER

Gao

Niger River

TO NIAFOUNKE

Ahmad Baba
institute

Petit Marché

Sankoré

BMS bank

Grand Marché

Al-Wangari

Governorate

Sidi Yahya

Jingere Ber

Place de l'Indépendance

Military camp

Mairie

Rue de Chemnitz

Mamma Haidara

Fondo Kati

Old Ahmad Baba
building

Hospital

TO BER →

Stadium

Route de Kabara

Savama office

TIMBUKTU

TO AIRPORT AND
RIVER CROSSING

Gaddafi mansion
↓

PROLOGUE: A MAN OF ENTERPRISE AND GENIUS

In among the millions of documents held by the British government's National Archives is a slim dossier known as CO 2/20. The volume is not much requested. These archives, after all, hold papers that cover a thousand years of British history, and most visitors to the airy reading rooms at Kew come in search of more obvious treasures: *Domesday Book*, Shakespeare's will, or the newly opened files of cold war traitors and spies. Every couple of years, however, someone will demand Colonial Office file 2/20, and a message will be passed to the Cheshire town of Winsford, where the dossier is held in a storage facility deep within Britain's largest salt mine. There, an employee will venture into the arid darkness, pluck the file from more than twenty-two miles of shelving given over to the National Archives, and dispatch it south.

The box that arrives days later at the reading room is made of thick cardboard and bound with white cotton tape. Inside is a sheaf of a hundred or so handwritten communications—manuscripts, we might say—that were sent from the British consul in Tripoli to London in the mid-1820s. Each piece of ragged, well-traveled paper illuminates a small corner of time and place, and a handful have special relevance for our story. These are the last letters of a neglected explorer, Alexander Gordon Laing, and encompass the period of his expedition to discover the "far famed Capital of Central Africa," as he described the city of Timbuktu.

Laing, a muttonchopped army major from Edinburgh, was fated to become the first European explorer to reach this elusive place. In the 1820s, Timbuktu dominated Europe's ideas about Africa as El Dorado had once colored its concept of the Americas. Timbuktu was believed to govern a rich sub-Saharan region called the Sudan, after the Arabic *Bilad al-Sudan*, "the land of the blacks." Rumors of the city's existence had circulated in Europe for hundreds of years, and its riches had been trumpeted since at least the fourteenth century. As Marco Polo's Zipangu was said to be a land where the king's palace was roofed with precious metal, Timbuktu's houses too were reported to be covered with gold. Scores of travelers had been sent to find it, but every attempt had ended in death or failure.

In 1826, it was the turn of Major Laing. Laing was a particular British sort, a product of that time between Waterloo and the Charge of the Light Brigade when military men sought death or glory, or a combination of the two. With his good looks and self-absorption, he could have slipped out of the pages of *Vanity Fair*, but it was a different novel, Daniel Defoe's *Robinson Crusoe*, that inspired his life of adventure. "The reading of voyages and travels occupied all my leisure moments," he once recalled. "The History of Robinson Crusoe . . . inflamed my young imagination." Like Defoe's hero, Laing was desperate to avoid the "middle station" of British life; like Crusoe he would cast himself into the world in order to find meaning and purpose. "I shall do more than has ever been done before," he wrote, "and shall show myself to be what I have ever considered myself, a man of enterprise and genius."

Not everyone shared Laing's immodest assessment of his abilities. While he was stationed in Sierra Leone in 1824, his commanding officer wrote to the minister for war and the colonies that Laing's "military exploits were [even] worse than his poetry." But this diatribe apparently had little effect; that year Laing was appointed leader of a new British mission to locate the city he believed it was his destiny to find. Becoming the first to reach Timbuktu would give him what he most desired in the world, as he explained in a poem:

> Tis that which bids my bosom glow
> To climb the stiff ascent of fame
> To share the praise the just bestow
> And give myself a deathless name.

Laing set out from Tripoli in the summer of 1825, riding into the 120-degree heat of the Sahara. The land at this time of year was so arid even his camels grew skeletally thin. His guide, a mild and agreeable presence on the coast, became greedier the farther south they traveled, and in the Tanezrouft, a burning plain the size of California, he appears to have betrayed Laing to a group of Tuareg. Heavily armed men surrounded the explorer's tent in the night, shot him, and hacked at him before leaving him for dead. Laing's account of the injuries he sustained in this attack is one of the most remarkable artifacts in the Colonial Office dossier. It was written on May 10, 1826, from a desert camp two hundred miles north of Timbuktu. Until this point, his dispatches were composed in a flamboyant, forward-leaning copperplate. This letter, dotted with mildew now, its folded seams darkened by Saharan dust, is an untidy up-and-down scrawl, written, as he explained, with his left hand.

"My Dear Consul," he writes, "I drop you a line only, by an uncertain conveyance, to acquaint you that I am recovering from . . . severe wounds far beyond any calculation that the most sanguine expectation could have formed." The detail of the incident is a surprising tale of "base treachery and war," but it must keep for another time. For now, he will acquaint the consul with the number and nature of the wounds he has suffered in the attack:

> To begin from the top, I have five sabre cuts on the crown of the head & three on the left temple, all fractures from which much bone has come away, one on my left cheek which fractured the Jaw bone & has divided the ear, forming a very unsightly wound, one over the right temple, and a dreadful gash on the back of the neck, which slightly scratched the windpipe.

He has a musket ball in the hip, which has made its way through his body, grazing his backbone. He also has five saber wounds to his right arm and hand, which is "cut three fourths across," and the wrist bones are hacked through. He has three cuts on his left arm, which is broken, one slight wound on the right leg, and two, including "one dreadful gash," on the left, to say nothing of the blow to the fingers of the hand he is using to write.

Scanning this butcher's bill, as the anxious consul must have done when the letter reached Tripoli six months later, the reader looks for signs of retreat. Laing is planning, surely, to return by the quickest possible route, as soon as he is fit, devising a way to avoid the bandits on the home leg? Not at all. The pull of Timbuktu, which lies over the horizon, as yet unmolested by European gaze, is too strong. He will not dishonor himself by giving up now. He is "doing well" despite his wounds, he tells the consul. He hopes yet to return to England with "much important Geographical information." He has discovered many things that must be corrected on the map of Africa, and he beseeches God to allow him time to finish the job.

Almost two months later, Laing writes again. His situation has become worse. The camp has been overwhelmed by a "dreadful malady" akin to yellow fever that has killed half the population, including his last remaining servant. "I am now the only surviving member of the mission," he informs the consul miserably. "My situation is far from agreeable." Still, so potent is his sense of destiny that he carries on:

> I am well aware that if I do not visit it, the World will ever remain
> in ignorance of [Timbuktu] . . . as I make no vain glorious assertion
> when I say that it will never be visited by Christian man after me.

Laing achieved his great ambition six weeks later, entering Timbuktu on August 13, 1826. Then something rather odd happened: he went quiet.

For five weeks he sent no word of his arrival to the consul. It was September 21 before he wrote again, and then the letter was barely five hundred words long. He is still holding the pen in his left hand, and his writing now is cramped, tense. His life is threatened, he tells the consul, and he is in a hurry to leave:

I have no time to give you my account of Tinbuctu, but shall briefly
state that in every respect except in size (which does not exceed four
miles in circumference) it has completely met my expectations. . . .
I have been busily employed during my stay, searching the records
in the town, which are abundant, & in acquiring information of
every kind, nor is it with any common degree of satisfaction that I
say, my perseverance has been amply rewarded.

The day after composing this letter, Laing left Timbuktu and
walked out of history. The consul forwarded the final dispatch to London with a covering note claiming a victory of sorts—it was the "first
letter ever written from that place by any Christian"—but in terms of
delivering information about the great object of European geography,
Laing's expedition was a flop. If Timbuktu had met his high expectations "completely," where was the detail? Most puzzling was Laing's assertion that there were abundant "records in the town," from which he
had drawn "information of every kind." What kinds of records could
warrant a soldier's attention? How could they be of use to the British
government?

ALMOST TWO CENTURIES LATER, it is clear that the "records in the
town" were some of the great quantity of mostly Arabic texts that are
now known collectively as the manuscripts of Timbuktu. The city's
documents, which Laing appears to have been the first European to
see, are so numerous no one knows quite how many there are, though
they are reckoned in the tens or even hundreds of thousands. They contain some of the most valuable written sources for the so-called golden
age of Timbuktu in the fifteenth and sixteenth centuries, and the great

Songhay empire of which the city was a part. They have been held up by experts as Africa's equivalent of the Dead Sea Scrolls or the Anglo-Saxon Chronicle, proof of the continent's vibrant written history.

In 2012 that history appeared to be under threat. After a coup in southern Mali, Timbuktu was overtaken by the fighters of al-Qaeda in the Islamic Maghreb (AQIM). The jihadists began systematically to destroy the centuries-old mausoleums of the city's Sufi saints. On January 28, 2013, the mayor of Timbuktu told the world that all of the city's ancient manuscripts had also been burned.

I recall that morning well. I was international news editor at *The Guardian* at the time, and Mali had a special resonance for me. Many years before, at eighteen, I had developed the idea of driving across the Sahara. I saved money, bought an old Land Rover, and set out from Yorkshire with a friend, traveling via Morocco and Algeria to Mali, which we reached in the spring of 1987. The desert town of Aguelhok marked the end of the crossing, our summit, and once there we cast about for a new idea. What if we traded the clapped-out car for three or four camels and rode to Timbuktu? The story we would tell! We found a vendor and negotiated for a week, but as he only ever managed to produce one small specimen we abandoned the plan and continued south. I sold the car in Gao, the capital of old Songhay, and traveled to Burkina Faso and Côte d'Ivoire and then home. I had not made it to Timbuktu, but I had fallen in love with the idea of the desert. I returned to the Sahara in 1989 in a different vehicle, but it was too unreliable to risk the drive to Mali. Once again, the City of 333 Saints remained tantalizingly out of reach.

In July 2012, with anger and sadness, I watched the footage of the jihadists trashing Timbuktu's monuments. The following January, when our correspondent was told that the rebels had torched the city's historic texts, we led *The Guardian*'s online edition with the news. Days later, it became clear that the manuscripts had not been destroyed after all; in fact, they had been smuggled to safety by the town's librarians. I became obsessed with the details of this operation. It seemed to me to echo the plot of Robert Crichton's comic novel *The Secret of Santa Vittoria*, in which the people of a small Tuscan town save a million bottles of wine from looting Nazis. Only it was far better than that: the treasure in Timbuktu was infinitely more significant; what was more, this evacuation was real. I left my job, determined to turn the story into a book.

Bruce Chatwin once observed that there are two Timbuktus. One is the real place, a tired caravan town where the Niger bends into the Sahara. The other is altogether more fabulous, a legendary city in a never-never land, the Timbuktu of the mind. I planned to give an account of both these Timbuktus by following two alternating strands: that of the West's centuries-long struggle to find, conquer, and understand the city; and that of the modern-day attempt to save its manuscripts and its history from destruction. The first narrative would explore the role of legend in shaping our view of Timbuktu; the second would relate the tale of occupation and evacuation.

What I didn't understand then was how closely these stories would mirror each other.

Charlie English
London, 2017

PART ONE

OCCUPATION

∖∖∖∖∖∖∖∖∖

If thou know not the way that leadeth to the City of
Brass, rub the hand of the horseman, and he will turn,
and then will stop, and in whatsoever direction he
stoppeth, thither proceed, without fear and without
difficulty; for it will lead thee to the City of Brass.

—*The Thousand and One Nights*

1.

A SEEKER OF MANUSCRIPTS

MARCH 2012

One hazy morning in Bamako, the capital of the modern West African state of Mali, an aging Toyota Land Cruiser picked its way to the end of a concrete driveway and pulled out into the busy morning traffic. In its front passenger seat sat a large, distinguished-looking man in billowing robes and a pillbox prayer cap. He was forty-seven years old, stood over six feet tall, and weighed close to two hundred pounds, and although a small, French-style mustache balanced jauntily on his upper lip, there was something commanding about his appearance. In his prominent brown eyes lurked a sharp, almost impish intelligence. He was Abdel Kader Haidara, librarian of Timbuktu, and his name would soon become famous around the world.

Haidara was not an indecisive man, but that morning, as his driver piloted the heavy vehicle through the clouds of buzzing Chinese-made motorbikes and beat-up green minibuses that plied the city's streets, he was caught in an agony of indecision. The car stereo, tuned to Radio

France Internationale, spewed alarming updates on the situation in the north, while the cheap cellphones that were never far from his grasp jangled continually with reports from his contacts in Timbuktu, six hundred miles away. The rebels were advancing across the desert, driving government troops and refugees before them. Bus stations were choked with the displaced; highways were clogged with motorbikes and pickups and ancient trucks that swayed under the weight of the fleeing population. Haidara had known when he left his apartment that driving into this chaos would be dangerous, but now it was beginning to look like a suicide mission. Soon he'd had enough: he spoke to his driver, and then they were pointing west again, back toward the skirts of the sprawling African metropolis.

Responsable is a French noun whose meaning is easy to guess at in English. There were few better words to describe the librarian then than as a *responsable* for a giant slice of neglected history, the manuscripts of Timbuktu, a collection of handwritten documents so large no one knew quite how many there were, though he himself would put them in the hundreds of thousands. Few had done more to unearth the manuscripts than Haidara. In the months to come, no one would be given more credit for their salvation.

In person the librarian was an imposing man with a handshake of astonishing softness, a drive-by of a greeting that left a hint of remembered contact, no more. He was well versed in the history and content of the documents, but appeared not so much a scholar as a businessman who controlled his affairs in a variety of languages via his cellphones, or in person from behind a desk the size of a small boat. He was not the only proprietor of manuscripts in the city, but as the owner of the largest private collection and founder of Savama, an organization devoted to safeguarding the city's written heritage, he claimed to represent the bulk of Timbuktu's manuscript-owning families.

Haidara had been raised in a large Timbuktu house made of banco and built around a courtyard, like a hundred thousand others in the region. He was one of fourteen children of Mamma Haidara, a Timbuktu scholar, and the town in which he grew up had changed little in a hundred years. At the heart of the city were the three large mosques: Jingere Ber, the "great mosque," in the west; Sidi Yahya in the center; and Sankore in the north. The spaces between the mosques were filled with houses and markets, and the old medina, in the shape of a fat teardrop, was a mile and a half around. The people had buried their relatives close to their houses, and as the city had grown, the burial grounds had been absorbed into the network of alleys and streets. The living and the dead now existed side by side, and in the tradition of mystical, Sufi, Islam, the divide between them had become blurred: the most holy ancestors, the scholars and judges and leaders of former times, lay in grand mausoleums where they were worshipped as saints. Someone had counted 333 such saints, and since it was an auspicious number, that was what Timbuktu had come to call itself, the City of 333 Saints.

There were no cars or trucks in Timbuktu when Haidara was growing up; the city did not get its first gas pump until the mid-1970s. Instead it was filled with animals. Sheep and goats and cattle and chickens picked at the sparse vegetation and at the scraps thrown in the streets. Caravans of donkeys brought cereals in from the river port to the south, while the biggest events of the year were the arrivals of the salt caravans, thousands of camels strong, from the mines in the desert.

At the age of six, Haidara had been sent to Kuranic school to learn the holy texts, and afterward to the Franco-Arab school to learn everything else. He remembered it as a childhood *sans souci*, free from worry, but like most Timbuktiens the family had little money. Their principal assets were the manuscripts. These were stored all over the house, Haidara would later recall, on shelves that bowed under the weight of paper, and in relatives' homes in and around Timbuktu. They were written mostly in Arabic, and were bound in cracking camel and gazelle hide, their fabric eaten by termites and stained with water. They covered almost every subject under the sun. There were works on astronomy, poetry, and medicine, as well as mundane documents of ownership, legal rulings, and bills of sale. More than anything, they were Islamic, commentaries on the holy texts and interpretations of their legal meanings.

Haidara's father used the manuscripts for teaching. Students came from around the region to learn from the scholar and his books, while his friends—the *grandes personnalités*, the neighborhood leaders and the notables of Timbuktu—came to sit and swap opinions. Sometimes his father would ask him to fetch a certain document, and Haidara would search through the rooms of the house to find the right work. Later he started to copy out parts of the manuscripts, and in this way he came to know and understand them.

His father died in 1981, when Abdel Kader was seventeen. It was tradition that the family of the deceased and the city fathers should meet to divide up the estate, and to this end a list of Mamma Haidara's possessions was compiled in an exercise book. The manuscripts, though, were kept apart: the collection was not to be divided, sold, or given away. Instead, one of the next generation would be tasked with looking after it. The elders, who had witnessed his inquisitive nature, chose Abdel Kader. He would be the *responsable*.

It was around this time that the Malian sage Amadou Hampâté Bâ came to speak in Timbuktu. Hampâté Bâ, who had lived since the early days of French colonization, was a gifted writer, a collector of traditions, an expert in West African culture, and a man of great intelligence and stature. Haidara went along to listen to him. Hampâté Bâ told his audience to imagine that in the cultural scheme of things the world's cities were in a line. At one time, he said, Timbuktu had stood at the front, but then God had ordered the queue to do an about-face, and now it was at the back. "We do not know how," Hampâté Bâ said, "but perhaps one day God will order another about-face so that Timbuktu finds its place again. You should not cross your arms and wait for that moment. You must help history. You must bring out your manuscripts. You must use them."

Hampâté Bâ's words sank deep into Haidara's consciousness. That day, he understood his purpose. He would try to revive the city through its manuscripts.

Timbuktu in the 1980s was already home to an organization devoted to studying Arabic texts. With the encouragement of the United Nations Educational, Scientific and Cultural Organization (UNESCO), the Malian government had endowed a research institute in the city in 1973, named after the sixteenth-century Timbuktu scholar Ahmad Baba, tasked with collecting and preserving Mali's written heritage. The Ahmad Baba center started out with fewer than one hundred documents and had added around 3,300 more by 1984, when its director approached Haidara and told him he should come to work there as a *prospecteur*, a seeker of manuscripts. Haidara agreed. He would become the most prolific manuscript prospector the center ever had.

He began by contacting friends and using his charm, his family name, and his natural persistence. Often people would deny that they had manuscripts, but Haidara would return again and again until he had won them over. He searched in Timbuktu but also in the wider region, crisscrossing northern Mali by donkey, camel, pirogue, and Land Rover. Sometimes he traveled with the salt caravans, trekking alongside them for fourteen hours straight. He went into towns and villages and hamlets, cajoling people into relinquishing the documents they had hidden or forgotten. He traveled to the borders of Mauritania and Senegal in the west, and to the frontiers with Burkina Faso and Niger in the east. He went to Goundam, Diré, Tonka, Niafounke, Niono, and all the places in between. He would pay as much as two hundred dollars for a valuable single-page document and three hundred for a complete manuscript, though sometimes he would pay in animals, which were often more valued than cash. Historical manuscripts were the most sought-after, followed by those that were elaborately decorated, very old, or written by local authors. If his haul was cumbersome, Haidara would hire a car or a riverboat to carry it back to Timbuktu. Little by little, he brought the books and documents in. In twelve years he added 16,000 manuscripts to the Ahmad Baba collection. He continued his prospecting after that, but stopped counting.

As he built up the state archive, Haidara increasingly thought about his own manuscripts, which lay in trunks stacked in small, dark rooms, exposed to damp and termites and the risk of fire. Even if he had wanted to, tradition did not allow him to sell them, so he decided to set up his own research library. He sent out faxes to international institutions and foundations and buttonholed influential visitors to the famous city, asking them for support. People offered to buy them, but no one wanted to pay him to keep them in Timbuktu.

In 1997, the eminent Harvard scholar Henry Louis Gates, Jr., came to Mali, and Haidara invited him to see his collection. Gates shed tears over the documents that were laid out in front of him. Why, Haidara asked, was Gates weeping? Because he had taught at some of the best universities in the world for almost twenty years, Gates explained, and had always told his students there was no written history in Africa, that it was all oral. Now that he had seen these manuscripts, everything had changed. On his return to the United States, Gates lobbied for funding for Haidara's project, which soon had the support of the Andrew W. Mellon Foundation. Other foreign donors—the Ford Foundation, the London-based Al-Furqan Islamic Heritage Foundation, the Juma al-Majid Center for Culture and Heritage in Dubai—would provide more money as the years went by. In 2000 the first modern private archive in Timbuktu, the Mamma Haidara Memorial Library, was opened at a ceremony attended by the First Lady of Mali. After that, Haidara helped his friends set up their own institutions, and soon libraries were springing up all over, as Timbuktu families brought out their collections.

The manuscripts by this time were becoming a cause célèbre. Increasingly they were being used to argue for a new interpretation of Africa's past that could combat the racism that had dogged the continent for so long. From Immanuel Kant to David Hume, Western philosophers and historians had cited the lack of written works from Africa as proof that the continent was too backward even to have a history. "There never was any civiliz'd nation of any other complexion than white," Hume wrote in 1748, "nor even any individual eminent in action or speculation. No ingenious manufactures amongst them, no arts, no sciences." This view was still being echoed by the British historian Hugh Trevor-Roper in 1963: "Perhaps in the future, there will be some African history to teach. But at present there is none. There is only the history of Europeans in Africa. The rest is darkness." Manuscripts existed all over West Africa, but Timbuktu's were the most famous, and now they were held up as counterevidence. In 2001, South African president Thabo Mbeki enlisted them in a campaign to help redefine the continent in African terms. He ordered the creation of a giant new Ahmad Baba building in Timbuktu with an exhibition space, a conference hall, restoration workshops, and an academic program of conservation. "[The manuscripts] open up possibilities for thinking in new ways about the world," Mbeki said, "the opportunity to look at history afresh."

Research into the growing numbers of documents reaching Timbuktu was meanwhile proceeding apace. In 2001, John Hunwick of Northwestern University, the leading international expert on the written Islamic heritage of West Africa, announced that a hoard of three thousand manuscripts he had been shown in one Timbuktu collection was "rewriting history." "My eyes were popping out of my head," Hunwick told the *Chicago Tribune*. "I'd never seen anything quite like them before." Hunwick's friend and colleague Sean O'Fahey said it was "like coming upon another Anglo-Saxon chronicle that gave us a new view of the early history of England." The find was simply "monumental," according to David Robinson, a professor of African history at Michigan State University.

By 2011, Haidara and his manuscript-hunting colleagues had made enormous progress with the task Hampâté Bâ had set them of restoring Timbuktu to its rightful status in the world. The number of manuscripts counted in the province now stood at no less than 101,820, Haidara estimated, and the figure for the whole country was close to a million. Had it not been for fire, war, and natural disaster, the number would be far higher.

Then the disturbance in the desert outside the city, which had rumbled along for decades, became a cacophony.

Northern Mali had long been a rough neighborhood, a refuge for bandits, smugglers, and revolutionaries. Militant leaders in the north had held grievances against rule from Bamako since colonial times, and these had erupted in periodic rebellions ever since. In 2003, Algerian jihadists fighting a war against their own government had taken refuge across the border in Mali, and soon afterward they received the blessing of Osama Bin Laden and adopted the name al-Qaeda in the Islamic Maghreb (AQIM). They put down deep roots in the desert, taking a cut from the smuggling trade, but their biggest money came from kidnapping. Between 2003 and 2010, AQIM made tens of millions of dollars by ransoming Western diplomats, energy workers, and tourists who strayed into the wrong territory.

In 2011, an extra ingredient was added to the simmering stew. That year, a rebellion in Libya, backed by NATO jets and cruise missiles, toppled the regime of Colonel Muammar Gaddafi, and hundreds of Malian Tuareg who had been employed in the dictator's armies returned home with all the weapons and ammunition they could carry. In Mali they joined forces with a political movement that had been campaigning for an autonomous Tuareg state called Azawad, and the National Movement for the Liberation of Azawad was born. The MNLA, as it was known, for its French abbreviation, declared war on the Bamako government and, with the aid of its al-Qaeda allies, inflicted a string of humiliating defeats on Mali's demoralized military. In mid-March 2012, a group of disaffected Malian army officers launched a coup, and in the political chaos that followed, the rebels took their opportunity, sweeping across the north as the army retreated in disarray.

Sitting in his car on the morning of March 31, Haidara once again changed his mind. At such a dangerous time there was only one place he should be. The cumbersome Land Cruiser made a U-turn once again, and headed northeast, toward Timbuktu and the war.

2.

A WIDE EXTENDED BLANK

The quest for Timbuktu began, as such things sometimes did, in a room above a London pub.

On June 9, 1788, a group of nine powerful men gathered at the St. Alban's Tavern, a rifle shot from the king's official residence at St. James's Palace, and settled in to discuss the future of exploration. This meeting of the exclusive Saturday's Club—it did not seem to matter that today was a Monday—included a former secretary of state, a future governor-general of India, and a lord of the king's bedchamber, as well as a smattering of knights of the realm. Eight of the club's full complement of twelve sat in Parliament; six were fellows of the elite scientific institution the Royal Society. One—the key player in this gathering of key players—was the society's president, Sir Joseph Banks.

Banks was forty-five then, bibulous, running to fat. Unlike his most famous predecessor, Isaac Newton, he was well liked: James Boswell described him as "an elephant, quite placid and gentle," who allowed you to "get upon his back or play with his proboscis." He had been educated at Harrow and Eton, where he discovered a hatred of the classics and a love of botany, and soon after leaving Oxford had embarked on his first scientific adventure, traveling as a naturalist on a Royal Navy frigate bound for Newfoundland and Labrador. This was a mere dress rehearsal, however, for the journey that would make his name: James Cook's first circumnavigation. He returned from that three-year voyage in 1771 with a staggering thirty thousand plant specimens and a fame that surpassed even that of Cook. He became a close friend of George III, developing his Royal Botanic Gardens at Kew into a major center of research, and by the age of thirty-five was leading the world's foremost scientific institution, the Royal Society. He would remain the society's president for the next four decades, building up a network of friends and acquaintances that included the most illustrious natural philosophers of the time—Benjamin Franklin, Carl Linnaeus—as well as creative thinkers and statesmen from Thomas Paine to Henri Christophe, the king of Haiti. From his house at 32 Soho Square he fired off thousands of letters dispensing patronage and advice to the projects that caught his enthusiasm. What a lot of enthusiasms there were.

Toward the end of the Age of Enlightenment, giant steps were being taken in every field of human endeavor, from geography and music to animal husbandry and rhubarb cultivation. It was a time of revolution in politics—in 1783, America had won independence from one monarch; in 1789, France would execute another—and in science too. Banks's contributions to the latter were immense. He would support William Roy, the founder of the Ordnance Survey; William Smith, the creator of the world's first geological chart; and William Herschel, the first person in history to discover a planet of the solar system, Uranus.

From his seats on the Board of Agriculture and the Board of Longitude, Banks would help modernize grain production and navigation, while as a trustee of the British Museum he would develop collections that would form the basis of the Natural History Museum and the British Library. Overseas ventures especially caught Banks's interest: he was behind HMS *Bounty*'s ill-fated mission to transplant breadfruit from Tahiti to feed slaves in the Caribbean, and promoted the establishment of a penal colony in Australia. Only that January, the first fleet of convicts had arrived on a shore he had once searched for new plant species, which Cook had christened Botany Bay.

In the summer of 1788, Banks and his friends were about to turn their attention in a new direction. Africa at that time was an obscure continent to Western geography, and Banks was unusual in having set foot on it, when Cook's ship *Endeavour* dropped anchor in the bay of Cape Town in 1771. Explorers might have crossed the Antarctic Circle, but what they knew of nearby Africa was a joke, as a satirical ditty penned half a century earlier by the satirist Jonathan Swift made clear:

> So Geographers in Afric-maps,
> With Savage-Pictures fill their gaps;
> And o'er unhabitable downs
> Place Elephants for want of towns.

Interest in this neglected continent had been sparked in the mid-1770s by James Bruce, a Scottish squire who had set out to discover the source of the Nile and ended up living in Ethiopia for two years. "Africa is indeed coming into fashion," Horace Walpole wrote in 1774. "There is just returned a Mr. Bruce, who has lived three years in the

Court of Abyssinia, and breakfasted every morning with the maids of honour on live oxen." As a result, Banks's own exploits, Walpole noted cattily, were "quite forgotten."

If Africa was indeed in fashion in London, it was also the subject of a looming moral crisis that would shape British foreign policy for the next half century. By the late 1700s, trade on the Guinea coasts—which had been named for their principal commodities of ivory, gold, slave, and grain—had become a key plank of the British economy. In the half century to 1772, the value of the African trade had increased sevenfold, to almost a million pounds a year. "How vast is the importance of our trade to Africa," wrote an anonymous English merchant that year, "which is the first principle and foundation of all the rest; the main spring of the machine which sets every wheel in motion." Much of the trade was in humans: sea captains based in London, Liverpool, and Bristol swapped guns made in Birmingham and East Anglian cloth for slaves, who were shipped to the West Indian tobacco and sugar plantations that kept the British economy afloat. In the 1760s British vessels had carried forty-two thousand slaves a year across the Atlantic, more than any other European nation.

Now, though, Britain's conscience was beginning to be pricked, as people came into contact with the victims of slavery for the first time. There were ten thousand black people working as domestic servants in England in 1770, and by the 1780s a small spate of popular books appeared that set out the trade's evils, including *The Interesting Narrative of the Life of Olaudah Equiano*, which became a classic text for the Quaker antislavery activists who would found the abolitionist movement. For Saturday's Club members such as Henry Beaufoy, the finding of alternative African commodities held the prospect of bringing the trade to an end. Others, including Banks, sniffed new commercial opportunities that could be good for Britain.

These motives were not spelled out in the club's literature. The reason put forward for the new push into Africa, laid down by Beaufoy and approved by Banks, was the pure, age-old call of discovery:

> Of the objects of inquiry which engage our attention the most, there are none, perhaps, that so much excite continued curiosity, from childhood to age; none that the learned and unlearned so equally wish to investigate, as the nature and history of those parts of the world, which have not, to our knowledge, been hitherto explored.

Such was the success of British seafaring, and of Cook's voyages in particular, that "nothing worthy of research by Sea, the Poles themselves excepted, remains to be examined," Beaufoy continued. The future of exploration now lay onshore: at least a third of the habitable surface of the earth remained uncharted, including much of Asia and America, and almost the whole of Africa. Thanks to the efforts of George Forster, an East India Company employee who had traveled from Bengal to England through Afghanistan, Persia, and Russia, knowledge of Asia was likely to "advance towards perfection." The fur traders of Montreal could meanwhile be relied upon to deal with the problem of western Canada. The African interior, however, was still "but a wide extended blank" on which geographers had traced, with hesitating hand, "a few names of unexplored rivers and of uncertain nations."

Such ignorance, Beaufoy noted, "must be considered as a degree of reproach upon the present age." To remedy this geographical stigma, the Saturday's Club would establish a new body, the African Association, devoted to promoting the exploration of the continent:

> Desirous of rescuing the age from a charge of ignorance, which, in other respects, belongs so little to its character, a few individuals, strongly impressed with a conviction of the practicability and utility of thus enlarging the fund of human knowledge, have formed the plan of an Association for promoting the discovery of the interior parts of Africa.

The society's rules were quickly hammered out: a membership subscription of five guineas a year was agreed on, and a committee of five was chosen. Banks would be treasurer and Beaufoy secretary, while Lord Rawdon, the bishop of Llandaff, and the lawyer Andrew Stuart were appointed assisting members. It would be the task of these men to recruit "geographical missionaries" to undertake the first journeys of discovery.

The remaining question, then, was where on that great uncharted landmass they should be sent.

TIM-BUK-TOO. The toponymy of these three short syllables is disputed. Do they refer to the "wall" or "well" of Buktu, a slave woman who lived in this storied place, five miles beyond the northernmost bend of the Niger River? Or are they Songhay, meaning "the camp of a woman with a large navel"? Or do they signify simply a low-lying place, hidden among dunes? There are many theories, many pronunciations, and many spellings of this word, which Bruce Chatwin described as a "ritual formula, once heard never forgotten." What seems clear is that a settlement was established here around 1100, and it grew into an influential town thanks to its position at the juncture of the world's largest hot desert and West Africa's longest river.

The Sahara extends over 3.6 million sun-blasted square miles, stretching from the Atlantic to the Red Sea and from the Mediterranean to the Sahel. It covers more of the earth's surface than the contiguous United States, China, or the continent of Australia. In popular imagination it consists of an ocean of dunes, and although these sand seas do exist, they account for less than a sixth of the whole. The Tuareg call the Sahara *tinariwen*, meaning "deserts," plural, to reflect its many different personalities. There are skyscraping mountains 11,000 feet tall and salt flats the size of Lake Ontario where the quicksand can swallow a car. Mostly, there are hundreds of thousands of square miles of flat, bare rock.

Six thousand years ago, the Sahara was green; it was roamed by elephants, giraffes, and rhinoceros that drank from its lakes and ate its vegetation. Now much of it sees no rain for years at a time. When rain does fall, roaring torrents appear that scour deep trenches in the land before vanishing moments later. It is by some measures the earth's hottest place, where shade temperatures can approach 140 degrees, but on winter nights, without the blankets of cloud cover, soil, and plant life, the desert can freeze white. Above this naked expanse, colliding layers of hot and cold air create violent winds that blow for fifty days at a time, stirring a suffocating dust that blocks out the sun and kicking up sand spouts that kill animals and uproot trees.

If the desert abhors life, on its southwestern edge it encounters the vital force of West Africa, a body of water locally called Joliba, the "great river" or "river of rivers," and known to the rest of the world as the Niger. The Niger is born in a ravine 2,800 feet up in the Guinea highlands of Futa Jallon, one of the wettest places on earth. Futa Jallon is the source of three great West African watercourses, the others being the Gambia and the Senegal. Each of these gives its name to a country, but the mighty Niger gives its name to two. If it followed the shortest route to the Atlantic, this river would be a steep 150-mile torrent; instead it sets out confidently in the wrong direction, wandering northeast to slide miraculously among desert dunes in the great boomerang of the Niger Bend before emptying, 2,600 miles from its source, into the Bight of Benin.

Roughly a third of the way along its epic journey, the Niger becomes lost in a flat, 300-mile-long inland delta. From the air this looks like a stream running out across a beach: the water branches into dozens of shallow channels and creeks. Two-thirds of its flow evaporates here, and by the end of the dry season large tracts of riverbed are dead. In July, when the rain falls again and immense volumes of water pulse their way downstream, the dried-up channels and lakes fill, and life blossoms once more. Floating grasses and wild rice burst forth; fish and insects hatch; egrets and spoonbills arrive, joining hippos, crocodiles, and manatees. Cattle herders drive their animals to the grass that has grown along the river's edge; farmers harvest rice, sorghum, and millet.

Timbuktu lies at the downstream end of the delta, and at the most northerly part of the bend. It is at the crossroads of the river trade and the desert caravan routes: the meeting place, in the old dictum, "of all who travel by camel or canoe."

As the annual inundations of the Nile gave birth to the kingdoms of ancient Egypt, the Niger's fertile inland delta nurtured its own civilizations. Even in classical times, reports of these lands filtered back to

Europe. In the fifth century BCE, Herodotus noted the existence of a river on the far side of the desert that abounded in crocodiles, with a city on its banks that was inhabited by black sorcerers. Pliny the Elder, writing five centuries later, described monstrous tribes who lived there, including the Aegipani, who were "half men, half beast"; the Troglodytes, who couldn't speak except to emit a batlike squeaking noise; and the Blemmyes, who had "no heads, their mouths and their eyes being seated in their breasts." These malformed humans would survive long into the Middle Ages: the Hereford Mappa Mundi, created around 1300, depicts both Blemmyes and Troglodytes in Africa, while later historians would exaggerate Pliny's Africans into people with one eye in the center of their forehead, or one giant foot that was large enough to shelter them from the sun.

In the seventh century, Christian Europe's route to Africa was cut by the Muslim armies that swept west across the Mediterranean's southern shore to the Atlantic, and for twelve hundred years information from beyond the Sahara was reduced to echoes that filtered back via the merchants who plied the desert. These were often fantastical—several reports reached medieval Europe of giant ants that harvested gold from African riverbeds—but there was substance to the rumors of the region's wealth. Before the Spanish colonization of the Americas, two-thirds of all gold circulating in the Mediterranean came from the Sudan. The Muslim geographer al-Idrisi, writing in the twelfth century, related that the king of ancient Ghana was so rich he had "a Lump of Gold, not cast, nor wrought by any other Instruments, but perfectly formed by the Divine Providence only, of Thirty Pounds Weight," while in the fourteenth century, Ibn Battuta—one of the most widely traveled people in history—chronicled the exploits of the Malian emperor Musa I. Musa—sometimes known as Mansa Musa, meaning "King Musa"—was said to have performed the pilgrimage to Mecca in 1324 with an entourage of sixty thousand soldiers, five hundred slaves, and one ton of gold as spending money, and was so free with his wealth that he depressed the price of the precious metal in Cairo for a generation.

Timbuktu first appeared in European geography fifty years later, on the Catalan Atlas, a 1375 map of the known world prepared by the Mallorcan cartographer Abraham Cresques for the king of Spain. The city's name was spelled "Tenbuch," and from the beginning it was associated with riches, since Cresques placed Musa next to it, holding a giant golden scepter and a huge gold nugget and wearing a heavy gold crown. Later reports seemed to confirm Cresques's information: in 1454, a Venetian captain in the pay of the Portuguese prince Henry the Navigator reached Waddan, a trading oasis south of Tripoli, and brought back an account of how camel caravans took rock salt to "Tanbutu" and then to "Melli, the empire of the blacks," where it was exchanged for large quantities of gold. It wasn't until the sixteenth century, however, that a firsthand account of Timbuktu was published in Europe that put the seal on the gilded legend.

The traveler's name was al-Hasan ibn Muhammad al-Wazzan al-Zayyati. Details of his biography are sketchy, but he is thought to have been born in Granada and to have moved when he was young to Fez, where he was well educated. Sometime between 1506 and 1510, at age seventeen, he was said to have accompanied one of his uncles on a diplomatic mission to the Sudan and visited Timbuktu. A decade later he was captured by Christian corsairs, who took him to Rome, where he was freed by Pope Leo X and converted to Christianity, adopting the name Johannis Leo de Medicis, which later became Leo Africanus. Leo settled down in Italy and wrote several books, but it was his

Description of Africa, with its account of life in the Sudan, that was met
with the greatest excitement: he had discovered a new world for Europeans, it was said, much as Columbus had by finding America.

In Leo's description, Timbuktu was a wealthy and charming city.
Though its houses were made mostly of mud and thatch, in the middle
of the town there was "a temple built with masoned stones and lime-
stone mortar by an architect of Béticos [in southern Spain] . . . and a
large palace built by the same master builder, where the king stays."
The town's several wells provided sweet water, and there was an abundance of cereals, cattle, milk, and butter; salt, however, was very
expensive, as it had to be brought five hundred miles from the desert
mines. The city's inhabitants were "very rich," he noted, and instead of
using coined money they used pieces of pure gold. As well as keeping a
standing army of three thousand horsemen plus a large number of foot
soldiers who shot poisoned arrows, the king of Timbuktu owned "great
treasure in coin and gold ingots," one of which weighed thirteen hundred pounds, and his court was "magnificent":

> When the king goes from one town to another with his courtiers,
> he rides a camel, and the horses are led by grooms. If it is necessary
> to fight, the grooms hobble the camels, and the soldiers all mount
> the horses. When anyone wants to address the king, he kneels be-
> fore him, takes a handful of dust and sprinkles it over his head and
> shoulders.

The people of the city had a lighthearted nature: "It is their habit to
wander in the town at night between ten p.m. and one a.m. playing
musical instruments and dancing," Leo wrote. There were also many
educated people there. This meant there was a great appetite for manu-

scripts, which were valued more highly in the city's markets than were other goods:

> In Timbuktu there are numerous judges, scholars and priests, all well paid by the king, who greatly honours learned men. Many manuscript books from Barbary are sold. Such sales are more profitable than any other goods.

Leo's work was widely translated. An English version was published in 1600 that sparked a wave of interest in Africa: it was a probable source for Shakespeare's *Othello*, and its account of sub-Saharan wealth would have encouraged English adventurers to pursue the Portuguese farther down the Guinea coast. In 1620, an expedition led by the English gentleman Richard Jobson reached Tenda, on the Gambia; here an African merchant told him of a town farther upstream called Tomboconda, where there were "houses covered with gold." Jobson's account of his expedition was republished in 1625 by the anthologist Samuel Purchas, who exhorted his countrymen to further investigate the African continent. "The richest Mynes of Gold in the World are in Africa," Purchas noted, "and I cannot but wonder that so many have sent so many, and spent so much in remoter voyages to the East and West and neglected Africa in the midst."

By the late eighteenth century, the legend of golden Timbuktu was fixed in the European imagination. This was the magnet that would draw Europeans into the heart of West Africa.

The African Association committee did not waste time. Four days after the meeting at the St. Alban's Tavern, they gathered in Banks's house in Soho Square to discuss dispatching their first recruit "with all expedition" in search of new discoveries. It mattered little that, as one twentieth-century African statesman put it, "there was nothing to discover, we were here all the time."

WHAT KIND of character would walk out into the extended blanks of the African Association's maps? Who was brave, desperate, or arrogant enough to bet on the lottery of exploration, to chance his life—and it was always *his*—in a land whose principal features were unknown, never mind the nature of its inhabitants, its beasts, its climate and diseases? What reward could possibly entice a man to wander out among the Blemmyes and Troglodytes, armed with little more than a pistol and an umbrella? Any well-informed European asked in 1788 to travel into the continent's interior should have recognized the journey as the death sentence it was and stayed at home. But the African Association's recruits were not well informed. That, in many ways, was the point.

The geographical barriers were not insurmountable. Yes, the routes across the desert were littered with the skeletons of pack animals and slaves alike, but much like an ocean, the Sahara was crisscrossed with trade routes and had been traversed by caravans for centuries. In the tropics, the explorer could be brought to a halt by torrential rain, but there were no forbidding mountain ranges of the Asian sort, no impenetrable forests such as those in the Amazon basin. A traveler could move from one village to another via a network of established pathways and tracks.

More potentially dangerous was the reception a Christian explorer was likely to meet. After centuries of religious conflict, Muslims in northern Africa knew that Europeans wanted their trade and their land, while wandering infidels were a gift for desert tribesmen seeking legitimate sources of plunder. As the Senegal-based merchant Antoine Pruneau de Pommegorge noted in 1789, "It is impossible to have knowledge of the far interior of the country, because . . . the white who would be brave enough to attempt such a voyage would have his neck chopped off before he reached it."

Farther south, people were more tolerant of non-Muslims, but a far greater threat lurked here, as an old slavers' adage made clear:

> Beware, beware the Bight of Benin,
> For few come out though many go in!

Disease made West Africa the deadliest place in the world for Europeans. In the early nineteenth century, almost half of any company of soldiers stationed on the West African coast, which became known as the "white man's grave," could be expected to die within a year. The interior was reputed to be even more deadly: trade missions inland, which would have meant almost certain death for a European, were subcontracted to African-born merchants.

The region boasted such a rich ecology of burrowing parasites, viruses, bacteria, and insects that no explorer would escape. These included the Guinea worm, whose larvae entered the body in drinking water, then migrated to the tissue beneath the victim's skin, where they grew, over several months, up to three feet long. If the host survived this agony, intensely painful pus-filled blisters would appear on the lower leg a year later, then rupture as the giant worms forced their way out. The blood-sucking tsetse fly, meanwhile, carried sleeping sickness, whose initial symptoms of fever and weight loss gave way to personality changes and narcolepsy as the disease migrated to the brain, killing its host only after several years. Intestinal infections such as amoebic dysentery could be lethal too.

The most dangerous sickness by some margin, however, was malaria. The commonest form of this parasite in West Africa, *Plasmodium falciparum*, is also the most deadly: it still kills hundreds of thousands a year. The mosquito that carries it thrives around humans, and its larvae can grow in a puddle as small as an animal's footprint. Once injected into the body, malarial microorganisms enter the bloodstream and are carried to the liver, where they grow inside cells that pop eight to twelve days later, releasing tens of thousands of offspring, which then start to invade the host's red blood cells and eat them from inside. When each cell implodes, the parasites move on, until the host's blood is being eaten on a massive scale. Victims begin to vomit up bile, and their skin, fingernails, and eyes take on a yellow hue. Finally, their stools and urine turn black, by which time death is not far away.

In 1788, neither malaria nor its vector was understood: the disease was blamed on bad air, or "miasma." Though the bark of the cinchona tree was a known treatment, it wasn't used effectively and the quinine it contained wasn't isolated until 1820. West Africans had at least some resistance from being exposed to the disease in childhood; Europeans had none.

Like their explorers, the members of the fledgling African Association in London were largely unaware of these hazards. James Bruce's sojourn in Ethiopia had proved that African travel did not have to be lethal, while Cook and others had shown that the world was open to the right sort of cautious investigation: Why should traveling in Africa prove any more difficult than, say, navigating the Great Barrier Reef?

For the right sort of character, with the right sort of constitution, blessed with faith and good luck, anything was surely possible.

They were not short of volunteers. Within days of their first meeting, the African Association committee had found two highly suitable recruits.

Simon Lucas, the son of a London wine merchant, had been sent to Cádiz as a boy to learn his trade, but was captured by a mob of Barbary pirates, the Salé Rovers, who sold him as a slave to the imperial court of Morocco. He remained there for three years, and after his release went back to serve for sixteen years as a British diplomat, before finally returning in 1785 to England, where he was made Oriental interpreter at the Court of St. James's. He offered his services to the African Association on condition that the committee secure paid leave for the duration of his mission.

Lucas was sick in June 1788, so the first departure fell to the association's second recruit, the thirty-seven-year-old American John Ledyard. Ledyard was also highly qualified, though in a very different way. Everyone who encountered this fine physical specimen appears to have been overwhelmed by his steady eye and his open countenance. He was "an extraordinary man," Beaufoy noted, who "seemed from his youth to have felt an invincible desire to make himself acquainted with the unknown, or imperfectly discovered regions of the globe."

Ledyard had been raised in Hartford, Connecticut, and showed an early penchant for adventure by escaping from the newly founded Dartmouth College and paddling a forty-foot dugout canoe 150 miles down the Connecticut River. He quit Dartmouth for good after that, joining an Atlantic merchantman that took him to Europe, where, in 1775, he enlisted as a marine in order to secure an introduction to Captain Cook. Cook took Ledyard on his third and final voyage, during which, it is sometimes claimed, Ledyard became the first re-corded Euro-American to get a tattoo. On his return, he deserted rather than fight with the Royal Navy against his own country, and settled down to write an account of the circumnavigation that became a bestseller.

The mid-1780s found him in Paris, where he made friends with John Paul Jones and Thomas Jefferson. Jefferson, then United States ambassador to France, was as impressed with Ledyard as everyone else: he was "a man of genius, of some science, and of fearless courage and enterprise," Jefferson wrote. He suggested that Ledyard try to find an overland route from Europe to the Americas via Saint Petersburg, Kamchatka, and Nootka Sound, and signed up his friend Joseph Banks as a sponsor. The explorer set out for the Siberian wastes and reached Yakutsk before being arrested as a spy, on Catherine the Great's orders. He was deported, paying for his passage to London with a check drawn on Banks's name, and showed up at the Royal Society president's London house in June 1788, dressed in rags. His timing was perfect. Banks immediately suggested "an adventure almost as perilous as the one from which he had returned"—in Africa. The penniless Ledyard was keen, and Banks sent his potential recruit to Beaufoy for a second opinion. Needless to say, Ledyard quickly won him over, as Beaufoy recorded:

> I was struck with the manliness of his person, the breadth of his chest, the openness of his countenance, and the inquietude of his eye. I spread the map of Africa before him, and tracing a line from Cairo to Sennar, and from thence westward in the latitude and supposed direction of the Niger, I told him that was the route, by which I was anxious that Africa might, if possible, be explored.

He said, he should think himself singularly fortunate to be entrusted with the adventure.

Another promoter of exploration, in a different age, might have asked whether a traveler who had just returned in rags from a two-year, 7,000-mile journey was ready for a mission that, if all went well, would last a further three years. Ledyard was required to travel from Marseilles to Cairo, Mecca, and then Nubia, cross the desert lengthways, find the Niger, and make his way home. It meant covering at least 12,500 miles, mostly overland, through some of the most hostile territory on earth. But Beaufoy recorded no qualms. When, he asked the candidate, would he be able to set out?

"Tomorrow morning," Ledyard responded.

In fact, the association gave him several more days. He left London on June 30, 1788, telling Beaufoy that he was "accustomed to hardships" and evils that were "terrible to bear," but they had never prevented him from his purpose. To Banks he said, "If I live, I will faithfully perform, in its utmost extent, my engagement to the society; and if I perish in the attempt, my honour will still be safe, for death cancels all bonds."

RICHARD FRANCIS BURTON, writing sixty years later, described the moment of setting out on a journey of African exploration as one of the gladdest moments in human life: "Shaking off with one mighty effort the fetters of Habit, the leaden weight of Routine, the cloak of many Cares and the slavery of Home, man feels once more happy. The blood flows with the fast circulation of childhood." Ledyard was equally exalted by his departure. "Truly is it written, that the ways of

God are past finding out, and his decrees unsearchable," he wrote to his mother. "Is the Lord thus great? So also is he good. I am an instance of it. I have trampled the world under my feet, laughed at fear, and derided danger. Through millions of fierce savages, over parching deserts, the freezing north, the everlasting ice, and stormy seas, have I passed without harm. How good is my God! What rich subjects have I for praise, love, and adoration!"

His route south took him through Paris, where he stayed for a week, meeting up with his friend Jefferson, who evidently disapproved of his working for the British but helped make arrangements for the onward journey; Ledyard thereafter sent regular updates to his fellow American. In Marseilles he boarded a ship bound for Egypt, which presented him with immediate difficulties. Alexandria was "more wretched" than anything he had seen, he told Jefferson, filled as it was with "poverty, rapine, murder, tumult, blind bigotry, cruel persecution [and] pestilence!" He reached Cairo in the oppressive heat of mid-August and found it to be "a wretched hole, and a nest of vagabonds," half the size of Paris, while the mighty Nile was "a mere puddle compared to the accounts we have of it," no more impressive than the Connecticut River:

> Sweet are the songs of Egypt on paper. . . . Who is not ravished with gums, balms, dates, figs, pomegranates, circassia, and sycamores, without recollecting that amidst these are dust, hot and fainting winds, bugs, musquitoes, spiders, flies, leprosy, fevers and almost universal blindness?

He spent three months in Cairo, preparing for his role as a Muslim traveler dressed in a "common Turkish habit" and gleaning what he could about the route ahead. He abandoned his plan to go to Mecca and instead began researching the route west via Sennar, a sultanate in the north of the modern state of Sudan. His greatest source of information was the slave market. Twenty thousand slaves would be imported to Egypt that year, he was told, and it was from these people that he began to get an idea of the scale and danger of his journey. "A caravan goes from here [Cairo] to Fezzan," he discovered, "which they call a journey of fifty days; and from Fezzan to Tombouctou, which they call a journey of ninety days. The caravans travel about twenty miles a day, which makes the distance on the road from here to Fezzan, one thousand miles; and from Fezzan to Tombouctou, one thousand eight hundred miles. From here to Sennar is reckoned six hundred miles." If he were to remain healthy and unmolested and to travel nonstop—three enormous suppositions—it would take at least six months to reach Timbuktu.

There was great promise in the countries along his route, however: "Wangara is talked of here as a place producing much gold," he noted. "The King of Wangara (whom I hope to see in about three months after leaving this) is said to dispose of just what quantity he pleases of his gold; sometimes a great deal, and sometimes little or none; and this, it is said, he does to prevent strangers knowing how rich he is, and that he may live in peace." Nevertheless, the strain of the Cairene environment and the task ahead was apparent as he prepared to leave the city on November 15. By the time of his final letter to Jefferson he was in a very different mood from the one in which he had set out:

I have passed my time disagreeably here. . . . I assure myself, that even your curiosity and love of antiquity would not detain you in

Egypt three months. . . . From Cairo I am to travel southwest, about three hundred leagues, to a black king. Then my present conductors will leave me to my fate. Beyond this, I suppose I shall go alone. . . . I shall not forget you; indeed, it will be a consolation to think of you in my last moments. Be happy.

Ledyard never reached the black king. He was still in Cairo when he fell ill with a "bilious complaint," probably stomach cramps caused by dysentery or food poisoning, later that month. The sickness didn't kill him, but the treatment did: he took the common remedy of vitriolic acid, but consumed so much that it produced "violent burning pains" that threatened to be fatal. He tried to cure these with tartar emetic, a potassium salt that was intended to induce vomiting but instead made him much worse. "All was in vain," recorded his biographer, Jared Sparks. "The best medical skill in Cairo was called to his aid without effect." Three days later, Ledyard was dead.

A correspondence ensued among Banks and Beaufoy, Jefferson, and Banks's acquaintance Thomas Paine. The men of the African Association told Paine that the caravan with which Ledyard intended to travel had been continually delayed, and at last he was thrown "into a violent rage with his conductors which deranged something in his system." Several years later, Banks reflected that they had been unlucky with this first mission, "for it failed by the death of Our Traveller Ledyard, whose health when he left England appeared to promise a long life, and whose strength of Body to overcome the fatigues of Travel . . . had been before fully tried."

In a eulogy, Beaufoy noted that Ledyard had been "adventurous beyond the conception of ordinary men, yet wary and considerate, and attentive to all precautions." He appeared, Beaufoy wrote, "to be formed by Nature for achievements of hardihood and peril." It was impossible to gloss over the truth, however: the African Association's first wandering hero had died by accident, in extreme pain, without getting farther than Cairo.

3.

HELL IS NOT FAR AWAY

MARCH 2012

By 2012, the Timbuktu of Haidara's youth had been transformed in the usual modern ways. It was now a place of snorting trucks and diesel fumes, 4x4s and flatulent motorbikes, electric lights, and fifty-four-inch flat-screen plasma TVs with a hundred satellite channels showing *Star Trek* reruns. Billboards advertised Coca-Cola and pay-as-you-go cellphones, while shoppers in jeans and T-shirts browsed the streetwear in Almadou Dicko's Harlem Shop and the Victoria Emporium with its "Prêt-à-Porter Fashions." The kids playing in the streets were as likely to be wearing Barcelona and Real Madrid strips as the red, green, and gold of Mali.

Even now, though, some things remained as they had always been. The festivals were still counted by the cycles of the moon, and the days were governed largely by the height of the sun and measured out in calls to worship. An hour before dawn, the muezzin announced the *fadjr* prayer, and the faithful washed the sleep from their eyes and bent their heads toward the east. The women who ran the city's bakeries loaded the communal ovens built on every street corner with flat rounds of dough, filling the air with the ancient aromas of wood smoke and baking bread. Donkeys still pulled wagons, and sheep and goats still grazed among the scraps in the street, having been released from pens made of sticks and string and—an innovation, this—old automobile fan belts.

Down by the river, transporters disembarked from the boats carrying cargo destined for the Grand Marché. On the way into town they passed farmers tilling their fields and women beating their washing and arranging it on bushes to dry. Although they were brought by truck these days, slabs of salt were still for sale in the Petit Marché, alongside fresh and dried fish, goat, mutton, beef, and camel.

After the *duha* prayer, the people of Timbuktu went home to eat, and after that, as the sun reached its brutal zenith, they found a shaded place to sleep. At *asr* they woke up and worked again until *maghrib*, at dusk. Their habit then, in the cooling evening, was to go to meet their friends, to gossip, drink tea, make music, play games, and talk politics and poetry until *isha*, when they would prepare for bed.

For weeks, these evening gatherings in Timbuktu had been dominated by talk of the crisis. Few people in the early days of the year had believed that the fighting would reach Timbuktu. In January, Mohamed Diagayeté, a senior employee at the Ahmad Baba institute, asked a soldier friend for advice: should he keep his family here or head for safer country in the south? There would be no problem in Timbuktu, the soldier had said. The town itself would remain secure. More recently, though, the soldier's opinion had started shifting. Things had gone awry, and like everyone else he now had a "little bit of fear."

Then things had begun to move very quickly. To Diagayeté it seemed unreal, like a dream.

On Thursday, March 29, a week after the coup in Bamako, the city leaders announced a meeting in the broad acre of sand by the Sankore mosque to try to pull the different communities together behind the town's ragtag Arab militia, Delta Force. People of all Timbuktu's ethnic groups—Songhay, Fulani, Bambara, Tuareg, Bella, Dogon—were invited to bring forward whatever they could spare to support the fighters who were now their best hope. They gave money, cereal, cattle, and bolts of cloth, all of which was handed over with a great show of solidarity, and they felt a little more secure.

The next day, the news again took a bad turn. The garrison town of Kidal in the far northeast had fallen to the rebels. A new ripple of fear ran through Timbuktu, and people started packing up to move south. That morning, the director of the Ahmad Baba institute, Mohamed Gallah Dicko, told his seventy employees to take as much of the organization's office equipment home as they could. If Timbuktu fell, at least the computers, cameras, and hard drives wouldn't be looted. Some, like the researcher Alkadi Maiga, didn't bother: Kidal was a far-flung town in a hostile region, a much more vulnerable outpost than world-famous Timbuktu.

Other people said the city was already surrounded.

At six that evening, just as the sun was setting, a small convoy of 4x4s set out from Timbuktu, heading east along the river into the desert. Word had been passed through the Arab militia that the MNLA rebels wanted a meeting, and so a delegation of city elders had been chosen, along with a number of fighting men from Delta Force. Among the four delegates was Kader Kalil, a sixty-five-year-old with a long Lee Marvin face whose gravel voice and lively opinions were often heard on Radio Bouctou, the community station he ran out of a brick box behind the mayor's office.

As the vehicles bounced along the rough track, Kalil was deeply unhappy. He was tired and scared, his ulcers were playing up, and he thought he and his fellow Timbuktiens were being led into a trap, but they had no choice: if the people wanted you to do something, you couldn't refuse.

At seven-thirty p.m. they stopped in the village of Ber to await the rebels' instructions, and Kalil called his wife to tell her he would not be home for dinner. "This may be the last time you hear from me," he said.

It was almost midnight when the little convoy of 4x4s set out again, driving now to the northeast. Six miles from Ber, the militia leader's cellphone rang and the suspicious Kalil listened to the tone of the conversation. Was he a bit too polite, a bit too eager to please? They must douse their lights, the militiaman said when the call was finished, so the position of the rebel camp wasn't given away. The blacked-out vehicles continued for another three miles, coming to a halt in an area of soft sand, desert grasses, and acacia thorns.

The men climbed down from the cars, treading carefully over the dark earth. The only flecks of brightness came from the glow of a cigarette or a struck match, but even in the gloom Kalil could make out a large number of armed men, with their ubiquitous Kalashnikovs and heavy turbans, and pickups parked beneath camouflage nets or hidden from the sky by the low desert trees.

They were led up a dune to where a carpet had been spread. After some time a group approached, led by a pale-faced Tuareg man in his fifties with a smear of dark mustache. He was Mohamed Ag Najim, the ex–Libyan army colonel who was now the senior military commander of the MNLA. He spoke in Arabic, which the leader of the Timbuktu militia translated into French.

"Welcome," said Ag Najim. "Please, consider yourselves at home."

With the sand and the vehicles and the open sky, the murmuring of conversation, and the calling of a bird in the desert, the delegates felt they were on a film set.

"What we ask is this," Kalil said. "Can you spare Timbuktu?"

"Out of the question," replied Ag Najim.

"Then you must give us time to prepare the people so they can decide whether to stay or leave."

"How much time?"

"A month."

"Out of the question," Ag Najim repeated. His men were mobilized and would have been in Timbuktu that night if the city's leaders hadn't agreed to parlay. Since they had shown the courage to come, however, he would offer them five days, as long as they met certain conditions, namely that all those who did not want to live in the independent state of Azawad must leave, as must all the Bambara, the dark-skinned southerners who dominated Mali's administrative class and military. Only then would he promise to enter Timbuktu without shelling it.

"By Thursday, those who can stay with us in Timbuktu will remain, but those who want to flee must flee," said Ag Najim.

It was almost dawn when the delegates hurried back down to their vehicles for the drive to town.

THAT MORNING, Saturday, March 31, Timbuktu awoke to another piece of terrible news: Gao, the largest town in the north and the headquarters of the Malian army in the region, had now fallen.

Alkadi had a simple thought when he heard this: "Timbuktu is finished."

Kalil at this time was racing to find the mayor, Halle Ousmane

Cissé, to relay the MNLA's ultimatum. The rebels were on their way to Timbuktu, Kalil told Mayor Cissé, there was now no question. They had promised not to come till the following Thursday, but Kalil didn't trust them: they could be here anytime, even today. Mayor Cissé was soon hurrying in turn to meet the senior representatives of the administration—the governor of Timbuktu, Colonel-Major Mamadou Mangara, and the regional military commander, Colonel Gaston Damango—to relay what the MNLA had said: the rebels would enter the town peacefully only if all the soldiers and state workers had left.

"We must not sacrifice the population," Mayor Cissé told them. "You have to leave now. If you don't, who is going to save us?"

The colonels' resistance didn't last long. There was little that they could do, in any case. The junta in Bamako had ordered Malian troops to withdraw from their base at Gao to prevent civilian casualties, and a reinforcement column that reached Timbuktu in the early hours had immediately been ordered to fall back toward the south. It was now retreating in disarray. What hope did that leave for the garrison, already demoralized and weakened by defections and desertions? "After the coup d'état there was no immediate force that could defend Timbuktu, despite the desire that was there," Mangara recalled. The governor agreed to abandon the city.

Senior representatives of the state were now informed they should leave and take with them what they could. As word spread that the government was pulling out, panic began to set in.

That morning, Alkadi was anxious enough to heed his director's request to remove all the valuables from the Ahmad Baba institute. He climbed on his motorbike and set off from the house he shared with his wife, their two small children, and his brother in the northwestern neighborhood of Abaraju. As he rode through the market to the Ahmad

Baba building on the Rue de Chemnitz, he saw people running in every direction, some to pack their families and belongings on the trucks, buses, and 4x4s that were heading south, others to drop their children with friends or relatives who lived in safer areas of town, away from the military camp. Wherever Alkadi stopped, he heard people talking about the best ways to escape. When he reached the institute, he grabbed his laptop, a Canon camera, and a hard drive he had been using to digitize manuscripts, packed them in a bag, and then drove back through the chaos of the market to his house, where he stayed for the rest of the day.

His brothers in Saudi Arabia, Burkina Faso, and Côte d'Ivoire had been calling for days, urging him to flee the terrorists. His wife, Fatouma, wanted to leave too, but Alkadi thought these moments of panic were the most dangerous, as that was when people lost their heads. The situation would settle down, he told her, she would see. They sat in front of the TV, flipping between Al Jazeera, France 24, and BBC World News. Sometimes—when their anxiety became too great—they didn't watch anything at all.

As afternoon turned to evening the road south from Timbuktu became clogged with people trying to escape, fleeing toward the ferry at Koriume, and the long desert crossing to Douentza and the south. Mangara and Damango left at six p.m. Other soldiers, who couldn't escape or didn't want to abandon their families in Timbuktu, quit the army camp and tried to hide among the population. In the hurry to flee their base, they left behind their belongings and equipment: livestock, cooking utensils, television sets. Since there were no clear orders, they also left their stockpiles of weapons and ammunition.

At dusk, Ismael Diadié Haidara, the proprietor of the Fondo Kati library, went to Sankore to meet his friends, who gathered there every night. The town was now gripped by a sort of "social psychosis," recalled Ismael, an affable man with small round glasses. Some said the rebels would arrive at any moment; others, that it wasn't true, they wouldn't come at all. More than anything, they felt powerless. He thought of his two youngest children, who were with him in Timbuktu, and of the thousands of manuscripts in the library across the courtyard from his house in the eastern neighborhood of Hamabangou.

At seven p.m. Ismael returned home. When the children were in bed, he went across to the library. He had already moved some of his manuscripts to a hiding place, and now he started to move the rest off the shelves and into lockers. He found it impossible to prioritize— "Which manuscripts can I take? Which ones will I leave for destruction? It is as if you have asked a father to choose between his children, whom he would save and whom he would sacrifice." He worked until eleven p.m., then went to bed. Across Timbuktu people lay awake, listening to the sounds of the city emptying itself.

IT WAS STILL DARK when Ismael left his house the following morning for a walk in the dunes. He had developed the habit of spending an hour at the break of each day on a circuit of the city, taking in the cool dawn air, the first pale light, and the daily resurrection of life. The street was deserted as he slipped through the door in the outer wall of the compound and set off toward the edge of town. He had not taken more than a few hundred steps when a neighbor spotted him. It was not safe to be out, said the man. "I'm going just for a short walk," Ismael protested, but the neighbor was insistent, and he decided to turn back. He reentered the courtyard a few minutes later, just as the sun was beginning to rise. When his fourteen-year-old son came out of the house to meet him, they heard the sharp report of two gunshots.

"Papa, did you hear that? The rebels have come."

"I heard it," Ismael said.

It was a little after six a.m.

Minutes later, the rattle of gunfire was shaking people awake all across Timbuktu. Diadié Hamadoun Maiga, a former deputy mayor, woke up at home in Sarakeyna, in the east of the city, to hear shots ringing out "all over." In Abaraju, Alkadi, who had been awake since five, found his morning routine of getting up, praying, and listening to the news interrupted by the crackle of gunfire. Someone told him it was the sound of an airplane, but he knew it wasn't.

At Diagayeté's house near the Sidi Yahya mosque, the family had been woken before dawn by an urgent banging at the door. A neighbor, a military man, pushed in without taking off his shoes or setting down his rifle. "You need to look to save your family," he said. "We have been instructed to abandon the town." He left again, to ditch his gun and change out of his uniform, and minutes after that Diagayeté heard a sound he would clearly recall years later: the *bok! bok! bok! bok! bok!* of an automatic weapon.

After Ismael had ushered his son inside, he returned to the doorway. From up the street came the roar of vehicles, and then a convoy raced past, heading for the Place de l'Indépendance, the governorate, and the military camp. Others saw gunmen arrive on foot: a group marched up the sandy drive at the low, gray-painted Hôtel Bouctou on the western edge of town and started shooting over the heads of the hotel workers. The men walked into the reception area, with its neat dining tables and red-and-white checkerboard floor, robbed the till of its contents—a measly fifty dollars' worth of francs—then demanded the keys for the new Land Cruiser that was parked out front, next to a garden planted with Madagascar periwinkle. The owner of the vehicle hurriedly found them, but it soon became clear the gunmen didn't know how to drive.

As the shooting escalated, people shut their doors and tried to keep themselves and their children calm. Some prayed. Ismael took his son and daughter into the library, then locked the door and continued the task he had begun the night before, of transferring his manuscripts carefully into lockers. Others went into the street to see what was happening and found pandemonium. Armed men were haring around in pickups, shooting and yelling, while civilians were running in all directions, some trying to leave the city any way they could: by car, motorbike, or donkey, even on foot, though it was 130 miles to the nearest stretch of tarmac road.

The hysteria caused by the gunmen was "total," according to Houday Ag Mohamed, one of the few state officials who had not yet fled. It seemed to him a deliberate strategy to scare any remaining Malian soldiers who wanted to fight, and it was working: when he went into the street, he found distressed army recruits struggling to get out of their uniforms, ditch their weapons, and find a hiding place. With his southern neighborhood of Sans Fil vibrating to rhythmic explosions, he hurried back inside and shouted at his family to lock themselves in their rooms since "Hell is not far away!" Soon afterward he heard the low murmur of conversation beneath his window and found a group of soldiers had sneaked into his compound. Anticipating a pitched battle inside their home, his wife announced there was nothing left to do but wait for death. Houday instead cautiously approached the young men, who offered him several chickens and their military vehicles to look after. He refused these gifts and persuaded them to hole up instead in the house of a neighbor who had left.

All over town soldiers were trying to find shelter. One group showed up at Ismael's. Thinking his building was already target enough, with its well-known manuscript library and a telephone mast on the roof, he persuaded them to go elsewhere. Other people took soldiers in: Diagayeté, sitting tight with his family, welcomed back his army friend, who was now weaponless and in a civilian T-shirt and trousers. He would stay for several days, along with one of Diagayeté's colleagues and some students from the Franco-Arab school.

The looting that had begun at the Hôtel Bouctou was now spreading. The militiamen knew the army camp well from the days when they had trained with government troops, and so they set about taking everything the soldiers had left, from refrigerators and chairs to weapons and crates of ammunition, and loading their loot in pickups and on motorbikes and carrying it off into the desert. The 4x4s were piled so high that one resident watched boxes of grenades topple off, the explosives hitting the ground and rolling around like mangoes fallen from a tree. Vehicles were a particular target for the looters. A line of 4x4s that the Malian military had parked next to the army camp vanished, as did most NGO- and state-owned vehicles.

That morning, Fatouma Harber, a teacher at the Franco-Arab school, spotted a young man gearing himself up for looting. "If they break open the banks I'm going to look for my share of the money," he declared. "Otherwise a weapon would do." He set off in the direction of the camp. A few minutes later, outside a mosque, he fell into an argument with a teenager over a stolen rifle: they were both tugging at it when the boy pressed the trigger and shot him dead.

Once they had taken as much as they could carry, the gunmen urged the bystanders to help themselves to what remained. Ismael saw people hurrying away with pieces of furniture on their heads. Even small children were among the looting crowds.

At nine a.m., the town was rocked by a huge explosion. Alkadi heard "one massive bang" and ran into the yard to find the sky filling with black smoke. Ismael, who was much closer to the army camp, felt the house shake. Boubacar Mahamane, a city elder nicknamed "Jansky" after a West African football star of the 1970s, was sitting on his roof terrace in the Grand Marché when he heard the detonation. "Oh, yes," he thought. "Now the party has really started." Gunmen trying to shoot the lock off a magazine in the camp had hit the explosives inside, and now shells were flying out in every direction, knocking down sections of the camp wall and landing in houses nearby. Clouds of foul-smelling smoke and fumes drifted south on the breeze, making the air in Sans Fil almost unbreathable.

For Ismael, this was the bitterest moment of the day, the moment when he realized the town had fallen. "I told myself, there is nothing we can do, truly, everything is lost," he said.

When Diadié, the former deputy mayor, saw who was doing the shooting, he immediately recognized them as the men of the Arab militia, Delta Force, and knew that Timbuktu had been betrayed. The MNLA were not far behind. On the advice of his brother, a high-ranking police officer, Kalil and his family were taking cover on the ground floor of his house in the Grand Marché when they heard a vehicle pull up outside and a knock at the door. He opened it to find a man wearing the heavy turban of the deep desert.

"Mohamed Ag Najim is at the entrance to the city and wants to see you now," the messenger said. "He has some very important information."

This was not a good moment, Kalil pointed out, perhaps he could come back another time. But the messenger insisted, and after Kalil's twenty-five-year-old son volunteered to accompany him, the aging broadcaster reluctantly followed the rebel out into the street.

They drove out through the chaos—a scene Jansky described as "looking like the end of the world"—to the south of the town, Kalil in a state of growing agitation. Near the stadium on the Kabara road, as they passed a group of pickups filled with masked gunmen careering into the city, he demanded that they go back: "If you do not take me home, I will get out!" The driver refused to stop, so Kalil called Ag Najim at the cellphone number he had been given on the dune outside Ber.

"I have to go back!" he told the MNLA leader.

"Come for five minutes," Ag Najim told Kalil over the din. "I have a very urgent statement that I want you to broadcast."

"Brother," said Kalil, "I do not want to be caught in the crossfire! Tomorrow or the day after tomorrow, when things will be calmer, you can call me."

Ag Najim agreed, and the driver turned around.

MNLA trucks were now circling along with the Arab militia. Though it was difficult to tell one armed man from another, the MNLA vehicles carried independence slogans in Arabic and sometimes the green, red, black, and gold MNLA flag, which the fighters raised over the mayor's office, the governorate, the police station, and the military camp. The looting now gathered pace as the different groups of gunmen raced one another to the most valuable prizes: state offices, large shops, banks, and public services. Even the governor's house was stripped.

By one p.m., the city was exhausted. Seydou Baba Kounta, an unemployed tourist guide known universally as Bastos, watched a group of MNLA arrive at the bank opposite his house and begin to raid it, shooting into the air as they did so. His wife and seven children were in the house, so he marched across the road. "Loot the whole bank, I don't mind," he told the gunmen. "But can you stop shooting everywhere?"

Bursts from small arms continued to rattle across the city into the evening, mingling with the black smoke emanating from the burning camp.

At four minutes to six, a time that coincided with a lull in gunfire, a statement was released on the rebel Toumast Press website announcing that the MNLA had just put an end to the Malian occupation of Timbuktu. Now, they said, the MNLA flag flew everywhere in the region.

HAIDARA HAD BEEN on the road all day. On Saturday night he had slept in Mopti, the major town of central Mali, and in the morning he pushed on toward Timbuktu. He left his car at Sevare—he had been told that if he took it farther, it was likely to be stolen—and continued on public transport with his driver, moving against the flow of refugees and soldiers heading south. At Douentza, 130 miles from Timbuktu, where the main route to the city left the tarmac and cut across the desert, they found a 4x4 bush taxi that would take them to the river crossing at Koriume. They seemed to be the only people heading north.

They reached the ferry at one p.m. but were told it was too dangerous to cross: the fighting on the other side was too hot. So they followed the river downstream for a short distance and hailed a fishing canoe. The fisherman took them to the village of Hondoubongo on the north bank, where Haidara called a friend in Timbuktu.

"There is shooting everywhere," the friend told him. Even so, if they waited, he would see what he could do.

At four p.m. the friend arrived in a Mercedes he had managed to borrow. Getting out of the city had been difficult; getting back in was harder. Every few hundred yards they were stopped by armed men who fired in the air when they approached, Haidara remembered, and at every halt they faced a barrage of questions. Who were they? Whose car was this? Why were they coming into the city? How did they get here? Where was the vehicle that brought them to Timbuktu? It took them two hours to travel the eight miles to the gateway that marked the entrance to the city.

Driving into Timbuktu in the dark, Haidara got a first glimpse of the anarchy that had reigned for much of the day: the *pa-pa-pa-pa-pa-pa* of gunfire was continuous, though he couldn't even tell which groups were shooting. He hurried to his house on the east side, a short distance from his library in Hamabangou, and closed the door.

He wouldn't go out again for a week.

4

THE FOURTH TRAVELLER

On May 1, 1797, Joseph Banks wrote a note to his friend the French commissary in London that briefly outlined the state of the African Association. The business of sending "Travellers" to explore the interior regions of Africa was proving more difficult than he had hoped. "[We] have already Lost 3 well Qualified men," he wrote, "without having much Elucidated the internal Geography of the Country, but [we] Still persevere."

In truth, only two explorers had been definitively "Lost." Lucas had set out shortly after Ledyard, leaving for Tripoli in August 1788, but a rebellion in southern Libya blocked his route south and he had returned safely without leaving the Mediterranean coast. Next came the indebted Irish soldier Daniel Houghton, who offered to try the interior from the Gambia, find the reputed city of "Tombuctoo," then trace the unknown course of the Niger—all for the modest sum of £260. The association gladly accepted his proposal, and Houghton set out in 1790. On September 1 of the following year he wrote a note in pencil from Simbing, in the Sudanese kingdom of Ludamar, saying he was in good health, and was never heard from again.

There was a fourth traveler already in the field, however, who Banks very much hoped was now on his way back from "Tambuctoo." This was the twenty-five-year-old Scotsman Mungo Park, who at that very moment was battling his way toward the West African coast after a two-year journey in which he had lost everything bar his beaver-skin hat. Unpromising as this sounds, Park's mission would prove to be the African Association's greatest success, laying down a new archetype of the heroic white-man-in-the-dark-continent against which later explorers would be measured. Park traveled through lands filled with murderous "Moors" and savage beasts, armed with little more than his British pluck, his unwavering faith, and a formidable constitution. Most important of all, he would come back alive.

The son of a prosperous farmer, Park trained as a surgeon, but it was botany that drew him to Banks's attention. The Royal Society president arranged for him to travel to the Dutch East Indies to hunt for specimens, and he was hired by the African Association after returning with eight new descriptions of Sumatran fish. He was brave and persistent, even after being told of Houghton's disappearance: "I knew that I was able to bear fatigue," he wrote, "and I relied on my youth and the strength of my constitution to preserve me from the effects of the climate."

He sailed from Portsmouth on May 22, 1795, carrying a letter of credit for £200 and instructions "to pass on to the river Niger, when arrived in Africa, . . . ascertain the course, and, if possible, the rise and termination of that river," then use his "utmost exertions" to visit the principal towns or cities in its neighborhood, in particular "Timbuctoo and Houssa"—although Houssa, or Hausa, was not a town but a people. With those tasks complete, Park could return by any route of his choosing.

On June 21, the little trading brig carrying him reached the mouth of the Gambia, then began to work its way slowly upriver to the community of European traders at Jonkakonda, where it would deliver mail and take on goods of beeswax and ivory. Park was invited to stay sixteen miles farther east, at the village of Pisania, with an English contact of Beaufoy's, the slaver John Laidley. There he settled down to learn Manding and gather any information he could about what lay ahead. After three weeks he was hit by his first attack of malaria and became delirious, and for much of August and September he was confined to the house, whiling away the "tedious hours" listening to the horrible sounds of the strange world into which he was about to venture:

> The night is spent by the terrified traveller in listening to the croaking of frogs (of which the numbers are beyond imagination), the shrill cry of the jackal, and the deep howling of the hyæna; a dismal concert, interrupted only by the roar of such tremendous thunder as no person can form a conception of but those who have heard it.

Lesser spirits would have given up there, but Park always demonstrated phenomenal drive, and by early December, when the rains had given way to hot sunshine and the river had dropped, he felt well enough to set out. He left Pisania in the company of a freedman named Johnson, who had once been transported to Jamaica and England, and one of Laidley's house slaves, Demba, who was promised liberty if the explorer returned alive. Park had a horse; a small assortment of beads, amber, and tobacco to barter; an umbrella; and his beaver-skin hat. At one p.m.

on December 3, 1795, he took leave of his European companions and rode out into the African woods. By now, his excitement at the idea of becoming a "Traveller" had given way to dangerous reality, much as it had for Ledyard, and he was in a gloomy and introspective mood:

> I had now before me a boundless forest, and a country, the inhabitants of which were strangers to civilized life, and to most of whom a white man was the object of curiosity or plunder. I reflected that I had parted from the last European I might probably behold, and perhaps quitted for ever the comforts of Christian society.

Park's despondency didn't last long. By February he had traveled three hundred miles inland, reaching the state of Kaarta, where he was well received by the king, Daisy Koorabarri. To avoid the imminent outbreak of war between Daisy and his neighbor Mansong Diarra, the king of Bambara, the explorer turned north toward Ludamar, the land in which Houghton had disappeared. This territory, located near the modern Mali–Mauritania border, was inhabited by "Moors," the blanket European description for North African Muslims of Berber or Arab origin, and Park's experiences there would mark him for the rest of his life.

In his first days in Ludamar he at least learned what had become of Houghton. The Irish soldier had paid some Moorish merchants to guide him toward Timbuktu, Park was told, but after two days he became suspicious of their intentions and insisted on turning back, whereupon the merchants robbed him and went off, leaving him without food or water. After walking for several days Houghton reached a well, but the people he encountered there refused to give him any food. "Whether he actually perished of hunger, or was murdered outright by the savage Mahomedans, is not certainly known," Park recorded. The soldier's body was dragged into the woods, and Park was shown the very spot where it had been left to perish.

This macabre story did not dissuade Park from proceeding deeper into Ludamar, and neither did Johnson's declaration that he would relinquish every claim to reward rather than go one step farther. Park gave him copies of his papers to take back to the Gambia and continued with Demba, but they were increasingly harassed by the people of the territory, who tried to provoke the explorer by hissing and shouting at him and spitting in his face, and telling him that as a Christian his property was their lawful plunder. On March 7, a group of them entered the hut where he was staying and arrested him. They took him to Benowm, to the camp of Ali, the country's ruler—a "tyrannical and cruel" man, according to Park. Ali imprisoned the traveler and as an added insult tethered a pig outside the hut where he was held. Ali's camp followers— "the rudest savages on earth," in Park's view—then tormented both the unclean animal and the Christian from sunrise to sunset:

> The rudeness, ferocity, and fanaticism, which distinguish the Moors from the rest of mankind, found here a proper subject whereupon to exercise their propensities. I was a *stranger*, I was *unprotected*, and I was a *Christian*; each of these circumstances is sufficient to drive every spark of humanity from the heart of a Moor; but when all of them, as in my case, were combined in the same person, and a suspicion prevailed withal, that I had come as a spy into the country, the reader will easily imagine that, in such a situation, I had everything to fear.

Arguably, given the future behavior of Europeans in Africa, Park *was* a spy, though Banks would have said his journey was being made for the purer motive of increasing human knowledge. In any event, this was the worst period in the young man's life, and it would haunt his dreams for years to come. While suffering bouts of malaria, he was variously told that he would be put to death or have his hand chopped off and his eyes put out, and was subjected to a mock execution. He was deprived of food and, as the hot season arrived and water became scarce, was reduced to drinking from a cattle trough, since the Muslims feared his Christian lips would poison their drinking vessels. If it wasn't clear to him already, in April, a sharif—a man who claimed direct descent from the Prophet—arrived in the camp and explained the desert tribes' attitude to Christians. The sharif had spent a number of years living in Timbuktu and asked if Park intended to travel there. When Park replied that he did, the man "shook his head, and said, it *would not do*; for that Christians were looked upon there as the devil's children, and enemies to the Prophet."

The sharif evidently took pity on the young Scot, however, and told him where the legendary city was. To reach it, he would first have to go to Walata, ten days hence, and Timbuktu was eleven days beyond that. Park asked again and again in which direction the city lay, and the sharif always gestured to the southeast, never varying the direction by more than half a point.

In late June 1796, after three months in captivity, Park managed to escape, though he had to leave behind Demba, who had been taken into Ali's army of slaves. He traveled through the savanna, dodging groups of "Moors," and approached the Niger near the Bambara capital of Segu. On July 20 he was told by his traveling companions that he should see the great river itself the following day. He was too excited to sleep and saddled his horse before daylight, but the gates of the village where he was staying were kept closed at night to keep out lions, and he waited impatiently for dawn. Finally the gates were opened, and after two hours' travel he set eyes on his prize:

> As I was anxiously looking around for the river, one of [my companions] called out, "geo affili" (see the water), and looking forwards, I saw with infinite pleasure the great object of my mission—the long sought for majestic Niger, glittering to the morning sun, as broad as the Thames at Westminster, and flowing slowly *to the eastward*.

He had become the first European explorer to set eyes on a river whose existence had been the source of speculation since the time of Herodotus. He was not surprised to find that it flowed toward the rising sun—in the direction opposite to that the African Association's scholars believed—since he had been told as much by many of the people he met. As for its outlet: even the merchants who traveled on it did not appear to know where it reached the sea, but said only that they believed it ran "to the end of the world."

He hurried to the river's edge, drank some of its water, then lifted his fervent thanks in prayer to God for having crowned his endeavors with success.

On the far bank was Segu, the great capital of the Bambara nation, which formed a prospect of "civilization and magnificence" of a sort Park had not expected to find in Africa. Word of his arrival was passed to the Bambara king, but Mansong was suspicious of Park and refused him entry, so the explorer sought shelter in a nearby village. All day he waited beneath a tree, the traditional place for strangers to sit until a host came forward, but the people of the village looked on him with astonishment and fear and refused to take him in. By dusk he was hungry and worried: the wind was rising, rain threatened, and the many wild beasts in the area meant he would have to try to sleep in the tree's branches. At last a woman returning from her work in the fields took him in, giving him water, a very fine fish for supper, and a mat to sleep on, and while he rested, the girls in the family spun cotton and sang a sweet and plaintive song in his honor that he was moved to record:

The winds roared, and the rains fell.
The poor white man, faint and weary,
Came and sat under our tree.
He has no mother to bring him milk;
No wife to grind his corn.
Chorus:
Let us pity the white man;
No mother has he.

Perhaps because of what he had suffered in Ali's camp, Park was deeply affected by this act of compassion. After six months of threat and anxiety, the generosity of this stranger unleashed a powerful emotion. "The circumstance, was affecting in the highest degree," he noted, through a less-than-stiff upper lip. "I was oppressed by such unexpected kindness; and sleep fled from my eyes." It was one of many acts of charity he was shown in West Africa, and typical of his treatment by women. "I do not recollect a single instance of hardheartedness toward me in the women," he recalled. "In all my wanderings and wretchedness, I found them uniformly kind and compassionate."

When the Bambara girls' words reached Britain, they became a subject of curiosity and delight. They were "simple and pathetic sentiments," some said, but they demonstrated that these pagans could exhibit a humanity that many believed to be the exclusive preserve of Christians. The author and political activist Georgiana Cavendish, Duchess of Devonshire, was moved to rework them into a rhyming poem, which she had set to music:

> Go, White Man, go; but with thee bear
> The Negro's wish, the Negro's prayer,
> Remembrance of the Negro's care.

In the morning, Park gave his hostess the only things of value he still possessed: two brass buttons from his waistcoat.

PARK REFERRED NOW to his plain but demanding instructions. He had achieved one of the African Association's principal objectives: finding the Niger and determining its direction. What remained—apart from the impossible request that he also discover the river's source and its termination—was the task of using his "utmost exertions" to visit the towns along it, especially Timbuktu. It was this goal that Park now set out to achieve. He followed the river's course for a hundred miles northeast, reaching Silla at the end of July. There, the strain of his exertions finally overtook him. He was "worn down by sickness, exhausted by hunger and fatigue, half naked, and without any article of value by which I might procure provisions, clothes, or lodging." Above all he recognized that he was heading deeper into the territory of those "merciless fanatics," the Moors. Fearing that if he was killed his discoveries would die with him, he decided to turn back, but first he would wring from the traders of Silla all the information he could about Timbuktu, "the great object of European research," which he was told lay farther to the northeast. Park's questions doubtless focused on his persecutors, and he was duly told the city was filled with Muslims who were "more severe and intolerant in their principles than any other of the Moorish tribes in this part of Africa." One old black man related how, on his first visit to Timbuktu, the landlord at his lodging house had spread a mat on the floor and laid a rope on it, saying: "If you are a Mussulman you are my friend, sit down; but if you are a Kafir, you are my slave, and with this rope I will lead you to market."

If anyone could overcome these difficulties, however, the rewards would be great, since Park's inquiries about the city's wealth seemed to confirm the rumors:

> The present king of Timbuctoo is named Abu Abrahima; he is reported to possess immense riches. His wives and concubines are said to be clothed in silk, and the chief officers of state live in considerable splendour. The whole expense of his government is defrayed, as I was told, by a tax upon merchandise, which is collected at the gates of the city.

His researches complete, the weary Park turned for home. He followed the Niger southwest to Bamako, then little more than a village, where he left the broad river to strike west to the coast. It was the rainy season and traveling was difficult: three times he had to swim streams in spate, pushing his horse ahead of him, with his journal tucked in the crown of his hat. A short distance from Bamako, robbers stripped him of what little he had left, returning only his worst shirt and a pair of trousers, but he refused to despair, and the headman of the next village ordered an attendant to find and recover his clothes and his horse. Park gave him the emaciated animal as thanks, before struggling on to the small town of Kamalia. By now he was in a dangerous condition: feverish, with an injured ankle that meant he could only hobble, and no food or items for barter. It was five hundred more miles to Pisania, and his route would soon take him through the gloomy wilds of Jallonkadoo, where there were further dangerous rivers to cross and no shelter for five days. "I had almost marked out the place where I was doomed . . . to perish," he wrote.

In Kamalia, Park was lucky to stumble upon another exemplary act of hospitality.

He saw a group of people listening to a man reading from an Arabic text. The reader, a slave trader named Karfa Taura, noticed Park and asked with a smile if he understood what was written in the book. Park didn't read Arabic, so Taura asked one of his companions to fetch a little volume that had been brought from the west. When Park opened it, he found it was *The Book of Common Prayer*. Both men were overjoyed by this moment—Taura by the fact that this ragged stranger could read the English words no one else could understand; Park by the discovery of a Christian text *in English* in West Africa—and an immediate bond was established. Taura offered to put Park up for free until the rainy season was over, and said he would then escort him to the Gambia with the party of slaves he was taking to the coast. Park accepted. Three days later he fell so severely ill he couldn't walk, and he remained at Kamalia for the next seven months, making notes about the life in the town as he recovered. It was during this time that he became the first European to record how manuscripts were used in the West African interior.

When Taura went away on business, he left Park in the care of a Muslim teacher named Fankooma, who owned a large number of manuscripts. Park had been shown similar documents at other places during his travels, but now he had time to discuss them in detail:

> Interrogating the schoolmaster on the subject, I discovered that the Negroes are in possession (among others) of an Arabic version of the Pentateuch of Moses [the first five books of the Old Testament], which they call Tauret la Moosa [the Torah of Moses]. This is so highly esteemed that it is often sold for the value of one prime slave.

The Sudanese also had copies of the Psalms and the Book of Isaiah, which were held in very high esteem, and Park discovered that many people in Kamalia knew the Old Testament stories, including those of Adam and Eve; the death of Abel; Noah's flood; the lives of Abraham, Isaac, and Jacob; the story of Joseph and his brethren; and the histories of Moses, David, and Solomon. He was surprised to find a number of people who could relate these stories to him in Manding, and they were shocked to discover that he knew them too.

Fankooma used his manuscripts to teach the seventeen boys and two girls in his school. The boys were educated in the mornings and evenings and performed domestic duties for their master during the day, which was when he taught the girls. The pupils learned to read the Kuran and say a number of prayers, and when they were ready, a feast was prepared and the student sat an exam, or "[took] out his degree," as Park put it. The explorer attended three of these ceremonies, listening with pleasure to the "distinct and intelligent answers" each of the students gave. When the examiners were satisfied, the last page of the Kuran was put into the student's hand, and he or she was asked to read it aloud. Finally, all the scholars rose, shook each student by the hand and bestowed on each the title of "Bushreen," or scholar.

The boys' parents paid the schoolmaster with a slave or the equivalent price on their children's graduation. (Park did not say whether the same was true for the girls.) This was always done, Park noted, if the parents could afford it; otherwise the boy would remain the domestic slave of the schoolmaster until he could collect sufficient goods to ransom himself. Although they were given an Islamic education, Park noted that most of Fankooma's pupils were not Muslims, and their parents' aim in putting them into school was solely their child's improvement. Kamalia was far from unusual in having a school. He had noticed that "encouragement . . . was thus given to learning (such as it is) in many parts of Africa."

After making these observations on a working eighteenth-century African education system, Park left Kamalia in April 1797. He traveled with Taura's caravan of thirty-five slaves, some of whom had been kept in irons for years and could scarcely walk, but were now bound for a miserable life in the Americas or a terrible death on the middle passage. It took two months to cover the "tedious and toilsome" miles. As they approached Pisania, Park met an English-speaking woman who had known him before he set out but who now mistook him for a Muslim. When he told her who he was, she looked at him "with great astonishment, and seemed unwilling to give credit to the testimony of her senses." The Gambia traders had been told long before that Park had been murdered in Ludamar, and had never expected to see him again.

PARK REACHED FALMOUTH just before Christmas 1797, after an absence from England of two years and seven months. Britain was thrilled with his discoveries, none more so than the members of the African Association, who had something to celebrate at last. Beaufoy had died in 1795, so the traveler worked up an account of his expedition with the association's new secretary, Bryan Edwards. *Travels in the Interior Districts of Africa*, which included new maps drawn by the noted cartographer James Rennell, was published in 1799. It was a gripping real-life adventure story, in which Park gave European readers their first proper account of the Sudan and its people, and it quickly became a bestseller. Timbuktu and the Niger were the talk of Europe.

The African Association had grown hugely in the decade since its founding. On May 25, 1799, its members met at the Star and Garter in Pall Mall, where Banks congratulated the assembly on Park's book, "which has been so well received by the public." While Lucas and Houghton had not been well chosen, Park had shown "Strength to make exertions, Constitution to endure fatigue, and Temper to bear insults with Patience, Courage to undertake hazardous enterprises where practicable, and judgement to set limits to his exertions when his difficulties were likely to become insurmountable."

Europe's attitude to Africa had changed in the decade since the Saturday's Club had created the association. Britain and France were in the middle of a long series of wars, and Napoleon had seized Egypt to try to threaten the Suez Canal and British trade in India. One corner of the African continent, at least, had a strategic value, and Banks, who always worked to promote the nation's interests, now talked frankly of exploiting Park's new information for profit, and by military means. Park had opened "a Gate into the interior of Africa," Banks said, through which "every Nation" could enter and extend its commerce. "A Detachment of 500 chosen Troops would soon make that Road easy, and would build Embarkations upon the [Niger]—if 200 of these were to embark with Field pieces they would be able to overcome the whole Forces which Africa could bring against them." With European technology, the "ignorant Savages" of the interior could be taught how better to pan for their gold, and the value of the annual return, which he estimated to be currently worth a million pounds sterling, would likely be increased a hundredfold.

The meeting drew up a memorandum to the Committee of the Privy Council for Trade and Plantations, setting out an unabashed colonialist agenda. They advised that "the first step of Government must be to secure to the British throne, either by Conquest or by Treaty, the whole of the Coast of Africa from Arguin to Sierra Leone; or at least to procure the cession of the River Senegal."

Park married that year and moved back to Scotland to work as a doctor, but the work didn't suit him and he was soon longing to return to Africa. He told the novelist and poet Sir Walter Scott that he was troubled by a nervous disorder that meant he would awake suddenly in the night and believe he was still a prisoner in Ali's tent in Ludamar. When Scott expressed surprise that he should still want to return to the continent, Park answered that "he would rather brave Africa and all its horrors than wear out his life in long and toilsome rides over the hills of Scotland, for which the remuneration was hardly enough to keep soul and body together."

By the winter of 1803–1804, increasingly alarmed by French claims on West Africa, the War and Colonial Office was seriously discussing sending a military force to capture Timbuktu. In the end it was agreed that the African Association's most successful traveler should be sent back with a small detachment of soldiers. This second Park expedition sailed from England on January 30, 1805, charged with following the course of the Niger "to the utmost possible distance to which it can be traced."

If the key to the success of his first journey was its unthreatening nature—bolstered by the kindness of Park's hosts, dollops of good luck, and immense personal fortitude—the second expedition was designed to fight. Park went with a captain's commission, a £5,000 salary, £5,000 for expenses, and a party of forty-five, including a company of soldiers, sailors, and carpenters, his brother-in-law Alexander Anderson, and a friend from Selkirk, George Scott. The soldiers were recruited from Goree, an island off the coast of Senegal that had recently been captured from the French, so they were partially acclimatized to West Africa, but disease still killed them quickly in the interior. By the time they reached Bamako, thirty-one of the Europeans had died. But the stakes were higher than ever for Park, and he pressed on. He reached Sansanding in October, where he built a forty-foot sailing boat he christened His Majesty's Schooner *Joliba*, the Manding name for the Niger. He hired a guide, Amadi Fatoumi, and bought three slave boatmen to help work it, but by the time they were ready to leave Sansanding there were only five Europeans left, and Anderson and Scott were both dead.

The survivors must have known by now that they were unlikely to escape the interior alive, and at least one of the soldiers was deranged. Even so, Park would not be swayed from his course. He informed London in his last dispatch that he had "the fixed resolution to discover the termination of the Niger or perish in the attempt," adding that if he did lose his life, at least he would die on the river. HMS *Joliba* set sail in November 1805, and Park was never heard from again.

It took the British government six years to work out what had happened. In 1811, one of Park's former guides tracked down Fatoumi, who had written his own account in Arabic of the expedition's last days. The *Joliba* had sailed downriver for 1,500 miles, with Park, still haunted by his experience of "Moors," electing not to land until they reached the coast. Whenever they encountered a threat they shot their way through it, and as reports of the Christians' aggression spread, so did resistance to their progress. Fatoumi's bald account of the *Joliba*'s passing of Timbuktu only hints at the last days of the disease-raddled crew as they teetered on the brink of madness:

[We] came to [Kabara]; on my passing there, three canoes came again to oppose our passage, we repulsed them by force as before; came to [Timbuktu]; on passing there we were again assailed by three other canoes, which we repulsed; passed [Gourma], after passing seven canoes [came] after us, which we likewise repulsed; we lost one white man, of sickness; there were then in [the *Joliba*] only four white men, myself, and three slaves we had bought, making eight hands; each of us had 15 musquets apiece, well loaded, and always ready for action. . . . [Sixty] canoes came after us, which we repulsed after killing many of the natives, which we had done in all our former engagements.

In this last action one of the few surviving soldiers, Lieutenant John Martyn, was in such a savage bloodlust and had needlessly shot so many that Fatoumi took hold of his hands and tried to restrain him. "We have killed enough," he told Martyn. "Let us cease firing!" The soldier turned his anger on the guide, but Park intervened to save him.

By a phenomenal effort of will, the bloodied boat reached Yelwa, in modern Nigeria, early in 1806, where Fatoumi left them. They were just five hundred miles from the Oil Rivers delta, where the Niger empties into the Gulf of Guinea, but they would not get much farther. Just above the steep rapids of Bussa, they were attacked from the shore. The boat ran aground, and Park and the three remaining Europeans jumped into the river, where they all drowned.

. . .

BY 1820 THE BRITISH GOVERNMENT had increasingly taken on the African Association's role of exploring the continent. The association's membership had dwindled along with its influence, from seventy-five in 1810 to forty-six by 1819. It had filled in many of the gaps on the maps of Africa and created a new model for exploration that would be built on by the geographical societies that were about to spring up all over the world. The association's findings had been won at some cost, however, as every one of its "travellers," apart from Simon Lucas, had died abroad. The young German Friedrich Hornemann reached Fezzan disguised as a Muslim in 1799 and sent back the intelligence that "Tombuctoo certainly is the most remarkable and principal town in the interior of Africa," before disappearing. Twenty years later a report reached Britain that he had died in 1801 in what is now Nigeria. Henry Nicholls was dispatched from the Gulf of Guinea in 1804 to find the termination of the Niger, without realizing that the object of his search was the very spot from where he had set out. He died in 1805, probably of malaria. In 1809 the association dispatched Johann Ludwig Burckhardt, who wandered the Middle East for nine years, learning Arabic and rediscovering the city of Petra, which had been lost for a thousand years, and the great temple of Ramses II at Abu Simbel, which had been buried by sand. As he finally readied himself to set out for the Sudan late in 1817, he contracted dysentery and died.

Banks was an old man by this time. He was fat and gouty and spent his waking hours in a wheelchair, though he continued to preside over the Royal Society until his death, which came on June 19, 1820. It would be another six years before a European explorer finally attained Timbuktu.

5.

AL-QAEDA TO THE RESCUE

APRIL 2012

Sunrise on Monday brought a new cavalcade of vehicles from the east. They filed along the sandy street that ran past Ismael's house, Toyota trucks painted the dun colors of the desert, each with a heavy machine gun mounted on the back along with a handful of swaying men. Unlike the vehicles Ismael had seen the day before, these picked their way along the road with deliberation. As they passed he could see that instead of flying the multicolored banner of the MNLA they carried black flags inscribed with white Arabic lettering. The new arrivals drove to the military camp and pulled down the MNLA's multi-colored standard and burned it before replacing it with their own oblong of dark material. "There is no God but Allah," the flags read.

By ten a.m. Jansky's phone was buzzing. A group of new arrivals had stopped in front of the mosque near the Flamme de la Paix monument at the northwestern edge of town, he was told, so he climbed into his car to go see who they were. Following the ring road he passed a group of rebel leaders driving in the other direction. His phone rang again. Another group had arrived at the hospital. He turned south.

The list of jihadists who arrived in Timbuktu that day would make a strong poker hand of "Most Wanted" playing cards. They included two senior al-Qaeda commanders: Yahya Abou al-Hammam, the "emir of the Sahara," and Mokhtar Belmokhtar, the leader of AQIM's Masked Brigade. Both were in their thirties, veterans of the Algerian civil war who had been sentenced to death in absentia, and by 2015 they would each have a $5 million bounty on their heads. Al-Hammam was said to have been involved in the murder of a seventy-eight-year-old French hostage in Niger, while Belmokhtar—a veteran of Afghanistan who went by an assortment of colorful nicknames including "One-Eye" and "Uncatchable"—was wanted for a string of killings and kidnappings.

But these men would play minor roles in the city's future, compared with two others who arrived in Timbuktu that day: Abdelhamid Abou Zeid and Iyad Ag Ghaly. Abou Zeid was also a veteran of the Algerian war, older than the others, most identifiable by his short stature: he was around five feet tall. The "Little Emir" was a rising star in AQIM thanks to the money he had made from kidnapping, which had earned the organization millions of euros. He was said to keep this money buried at a secret desert location, and was seen paying his fighters in brand-new euro notes. He could be ruthless—in 2009 his jihadist brigade had murdered a British man, Edwin Dyer, who had been captured near Timbuktu—and wherever Abou Zeid went, his Western hostages were held close by. Despite his wealth he led an ascetic life, and like a good jihadist he carried his Kalashnikov at all times. He spoke in a murmur that was said to be inspired by the soft tones of Bin Laden. He drank Coca-Cola and enjoyed milk mixed with rice and dates.

Ag Ghaly, meanwhile, was from the same Tuareg clan as Mohamed Ag Najim. Like Ag Najim, he had joined Gaddafi's military as a young man but returned to Mali in the 1980s to carve out a career as a revolutionary. He had a black beard and a babyish face, and though at one time he enjoyed whiskey and music, he had since become radicalized. In one U.S. diplomat's assessment, he cast a shadow over the north of the country and turned up "like the proverbial bad penny" to take his cut whenever a ransom was paid. His ability to play both sides was legendary: the Malian government once sent him as an envoy to Saudi Arabia, but he was expelled for making contact with extremist organizations. When his bid to lead the MNLA was rejected, he created a new jihadist group named Ansar Dine ("Defenders of the Faith"), which acted as a domestic branch of al-Qaeda. That day, he was in Timbuktu to hijack the MNLA's victory.

At eight a.m., Alkadi went to see a colleague, and together they decided to go into town on Alkadi's little motorbike to find out what was happening. In the Petit Marché they saw two Toyotas pull up next to a small mosque. Each vehicle was packed with gunmen wearing turbans that tumbled down to their waists, and in the lead truck was a man with distinctive bright teeth and a hennaed beard whom Alkadi recognized as Oumar Ould Hamaha. Known to most as Barbe Rouge, or "Redbeard," Hamaha was a Timbuktien and a jihadist commander.

"Come, gather round the car," Hamaha told the crowds in the market in good French, as his fighters jumped down from the 4x4s and began to usher people toward him. "We have not come to kill you," he said. "We have come in the name of Islam."

When a crowd had assembled, Hamaha began to explain their mission.

They were not looking for independence from Mali, he said, nor did they want to do people harm. Timbuktu had once been a great Islamic city, and they simply wanted it to become one again. The problems that people had—of poverty, unemployment, unhappiness—existed because they had been led astray from the laws of God. Now that God had allowed them to capture the town, it was His will that they ensure Timbuktu lived by the strict laws of Islam.

After his speech, Hamaha took questions, and when he had finished he moved on a short distance and his men went to round up a new audience. He continued in this manner for much of the day, and other jihadists did the same, so their message was broadcast to the people.

It wasn't long before these question-and-answer sessions became dominated by complaints about looting. The jihadists listened. Then they started handing out phone numbers that people with grievances could call, and from then on, whenever anyone had an issue with the MNLA—when their car or motorbike was taken or their shop looted—they phoned the jihadists, and if the stolen goods were private property, the jihadists would order the MNLA to hand them back. "Ansar Dine said that looting against private people was not normal," recalled Sane Chirfi Alpha, Haidara's childhood friend and a former head of tourism for the city. "If it was against the state, it was okay, but if it was against private citizens, they had no right to do it. Every time someone seized something private, Ansar Dine—and elements of al-Qaeda too—took it upon themselves to get it returned."

Some essential state-owned assets were also protected. The city was in a "catastrophic" condition after the looting, the Ansar Dine spokesperson Sanda Ould Bouamama said, so they set about trying to fix it. They made sure the utilities were secured—including the water supply, the Energie du Mali electricity plant, the telecommunications equipment—as well as Radio Bouctou and the hospital. On Sunday night the head of Timbuktu's health services had been called by an assistant and told that he had no office left: it had been looted and trashed. On Monday morning Ag Ghaly went to the hospital personally and asked the health workers what was missing. The vehicles, including the ambulance, had been stolen, along with medical machines and supplies, so Ag Ghaly found two trucks to replace them.

After the wave of destruction that had washed through the town on Sunday, people were impressed. "They were psychologists, they knew how to win people over," Diadié recalled. "They started listening. If there were frustrated people, or people who had lost things, they would make amends and try to buy their esteem." Even Jansky conceded that Ag Ghaly was a "boss."

The looting hadn't entirely stopped, though, and later on Monday the city elders went to see Ag Ghaly to complain: family homes were still being broken into, they said, and things were being stolen and destroyed. At that moment, the Ansar Dine leader ordered the MNLA out of the city center altogether. From then on, the town would be held by his jihadist fighters, while the southern districts, including the airport and the riverside, would be the domain of the secular MNLA. "The MNLA had the right to come and do its business here, to buy what it needed," said Sane Chirfi Alpha, "but they were not allowed to stay in the city after eight p.m." When they came into town, they had to come without weapons or flags, in vehicles without guns.

Timbuktu would pay a price for Ag Ghaly's protection, however. That evening, the Ansar Dine leader called the imams to the military camp to explain that they would "fight to the death" against those who wanted to speak of the creation of a secular republic—in other words, the MNLA—and he set out the requirements of the new theocratic regime.

Details of Ag Ghaly's political philosophy were broadcast on Radio Bouctou later in the week. He began by citing a controversial hadith in which the Prophet is alleged to have said that he had been "ordered to kill the people until they testify that there is no god except Allah, and that Muhammad is the Messenger of Allah, and they establish prayer and pay the *zakah* [give thanks to God]." Ansar Dine was not an ethnic, tribal, or racist group, he said, but an Islamic one that was the enemy of unbelievers and polytheists. The suffering of the Muslim people was the fault of the laws of Jews and Christians:

> It is not a secret, the scale of hardship our Muslim society is suffering, and the worst of it is disabling the Islamic sharia, which Allah has blessed us with, and replacing it with man-made laws that are taken from the Jews, Christians and their followers, which result in oppression, aggression, immorality, disobedience, poverty, deprivation and only Allah knows what.

For these reasons, he went on,

> your brothers from the mujahideen and the Ansar Dine organization have come together and vowed to uphold what is right, to implement the religion, to lift injustice from the oppressed, to reunify the Muslims, and to unite their efforts around the [belief] that there is no god but Allah, and Muhammad is his Messenger.

To succeed in his endeavor, Ag Ghaly required three things from the people of Timbuktu. First, he called upon "all segments of Muslim society to help . . . in establishing the religion," spreading justice and security, promoting virtue, and preventing vice. Second, he said, "our brothers the traders" must continue to supply the city with basic food-stuffs, fuel, and medicines, since "Allah will aid the slave as long as the slave aids his brother." Finally, the population of the city, especially those with "talents and capabilities," must pull together and help the community, either financially or by volunteering, since it was written in the scripture that:

He who has done an atom's weight of good shall see it
And he who has done an atom's weight of evil shall see it.

On Monday evening, Timbuktu began its first night under sharia law.

THE KEEPERS of the manuscripts met the jihadists' arrival with relief. Whatever strange ideas these people had about the Muslim faith, they would surely not threaten the safety of what were, after all, mostly Islamic texts. They might even help protect them from the looters.

Abdoulaye "Air Mali" Chabane—a portly figure, nicknamed after the national airline many years before because of his speed on the soccer pitch—was sitting opposite the new Ahmad Baba institute building in Sankore on Monday morning when he saw two vehicles pull up and several gunmen enter. After a moment's reflection he stood and followed them. Inside the compound, he saw two young men on the lower ground floor and several more in the offices above, all armed, and thought it prudent to leave. Sitting outside once more, he heard a good deal of shouting from the building, and soon the men reappeared, carrying a plastic sack full of loot. He watched them climb into their vehicles and drive away.

An hour later, another group arrived, in a pickup with a black flag. Their leader was a fat, bearded man who looked foreign. Air Mali approached and told him that the "lunatics" had come to visit. He had heard a lot of noise but did not know what they had done. "Are they still there?" asked the jihadist. When Air Mali said no, the commander said they should go in together.

Inside, they found the offices smashed up and the windows broken. Air Mali thought the men must have been searching for cash, because there were cellphones lying around that they hadn't bothered to take. They also appeared to have tried to get into the safe, without success.

"Where are the workers?" the commander asked.

"Gone," said Air Mali. "Fled."

The center must be preserved, the commander announced grandly, since it contained the history of the people; the stories of their fathers and grandfathers were all kept in here. Did Air Mali know anyone who could come to evaluate the damage?

Air Mali felt a wash of relief: it appeared that the jihadists could be made to understand. Even if everything else was looted, this place could at least be saved. He called the institute's accounts manager and explained the problem. At first he said he couldn't come, but Air Mali insisted, and the manager arrived that afternoon and checked the contents against his inventory. Everything valuable that was left should be removed to a safe place, he said: the computers, the furniture— everything but the manuscripts. Those were in a safe place and were not going anywhere. Anyway, the thieves had shown earlier that they were not interested in taking them.

When the inventory had been checked, the manager gave the list of missing items to the jihadists, who said they would investigate. They would also send people the following day to guard the building.

Several days passed, but nobody came.

Ismael Diadié Haidara meanwhile spent much of Monday in his Fondo Kati library, finishing the job of moving his manuscripts. In the afternoon he was sitting under the tree in his courtyard with a friend when a car pulled up outside. There were five armed men in the back and two in the front, and their leader asked who was the *responsable* for the house. Before Ismael could speak, his friend said that the director wasn't there.

"He has gone to Bamako," he said. "He fled."

"What is this place?" asked the rebel. "Is it an office?"

"No, a library."

"What is inside this library?"

"Books. Kurans."

"Ah," said the man. "If they are Kurans, then no one will touch them until the return of the owner."

The pickup moved off. Fifty yards down the street it stopped and reversed, and the jihadist went to speak to the man who owned the shop next door. Ismael thought they were trying to verify what his friend had said.

"We must keep calm," Ismael told his companion. "If they ask us again, this time I will speak."

The jihadists bought a few things from the shop, including sugar and tea, then came back. "It was a very delicate, very difficult moment," Ismael recalled. "They were no more than five meters from the library."

"I know you now, you two, I have seen you," said the leader. "If something happens to this house, I will come looking for you."

"No problem," said Ismael. "Everyone is calm. Nobody is going to touch anything here."

When the men had gone, Ismael's friend turned to him. "Those people are going to come back," he said. "You have to get out of here. Leave this town, because you are known—everyone knows you. In the end they will come to look for you."

"Perhaps," said Ismael. "Yes."

6

IT SHALL BE MINE

1824–1830

Joseph Banks might have been dead and the African Association in decline, but in the early 1820s a new European competitor was about to join the race for Timbuktu. On December 3, 1824, the central committee of the newly formed Société de Géographie in Paris was given a curious piece of information by one of its founding officers, the cartographer Edme-François Jomard. According to the society's minutes:

> M. Jomard announced that an anonymous member had donated a thousand francs . . . to recompense the first traveller who has penetrated as far as the city of Timbuktu via Senegal, and who has procured (1) positive and accurate observations on the position of this city, on the course of rivers that run in its vicinity, and the trade of which it is the hub; (2) the most satisfactory information about the country between Timbuktu and Lake Chad, as well as

the direction and height of the mountains that form the Sudan basin.

The idea of a Timbuktu prize evidently caught the imagination of the 217 savants who had established the Société de Géographie, since its value immediately began to snowball. A thousand-franc donation for "geographical discoveries" from Count Grigory Orlov, a Russian senator living in France, was immediately added to it, doubling the prize pot, whereupon the minister of the French navy doubled it again. Not to be outdone, the minister of foreign affairs added another two thousand, and the minister of the interior a further one thousand. Several other members came forward with more, so that by early 1825 it was worth a very healthy 10,000 francs, to which the society itself— which would judge the winner—added the promise of a prestigious Great Gold Medal of Exploration and Journeys of Discovery to go with the cash.

Still, it would not be easy to claim this substantial sum. As well as being "fortunate enough to surmount all perils attached to reaching Timbuktu," the society's *Bulletin* stated that the victorious contender would have to procure illuminating facts about the geography, produce, and trade of the country. In particular, the society required a map based on celestial observations, and a handwritten report containing information about the nature of the terrain, the depths of the wells and the water in them, the width and speed of streams and rivers, their color and clarity, and the produce of the land they served, the climate, the declination and inclination of the magnetic needle, and the breeds of animals that lived there. They should also return with specimens of fossils, shells, and plants, and a detailed study of the region's inhabitants:

By observing the people, [the explorer] will take care to examine their habits, their ceremonies, their costumes, their weapons, their laws, their worship, the manner in which they feed, their diseases, their skin colour, the shape of their face, the nature of their hair, and also different objects of their trade.

For anyone who lived in the Sudan, this would have made uneasy reading. Although, as with that of the African Association, the research was undertaken in the name of geography—it was "an immense field to cultivate for the knowledge of the human races," the *Bulletin* trumpeted, "for the history of civilizations, for their language, their customs and their religious ideas!"—this was also just the sort of information an imperial power would require. The relish with which ministers poured in government money would have been doubly suspicious. In fact, the "Prize for the Encouragement of a Journey to Timbuktu" looked very much like a late entrant's attempt to buy her way into the Africa exploration game begun by her long-standing rival. The *Bulletin* admitted as much: it was a British government mission to Central Africa in 1823 that had drawn European attention once again to the continent, and it was only natural that the three-year-old Société de Géographie also should turn its eyes in this direction. It would be to France's commercial advantage to find a route into the interior that followed Mungo Park, which would conveniently link up with long-established French settlements in Senegal.

As word of the prize spread, a half-dozen adventurers were rumored to be gearing up for attempts on the city, but there were two who became especially synonymous with the newly incentivized race for Timbuktu: René Caillié and Major Alexander Gordon Laing.

It was Laing who would send the "first letter ever written from that place by any Christian," as the British consul in Tripoli, Hanmer War-rington, put it. The son of an Edinburgh schoolmaster, Laing worked briefly as a teacher himself before escaping into the army and postings to the exotic territories of Barbados, Jamaica, and Sierra Leone, where he was sent in 1819. In West Africa he led a number of missions into the interior, demonstrating the courage, physical robustness, and talent for self-promotion that would be essential to the attempt on Timbuktu already taking shape in his head. "I have had for many years a strong desire to penetrate into the interior of Africa," he wrote to friends in 1821, "and that desire has been greatly increased by my arrival on the Coast [of West Africa]."

In 1824, in poor health, he was sent home to report the disastrous British defeat by the Ashanti at Nsamanko to the secretary of state for war and the colonies, Lord Bathurst. To the great irritation of his commanding officer in Sierra Leone, Sir Charles Turner—who com-plained that Laing was "unwize, unofficerlike, and unmanly" and that his "military exploits were [even] worse than his poetry"—the forty-year-old major ingratiated himself with Bathurst and was appointed to lead a "Timbuktu Mission." In May 1825 he arrived in Tripoli, where he was greeted by Warrington, a hard-drinking patriot who was ru-mored to be an illegitimate son of George III, and immediately embarked on a whirlwind romance with the consul's daughter, Emma. They were married at her father's large estate on the outskirts of the city on July 14, four days before the groom set out for Timbuktu. War-rington had seen too many explorers ride off to their doom in the desert and refused to let the couple consummate their partnership until his return. "I will take good care my Daughter remains as pure & chaste as snow," he wrote to Bathurst, in one of the more eccentric communica-tions received at the War and Colonial Office.

Laing engaged a merchant, Shaykh Babani, to take him to Timbuktu for the sum of $2,500, a thousand of which was paid up front. Both the explorer and the consul formed a positive view of Babani, who was said to have lived in the mysterious city for many years. He was a man "of the most sterling worth," Laing noted, "quiet, harmless, and inoffensive," while Warrington judged him to be "one of the finest fellows [he] ever saw, with the best tempered & most prepossessing Countenance [he] ever beheld." The shaykh would take Laing to Timbuktu in two and a half months, it was agreed, at the end of which he would pass Laing into the care of his particular friend, the "Great Sheikh, and Cheif Maraboot Mouckta," who was powerful enough to ensure the explorer's safe onward passage to the coast. Apart from Babani's caravan, the expedition included two West African sailors, who Laing hoped would one day build a boat to sail the Niger; a Jewish interpreter; and a much-traveled Caribbean-born army trumpeter named Jack le Bore who acted as the explorer's manservant. There was little subtlety to Laing's approach: they would travel in Muslim robes, but lest anyone mistake their true identity, he would read Christian prayers to his attendants every Sunday, when they would all appear together "dressed as Englishmen."

The expedition set out into the desert at the height of summer, when the thermometer regularly hit 120 degrees and the land was so arid that, according to Laing, "as little herbage was to be found as in the bottom of a tin mine in Cornwall." It took almost two months to reach the ancient oasis town of Ghadames, less than three hundred miles from Tripoli, after Babani led the caravan on a roundabout route of a thousand miles. Seven camels went lame on this first part of the journey, while the men ran out of food and were down to their last rations of water. Most of Laing's scientific equipment was also broken, as was his only rifle, which had been trodden on by a camel's "great gouty foot."

But it was Laing's romantic soul that provided the most significant early threat to the expedition. In Ghadames he received a packet of letters from his new bride, including a pallid portrait of her that had been commissioned in Tripoli. His sweetheart's consumptive appearance put Laing into a paroxysm. The following morning he wrote to Warrington, threatening to abandon his mission altogether as Emma was evidently pining for him:

> My Emma is ill, is melancholy, is unhappy—her sunken eye, her pale cheek, and colourless lip haunt my imagination, and adieu to resolution—Was I within a day's march of Tombuctoo, & to hear My Emma was ill—I wou'd turn about, and retrace my steps to Tripoli—What is Tombuctoo? What the Niger? what, the world to me? without my Emma?

By six p.m., though, he had recovered and was writing again, asking to be excused his "agitation of the morning." The following day he was pledging once again to perform his duty "like a Trojan."

After staying six weeks at Ghadames, Shaykh Babani's caravan left for the southwest, reaching In Salah, in the district of Tuat, on December 2. Here, far beyond the reach of the Tripolitanian authorities, Babani was changing: he was now "needy and avaricious in the extreme," wrote Laing. On January 9 they set out again. The caravan was jumpy. Every distant bush was taken for a mob of Tuareg marauders, and at one point Laing was mistaken for Mungo Park, but he paid little heed to the danger that implied. In the great arid plain of the Tanezrouft, which was "as flat as a bowling green, and as destitute of verdure as

Melville Island [in the Arctic Circle] in the depth of winter," a group of heavily armed Ahaggar Tuareg on fast camels joined them, riding side by side with the caravan. A few days later, after what Laing described as an act of "base treachery" by Babani, the Tuareg silently surrounded his tent at three a.m. and fell on him. The translator tried to run away but was caught and killed, as was one of the African sailors. The other was wounded in the leg, while Jack le Bore managed to escape. Laing, meanwhile, was shot and stabbed twenty-four times and left for dead.

Somehow, the gravely injured explorer managed to climb onto a camel that morning. He was carried a further four hundred miles to the territory of the powerful shaykh of the Kunta Arabs, Sidi Muhammad, where on May 10, 1826, he wrote to his father-in-law with his mangled left hand, detailing his appalling injuries. Even as Laing was convalescing, Sidi Muhammad's desert camp was overwhelmed with a catastrophe of its own. On July 1, Laing wrote again to Warrington with news, this time datelining his letter "Azoad":

> With a mind sadly depressed with sickness, sorrow, and disappointment, I lift an unwilling pen to acquaint you that I am no further on my Journey than when I last addressed you.

A sickness, "something similar to yellow fever," had swept through the camp and killed half the population, including Babani, Sidi Muhammad himself, and Jack le Bore. Laing had caught the fever too, but had recovered, and he was now the only one of his original party left alive. He was still suffering from "dreadful pains" in his head, arising from the severity of his wounds. Nevertheless, driven by a sense of destiny that bordered on madness, he determined to push on.

He was now only a few days' ride from Timbuktu, but the timing of his arrival in the region could hardly have been worse: the city was falling under the control of the Muslim ruler of the Fulani empire of Masina, Ahmad Lobbo. Lobbo had recently been warned by the sultan of the powerful Sokoto caliphate not to let Europeans visit the Sudan on account of the abuses and corruptions they had committed in Egypt and elsewhere, and now he wrote to the governor of Timbuktu, telling him ominously to "take from [Laing] all hope of returning to our dominions." The new Kunta shaykh, Sidi Muhammad's eldest son, al-Mukhtar al-Saghir, repeatedly warned the explorer not to continue, but Laing insisted. Shaykh al-Mukhtar did what he could: he provided an escort to Timbuktu and wrote to the town's governor, asking him to protect Laing.

Laing reached the city on August 13, 1826, a little over a year after leaving Tripoli, and five weeks later wrote his only letter from Timbuktu, to Warrington. He was not, strictly speaking, the first European ever to reach Timbuktu—Leo Africanus, after all, had been born in Europe and lived in Italy, and European mercenaries and renegades fought with the Moroccan army that invaded in 1591—but he was the first explorer to get there and send an account home, brief and cryptic though it was. If the city was a letdown, Laing was not going to say so now. It is likely that he spent weeks in Timbuktu filling his journals with observations he one day hoped to publish, but he didn't want to share these with the British government just yet, and suddenly there was no time: a party of Fulani was expected and he had been urged to leave immediately. He couldn't entirely disappoint his reader, however, so he stated simply that "the great Capital of central Africa" had "completely met [his] expectations" in every respect except size, and promised to write more fully from Segu, though the road ahead was "a vile one," and he knew his perils were not at an end.

Laing left Timbuktu around three p.m. the following day, September 22, accompanied by a freed slave, Bungola, and an Arab boy. He set out north into the desert, toward Arawan, on a roundabout route designed to avoid Lobbo's men. Then, like so many before, he disappeared.

THE SAHARA KEPT FEW SECRETS. Despite its immense size and small population, rumors traveled fast. Caravans picked up the gossip of every settlement they passed through, from the great markets to the smallest oases, and carried it with them to their destinations. It was always a surprise to students of the Sahara, the historian E. W. Bovill noted, that "in this tremendous desert everyone seemed to know what everyone else was doing." In the early nineteenth century, few pieces of information moved more quickly than news of an intruding European.

The first echoes of Laing's troubles reached Warrington in Tripoli in March 1826: there had been a treacherous attack on his party and the explorer had been badly injured. After that, the desert grapevine fell silent. As both consul and the explorer's father-in-law, Warrington was in a compromised position made worse by his daughter's distress and his own knowledge of the intrigue in the Tripolitanian court. Laing had traveled with the protection of the powerful pasha of Tripoli, Yusuf Karamanli, and now Warrington put Karamanli under great pressure to deliver news of Laing. In the spring of 1827, the pasha gave Warrington a copy of a report sent from Shaykh al-Mukhtar himself.

The leaders of Timbuktu had been embarrassed by their desire to look after their guest and the demands of their new sovereign, Ahmad Lobbo, the shaykh explained:

In order to reconcile the two interests, they permitted him to remain at Timbuctoo about a month . . . until he met with the enemy of God and his prophet, Hamed Ben Abayd Ben Rachal El Barbuchy, who persuaded him that he was able to conduct him to Arawan, from thence in order to embark at Sansandyng, and thence to continue his road to the great ocean.

The "enemy of God" was a shaykh of the Barabish (Bérabiche) Arabs who also went by the name Ahmadu Labeida. He and Laing left Timbuktu together, but halfway along the route the guide ordered his servants to seize Laing and kill him. Afterward they searched his baggage, whereupon "every thing of a useless nature, [such] as papers, letters, and books, were torn and thrown to the wind, for fear they should contain some magic, and the articles of value were retained." This, said Shaykh al-Mukhtar, was the faithful history of the circumstances of Laing's death.

Warrington forwarded the reports to the War and Colonial Office, without fully believing them. Some months later the British diplomat was aggrieved to hear of a letter sent on April 5 to the French newspaper *L'étoile*, which stated as fact that Laing was dead. There was no name attached to the letter, but it was datelined Sukkara-Ley-Tripoli, which happened to be the residence of the French consul, Baron Jean-Baptiste Rousseau. Warrington disapproved of the French in general and Rousseau in particular, and now he found a target for his wrath and grief. How could Rousseau know what Warrington did not? He conjured an elaborate plot among the French, Pasha Karamanli, and the pasha's foreign minister, a debt-ridden Francophile named Hassuna D'Ghies. This man, Warrington believed, had been in cahoots with the treacherous Babani all along, and may even have sponsored Laing's

eventual killer. As Warrington sent back reports hinting at this conspiracy, a Royal Navy frigate was diverted to Tripoli to persuade the
pasha to cooperate further with the consul's investigations. That day,
April 22, 1828, the pasha admitted for the first time that Laing was
dead. In August, Bungola arrived in Tripoli, where he confirmed that
the Barabish shaykh had "killed [the explorer,] being assisted by his
black servants by many cuts of sword when asleep." There was now no
doubt about Laing's fate.

The affair had a catastrophic effect on the already ailing Emma,
who remarried and moved to Italy, but died the following year, at the
age of twenty-eight, just four years after watching her beau ride out for
Timbuktu. Her desperate father, meanwhile, fixated on the explorer's
journals, refusing to believe Shaykh al-Mukhtar's assertion that they
had been destroyed. There was no doubt that they would contain vital
information about the interior that would make his son-in-law's name
and, equally important, prop up any future claim Britain might make
on the rich African interior. His suspicions once again turned on
D'Ghies and the French consul.

Rousseau in the meantime inadvertently fed his rival's paranoia by
declaring he had discovered the existence of a history of Timbuktu,
which he hoped would soon be in his possession. The baron's letters
announcing his findings were published in the Société de Géographie's *Bulletin* in 1827 and are almost certainly the first mentions in
European literature of the *Tarikh al-sudan*, although he didn't know
it was called that. Often misattributed to Ahmad Baba, the *Tarikh
al-sudan*, or "Chronicle of the Sudan," was written in the 1600s by
another Timbuktu scholar, Abd al-Rahman ibn Abd Allah al-Sadi.
Once found, it would become the essential text for historians of the
region.

In his first letter, Rousseau mused that the capital of the Sudan, "Tin-Buktou," had always escaped the most persevering investigations. "Everyone speaks of it, and no one has yet seen it." He hoped that, driven by the Société de Géographie's "noble and generous competition," there would come a traveler "who is happy to lift . . . the mysterious veil which will undress her to the eyes of European scholarship." In the meantime, the French consul continued, he had managed to collect a few pieces of information on the subject:

It seems there exists a detailed history of this town, which is written by a certain Sidi-Ahmed-Baba, a native of Arawan, a township of the [Kunta] country, a history which only puts its founding at 1116 AD. This is how, in this work, the circumstances which surrounded the foundation of Tin-Buktou are told:

"A woman from the Tuareg tribe, named Buktou, settled on the edge of the Nile of the Negroes, in a cabin sheltered by a bushy tree; she possessed some ewes, and liked to exercise her hospitality on the travelers of her nation who passed that way. Her humble house was not slow in becoming a sacred sanctuary, and a place of rest and of delight for the surrounding tribes, who called it Tin-Buktou, that is to say the property of Buktou (Tin being in their idiom a possessive pronoun for the third person). Next these tribes came from all sides to gather and made a vast camp, which was later transformed into a vast and populous city." This is, according to Sidi-Ahmed-Baba, the etymology of the name and the origin of the foundation of Tin-Buktou, of which, after all, the fame is perhaps only a chimera, which will vanish once we are able to surmount the many obstacles that prevent access.

More letters from Rousseau, dated March 3 and June 12, 1828, were published in the Societé de Geographie's *Bulletin* the following year. This time he or the *Bulletin*'s editors confused Ahmad Baba's name with that of the folk hero Ali Baba: "I hope to be soon in possession of the history of Timbuktu by Sidi Ali Baba of Arawan, which I am awaiting from Touat," Rousseau wrote.

For Warrington, this was further evidence of French dirty tricks. How could Rousseau be in a position to get hold of the "Ali Baba" history of Timbuktu when no Frenchman had reached the city? Was this the volume to which Laing had alluded in his sole letter from that place, in which he had written that he had been "amply rewarded" in his searches of the town's records? There was a simple explanation for the missing papers: the French had stolen them. The more he pursued this line of investigation, the more witnesses came forward to give him the answer he desired. Bungola told him D'Ghies had taken personal possession of Laing's papers, while an ex-employee of Rousseau's said he had seen D'Ghies handing over documents to the French consul in exchange for money. D'Ghies must have found the fruits of Laing's journey, Warrington surmised, and sold them to the French to help pay his debts.

As Warrington squared up to Rousseau over the missing Laing papers, news was about to break of a second European who had reached Timbuktu. The development was doubly bad for Warrington, since the explorer was French.

RENÉ CAILLIÉ was in many ways Laing's antithesis. He was modest, the son of a convict, orphaned at eleven, a neglected child with a dreamy, even melancholic character. One of his few pieces of early luck was the appearance in his life of a teacher who encouraged him to read adventure stories. Like Laing's, Caillié's imagination was inflamed by Robinson Crusoe, but nothing in the literature excited him as much as the map of Africa. As a child, he had scanned the continent's mammalian shape, from rounded rump to rhinoceros horn, and pored over its fantastical annotations. What undiscovered cities lay in those gaps? What unseen creatures? What unknown civilizations? His passion for geography grew into an obsession. He would make his name, he decided, with some important discovery on this little-explored continent. He cut himself off from his friends, renounced sports and other amusements, and devoted his spare time to books and maps. At sixteen—the same tender age as the nineteenth century—he left home with sixty francs, bound for Africa.

The first decade of Caillié's exploring career was an education in what could go wrong for European adventurers. The vessel on which he worked his passage south, the *Loire*, sailed from France in company with the frigate *Medusa*, a ship whose name lives in infamy. The *Medusa* was wrecked on the notorious shoals of Arguin, an island on the west coast close to Cape Blanco, whereupon her captain and officers took to the boats, consigning 147 lower ranks to a makeshift raft, which they cut adrift. Only fifteen people survived the scenes of drunken fighting, starvation, and cannibalism that broke out on board, which were immortalized by Théodore Géricault in his painting *The Raft of the Medusa*, a metaphor for the corruption of the French elite.

Caillié would soon find equally significant disasters were unfolding on land. Among these was a large British expedition to the interior and Timbuktu under Major John Peddie, which set out from a swampy malarial region at the mouth of the Nunez River. Peddie died of fever before he had even left the coast, and his expedition penetrated just three hundred miles inland before it was forced to return with half its officers dead. Undeterred, the British tried again, this time starting from the Gambia, but the expedition was so expertly milked by the king of Bondu that its commander, Major William Gray, soon had to send to the coast for more gifts. Caillié joined the resupply caravan, which carried too much baggage and too little water into the desert. The young man's eyes became hollow with dehydration, and he watched other men grow so desperate they drank their own urine. Later, he caught a fever, and was lucky to make it back to France alive. There he heard that these failed British military expeditions had cost the extraordinary sum of £750,000, worth about $3.4 million at the time.

Still, Caillié persevered. In 1824 he returned to Africa with his own idea for an assault on the interior. Unlike the failures he had witnessed, his mission would be low-cost and low-key. He would disguise himself as a poor Egyptian Arab who had been kidnapped by French troops as a child and was now heading home to Alexandria. He spent three years preparing for this role, studying Arabic and the Islamic texts, perfecting his cover story, learning how to dress, pray, and eat like a Muslim. Neither the French nor the British would sponsor his solo mission, but the Société de Géographie prize would be reward enough. He would give the money to his sister, who was living in poverty in France.

"Dead or alive," he swore to himself, "it shall be mine."

Caillié left the coast of Guinea on April 19, 1827, in Arab costume, carrying a Kuran and the essential umbrella. He climbed through the malarial swamps into the Guinea highlands, and struggled over mountain passes and ravines and torrents swollen by tropical storms. He took shade from the sun under spreading bombax trees and ate tamarind fruit to ward off the fever that always threatened to overtake him. In the uplands of Futa Jallon he crossed the Niger—even here, close to its source, it was two hundred yards wide—and at Kankan he survived an attempt by his guide to unmask him as a Christian. His feet broke out in bleeding sores and an attack of scurvy stripped the roof of his mouth to bare bone, but he recovered. He carried on. In March 1828 he reached Jenne, on the Bani River, where he found a boat that would take him north to the Niger, and then 250 miles farther to Kabara, the port of Timbuktu. On April 19, 1828, a year to the day after setting out, he was at last close to his objective.

At one p.m. that day, he was hiding in the bottom of the boat when the crew called down to tell him they were approaching Kabara, and he hurried out on deck. At first he could see nothing but marshland covered with aquatic birds; then the little port town that served Timbuktu appeared, perched above the floodline on a small hill. The water in the river was too low for the boat to get close, so he climbed into a canoe, which was dragged through the shallows by slaves.

It was no Le Havre or Marseilles, but there was a buzz about Kabara. The quay was busy with men and women carrying goods back and forth, while shipwrights worked to repair canoes that had been hauled out to the foreshore. The narrow streets of the town itself were filled with a hubbub of people selling fish, milk, cola nuts, and pistachios, while strings of donkeys and camels passed continually, carrying merchandise to Timbuktu. It was the last day of Ramadan, and at dusk the town celebrated with dancing and festivities.

At half past three the following afternoon, Caillié joined a small caravan assembling on the road to Timbuktu.

The path north was white with shining sand so soft it made walking difficult. It led past unexpected lakes whose banks were overgrown with vegetation, and through a dwarf forest of palms, mimosas, and gum acacias. For much of the journey they were followed by a Tuareg man mounted on a superb horse who eyed him narrowly and asked the caravan drivers where he had come from, but the horseman lost interest after being told Caillié was a poor Egyptian. Two and a half miles along the track, at the halfway point between Kabara and Timbuktu, they reached an infamous murder spot known as "They Hear Not," since from there cries for help could not be heard at either town. The caravan moved safely through it. The sun was touching the horizon when, two miles farther on, the track climbed a bare dune. From the top, at last, Caillié could see his destination.

The city lay long and low before him, stretched between an immense sky and an immense desert. "Nothing diminishes the vast landscape which is lighted by the throbbing glare of the veritable sun of the desert," a later traveler wrote of reaching this spot. "Truly she is enthroned upon the horizon with the majesty of a queen. She is indeed the city of imagination, the Timbuctoo of European legend." Caillié was overcome:

> I now saw this capital of the Soudan, to reach which had so long been the object of my wishes. On entering this mysterious city, which is an object of curiosity and research to the civilised nations of Europe, I experienced an indescribable satisfaction. I never before felt a similar emotion and my transport was extreme.

He was unable to share his joy for fear of giving away his identity. Instead he silently gave thanks to his God: the obstacles and dangers had appeared insurmountable, but with the Lord's protection he had achieved the object of his ambition.

As he approached more closely, however, his excitement began to fade. Timbuktu was not quite as magnificent as he had expected:

The city presented, at first view, nothing but a mass of ill-looking houses, built of earth. Nothing was to be seen in all directions but immense plains of quicksand of a yellowish white colour. The sky was a pale red as far as the horizon: all nature wore a dreary aspect, and the most profound silence prevailed; not even the warbling of a bird was to be heard.

Its buildings were not tall or especially large; most consisted of a single story. The town had no walls. There wasn't a breath of wind, and when he lay down to sleep the oppressive heat made him more uncomfortable than ever. The following morning, examining the town in daylight, he found it wasn't nearly as big or as busy as he had been led to believe. Its vaunted market was a desert compared with that of Jenne. Its atmosphere was soporific. "Everything had a dull appearance," he noted. "I was surprised at the inactivity, I may even say indolence, displayed in the city."

As Baron Rousseau had suspected, the great city of gold-roofed houses was a chimera. "Exaggerated notions" of this "object of curiosity for so many ages" had prevailed, Caillié wrote, including its population, civilization, and trade with the Sudan. It was small, three miles in circuit, and roughly triangular in shape, and it had been raised on soil that was "totally unfit for cultivation" and had no vegetation but stunted trees and shrubs.

Still, the city had a few redeeming features that would leaven his disappointment. Its streets were clean, and its inhabitants neat and—

contrary to what Park had been told—gentle and obliging to strangers. The women were not veiled like those in Morocco and were allowed to go out when they pleased and visit anyone they chose. There were seven mosques in all, two of which were large, and each was surmounted by a brick minaret. Climbing the tower of the great mosque of Jingere Ber, Caillié could only admire the fact that a town had been built here at all: "I could not help contemplating with astonishment the extraordinary city before me, created solely by the wants of commerce, and destitute of every resource except what its accidental position as a place of exchange affords."

The ruler of Timbuktu was a merchant named Osman, who had inherited a considerable fortune from his ancestors, and was, gratifyingly, "very rich." He received Caillié while sitting on a beautiful mat with a luxurious cushion:

The king appeared to be of an exceedingly amiable disposition; his age might be about fifty-five, and his hair was white and curly. He was of the middling height, and his colour was jet black. He had an aquiline nose, thin lips, a grey beard, and large eyes, and his whole countenance was pleasing; his dress, like those of the Moors, was composed of stuff of European manufacture. On his head was a red cap, bound round with a large piece of muslin in the form of a turban. His shoes were of morocco, shaped like our morning slippers, and made in the country. He often visited the mosque.

Trading was the lifeblood of this, "one of the largest cities" Caillié had seen in Africa, and "the principal *entrepôt*" of this part of the continent. There were many Moroccans here, who stayed for six to eight months to sell their goods and buy more to carry north. In trade, wrote Caillié, the people were industrious and intelligent; and the merchants were generally wealthy, occupying the finest houses in the city and owning many slaves. Merchandise consisted mainly of salt and other goods that reached Timbuktu by caravan or boat. There were even articles from Europe: Caillié found double-barreled guns with the mark of the state-owned French armament factory at Saint-Étienne, as well as European "glass wares, amber, coral, sulphur, paper &c." "Paper &c" was the closest Caillié came to mentioning manuscripts.

The Frenchman stayed a fortnight. He devoted his last few days to trying to work out what had happened to Laing, whose name he had heard in Jenne, and was shown the spot where he was said to have been murdered. Caillié secretly shed a tear—"the only tribute of regret I could render to the ill-fated traveller." He left Timbuktu on May 4, 1828, traveling with a caravan carrying ostrich feathers, ivory, gold, and slaves to the markets of Morocco. His host, Sidi Abdallahi Chebir, an "excellent man," gave him enough merchandise to fund his onward journey and awoke early on the day of departure to accompany him for some distance, before he affectionately pressed Caillié's hand and wished him well.

The men of the caravan were less hospitable. The drivers showed no mercy to the penniless traveler, and were worse with the slaves. Water was always so short that Caillié felt constantly to be on the verge of death, and the drivers refused to give him more even when he begged. Sandstorms threatened to bury the whole caravan, forming at times into great dust devils. Yet as they trekked beneath the burning sky, he couldn't help being awed by the immensity of the desert landscape, with its boundless horizons and immense, shining plains.

. . .

CAILLIÉ REACHED the French consulate at Tangier on September 7, 507 days after setting out. He was exhausted, ill, and dressed in rags, but was able at last to remove his disguise, put on European clothes, and find a ship bound for Toulon. There he wrote to Jomard at the Société de Géographie, who immediately sent five hundred francs to cover the cost of his journey to the French capital. In Paris, Jomard and his colleagues interrogated the explorer in order to verify his account, which they pronounced to be genuine: he had achieved "every thing possible . . . more than could have been hoped for with such resources," and had "completely succeeded." Despite British objections, Caillié was awarded the prize money and, in 1830, the gold medal, although it was agreed that this should be shared with Laing.

Caillié's victory was met with triumphalist crowing in France. "Here we have a subject of glory for France, and of jealousy for her eternal rival!" declared one French newspaper. "That which England has not been able to accomplish, with the aid of a whole group of travellers, and at an expense of more than twenty millions, a Frenchman has done with his scanty personal resources alone, and without putting his country to any expense." The British responded with fury. How could a humble, ill-educated Frenchman reach the goal they had been pursuing for decades? The intensity of Timbuktu fever had produced numerous false claims in recent years; surely Caillié's account was just another lie. Most likely he had been shipwrecked on the coast of Barbary and heard some vague intelligence about the interior that he had pretended was his own. His Muslim disguise only added to the British outrage: If an explorer was prepared to swap religion willy-nilly, how could his observations possibly be trusted?

"This eternal cant and whining about the 'jealousy' and 'rivalry' of England" implied only "a constantly-recurring consciousness of the intellectual and physical superiority of our countrymen over theirs," thundered *The Quarterly Review*, before going on to do its utmost to discredit Caillié's "imposture." Laing was the rightful discoverer of Timbuktu, while Caillié was "illiterate," and Jomard had been less than scrupulous in verifying his journey. "We shall offer no opinion whether M. Caillié did or did not reach Timbuctoo," stated the *Review*'s anonymous critic, "but we do not hesitate to say that, for any information he has brought back, as to the geography of Central Africa, or the course of the Joliba, he might just as well have staid at home." The diatribe concluded with a long and well-briefed account of the British conspiracy theory that held that Rousseau and D'Ghies had stolen Laing's papers.

Caillié was deeply wounded by these attacks, which affected him more, he said, than "all the hardships, fatigues and privations" he had encountered in the interior of Africa.

In Tripoli, the fêting of the Frenchman drove Warrington to scour the desert ever harder for Laing's journals, which now bore the double burden of rescuing his country's and his son-in-law's glory. October 1828 found him writing to the War and Colonial Office of the "Miserable Intrigue" in which he had "cause to suspect the French Consul may have purloined the Papers of Major Laing." By May 1829, he was informing the British government that D'Ghies was expecting not only a copy of the "History of Tomboucto" but also the arrival from Tuat of its author "Sidi Ali Baba d'Arowan." (This despite the fact that *Ahmad* Baba had been dead for more than two hundred years.)

At first, Warrington said, he had been inclined to ridicule the idea of a history of Timbuktu being produced in Africa, because he did not believe any African would be interested in his country's past. "Is it likely," he asked, "that this Sidi Ali Baba should have examined the Records and written the History of Tinbuctu—Believe me a Bowl of Cuscusou is more an object of Research to any Moor than such a history." However, he was now convinced that the "Ali Baba" history must have been obtained in Timbuktu by Laing, and was therefore evidence of the French plot. "We are surely justified," he announced, "in believing that Laing was in possession of the History of Tenbuctu." It was a short step from this fantasy to the conclusion that whoever possessed a copy of this "History" also possessed Laing's journals.

To force the pasha to produce the documents, Warrington broke off diplomatic relations in June that year and hauled down his Union Jack. The pasha, whose survival relied on playing British power off against the French, was horrified. On August 5 he let it be known that a group of people were coming from the desert who would indeed testify that Laing's papers had been given to D'Ghies and the French consul. D'Ghies, reading the political wind, decided to run: three days later he was smuggled out of Tripoli on an American corvette. Shortly afterward, the pasha ordered that the French flag be hauled down from Rousseau's consulate.

Warrington's state of mind is revealed in a letter he wrote to the undersecretary of state for the colonies, R. W. Hay, on August 10, 1829, announcing on his honor, "Should you wish to take any steps with the French authorities you may safely do it, as I am apprehensive Mr. Rousseau will fly to America also, as soon as he hears His Infamous Villany is detected. He has not only defrauded the English Government of the journals & manuscripts of Major Laing, but he has stole also Letters to His Wife, to me & my Family."

It was, concluded Warrington, "really too horrid to continue."

Two days later, Warrington's deranged assault on Rousseau culminated in the offer of a duel. The baron had already had enough: fearing for his life, he had appealed to the United States for help in fleeing Tripoli and, like D'Ghies, been smuggled aboard an American ship. With *l'affaire Laing* now a full-blown diplomatic crisis, the French government appointed a commission to investigate Warrington's claims. Later that year, it pronounced Rousseau innocent of all charges.

The fallout was not yet over. France had been made to look a fool and needed redress. In 1830, a French squadron arrived in Tripoli harbor and ordered the pasha publicly to retract all charges against their consul and repay debts to his French creditors of 800,000 francs. With his throne room in range of French guns, the pasha had to concede. Short now of both money and credibility, the rule of the Karamanli dynasty was nearing its end: in 1832 the pasha was overthrown and direct Ottoman rule was reinstated soon afterward. The once powerful ruler of Tripoli died in rags in a hovel a short distance from the palace he had occupied for so long.

Rousseau fared little better. No copy of the *Tarikh al-sudan*, the manuscript that could have made his name, seems to have reached him. After the French intervention, he returned to Tripoli, but suspicions remained in Paris and London about his conduct, and he died soon afterward, in 1831. Caillié's story ended a little more happily. He was made a member of the Légion d'Honneur and was awarded a pension, and the three-volume account of his travels, published at public expense in 1830, made him a famous man. Though he was unsuccessful in gaining support for further expeditions to Africa, he lived with his wife and children on a farm in western France until May 17, 1838, when he succumbed to tuberculosis. Warrington meanwhile remained in Tripoli until 1846, at which point he was forced to resign after arguing with the consul of Naples over a box of cigars. He moved to Patras, Greece, where he died the following year. Laing's journals had not been found.

As for the object of European lust: Timbuktu had been attained, but not in the way anyone would have wished. Caillié's public deflation of the gilded myth that had endured since the Middle Ages did, however, inspire a nineteen-year-old Cambridge undergraduate to verse. In 1829, the year after the French explorer's return, the young Alfred, Lord Tennyson, entered his poem "Timbuctoo" into the university's poetry competition. It told the tale of how "Discovery" had punctured the dream of argent streets and tremulous domes that were once thought to have existed in the Saharan city:

> O City! O latest Throne! Where I was rais'd
> To be a mystery of loveliness
> Unto all eyes, the time is well-nigh come
> When I must render up this glorious home
> To keen Discovery: soon yon brilliant towers
> Shall darken with the waving of her wand;
> Darken, and shrink and shiver into huts,
> Black specks amid a waste of dreary sand,
> Low-built, mud-wall'd, Barbarian settlements.
> How chang'd from this fair City!

By the end of the poem, "The Moon / had fallen from the night, and all was dark!"

7.

ISMAEL'S LIST

APRIL 2012

I t looked as if Timbuktu had been bombed with paper. Outside each state building—the mairie, the governorate, the banks—lay a carpet of typed, printed, or handwritten documents, the achievements of a hundred years of state bureaucracy. Administrators had worked since colonial times to collect details of every aspect of Timbuktien life, but in their trashing of the city's offices, the rebels had pulled the files from every bookshelf and cabinet and chucked them into the roads and alleyways, where they now lay trampled underfoot. Ismael Diadié Haidara, out near the southern entrance to town one day, passed a dune covered with sheets of paper that riffled in the warm wind. Houday Ag Mohamed, himself a government official of long standing, recalled: "The town's soul was laid bare. Its most closely guarded secrets lay in the streets." For those who viewed the world through the lens of manuscripts, it was a warning of what might come.

After his long drive north, Haidara remained with his wife and five children at their home in Hamabangou. During those days he spent much of the time on the phone, talking to his friends and colleagues, and occasionally to journalists too. Since the jihadists' arrival, the chaos in the city had been largely brought under control, he told a reporter for the magazine *Le point*. There had not yet been any serious threat to the libraries, but these were uncertain times: "The problem is that we do not know really what is happening, and still less about what tomorrow will bring," he said.

Heritage organizations outside Mali were growing increasingly alarmed. On Tuesday, April 3, the day after Ansar Dine's takeover, the director-general of UNESCO, Irina Bokova, issued an alert for the city's historic buildings: "Timbuktu's outstanding earthen architectural wonders that are the great mosques of Jingere Ber, Sankore, and Sidi Yahya must be safeguarded," she said, calling the city "essential to the preservation of the identity of the people of Mali and of our universal heritage." Others foresaw serious danger for the manuscripts. "I have no faith in the rebels," said Shamil Jeppie, the head of the University of Cape Town's Tombouctou Manuscripts Project. "They may have an educated leadership, but they are sending in footsoldiers who are illiterate and if they want something they will take it. . . . They won't have any respect for paper culture."

A petition begun by a group of fifty-one leading scholars and library directors now started to gain traction on the Internet. Calling for the manuscripts to be protected lest an important part of world memory be "annihilated," the petition attracted the names of more than 1,500 academics from universities in seventy-four countries, including Yale, Harvard, Oxford, Cambridge, and the Sorbonne. The head of the West African research institute IFAN, meanwhile, warned that the precious documents might be illegally sold or destroyed by the occupiers. "These manuscripts have survived through the ages thanks to a secular order," said the scholar Hamady Bocoum. "With the arrival of the Islamists, that secular order is broken, that culture is in danger."

Ismael was worrying about the end of the secular order too. Al-Qaeda had a long-standing threat against teachers of French in Mali, and the education system was one of the early targets for Ansar Dine's Islamification program. The jihadists ordered that boys and girls be separated, but there weren't enough teachers left to take the extra classes, so schools remained closed. A ban on teaching philosophy was also announced, which Ismael found personally threatening, since as far as he was aware he was the only one in the city who taught it. He had a large library of printed books devoted to the subject, including works by Plato, Aristotle, Seneca, Spinoza, and Montaigne, and he knew the red-bearded jihadist Hamaha was aware of its existence since he and his elder brother, a family friend, used to come round to read them.

Ismael's greater concern, though, was for his manuscripts. He had been busy in his Fondo Kati library, and by Wednesday the documents had already been hidden in places he refused to divulge even two and a half years later. "Like that, even if the men came into the building, they were not going to find anything," was all he would say.

He wasn't the only one hiding manuscripts. The al-Wangari library, which was said to be based on the original collection of the sixteenth-century Timbuktu scholar Muhammad Baghayogho, was in the care of its guardian Mohamed Cissé while its proprietor was abroad. At eleven a.m. on Thursday, Cissé was disturbed by an anonymous phone tip-off. "Be careful," the voice said, "bad people are in front of your gate."

The call put Cissé in a funk. What could he do? He had to go see who these "bad people" were and find out what they wanted. When he reached the library building, which stands at an intersection in the warren of streets behind the Sidi Yahya mosque, he saw two jihadist pickups parked out front. As far as he could tell, the armed men didn't intend to go inside, but even so he was worried. That night he called the patron, Mukhtar bin Yahya al-Wangari, to tell him what had happened, and they agreed the manuscripts should be moved. Two days later, Cissé and Mukhtar's elderly brother came to the library in the dark with a few sacks and some lockers to begin the process.

"I looked at the atmosphere [around the library], checking whether it was really calm and that there were no people with guns loitering on the corner," Cissé recalled. The street was empty, so they slipped inside and locked the door behind them, then began to take the manuscripts down from their shelves and place them in the sacks and lockers. They were too flustered to prioritize the more important documents; they just grabbed what they could. It took thirty minutes to an hour to fill each locker. "Every time we took a manuscript, we had to do it softly, to be careful that we didn't damage them, because the folios are very old. That was why it took a lot of time." When a box was full, it was closed with two padlocks. They put some manuscripts in sacks as well, but these were hard to carry.

They listened carefully before leaving, and when the street outside was quiet, they took a deep breath and unlocked the door. One man carried the lockers in a handcart, or *push-push*, while the other brought the cumbersome bags. Mukhtar's brother lived a short distance away, across the main road from the Sidi Yahya mosque, and they took the manuscripts to his house and placed them in a dark room, covering them with other household objects so that even if someone came in and looked around, they wouldn't be seen.

Hiding manuscripts was not an option at the most visible library, the new Ahmad Baba building in Sankore, which contained around 15,000 of the institute's total collection of 38,803 documents. The head of the institute had been working his last days in the job before handing it over to a new director, and he had fled the city that week. Abdoulaye Cissé, a tall man with an angular face, was now the organization's senior official in Timbuktu. On Thursday, he too received an anonymous tip-off. "There are bandits who want to come to destroy your library," he was told. There was only one thing he could do, he decided: ask the city's new occupiers for help.

He set off for the military camp, where the jihadists were now based, and asked a bearded sentry in combat fatigues if he could speak with Iyad Ag Ghaly. But the Ansar Dine leader wasn't there, and instead Cissé was passed to another commander, a Chadian called Adama who would become known for wearing a suicide vest wherever he went. Cissé explained that he had received a threat that the Ahmad Baba building was going to be looted, and told him it must be protected at all costs. Adama promised to see what he could do.

Two days later, a group of jihadists arrived in Sankore and started to deploy around the building. Cissé went to talk to them, telling them he worked for the institute and was a Timbuktien—"I am from the town and I will not leave the town," he said—and that he had to come in regularly to check that everything was safe, that was his job. They agreed to let him look around whenever he wanted, and he continued to visit the premises every few days to see that no more damage had been done.

At the old Ahmad Baba building on the Rue de Chemnitz, the caretaker Abba Traoré and his grandson Hassini had been trying to fend off groups of looters who asked them to open the storerooms, telling them they didn't have any keys. When they explained this problem to the jihadists, they were given a note in Arabic that said the building was under their protection and must be left alone. "If looters came, I would show them the paper, and they would go," recalled Hassini. "That was how we did it."

THROUGHOUT APRIL, as the days grew hotter, people drained out of northern Mali. Refugees packed their bags with a few essentials, locked their homes, and went to join whatever transportation they could find. Some set out for neighboring countries—Mauritania, Burkina Faso, Côte d'Ivoire—where they ended up in refugee camps; others went to southern Mali, stopping in Segu, Mopti, or Bamako. Almost half a million people would leave the north that year. Some went to stay with relatives, sharing small apartments with families who had been struggling to get by even before the crisis, living on handouts from the World Food Programme and charities that had been in the country for decades. Adults lost their jobs, children lost their schooling, and at every stage of their flight the refugees were robbed, by the rebels in the land they were fleeing and by the *militaires* in the territory they were running to.

They fled mostly because they were scared. "Everyone you saw, you could read the fear on their face," Diagayeté recalled. He remembered his family being so afraid they could barely eat. "Everyone was frightened. People didn't know what was going to happen that day, or what would happen the following day." Rumors of rebel atrocities ran around the town. "People said if you are an artist they would cut out your tongue, because they hate music and want to ban it," said Bintu Guerba, a singer. The jihadists didn't cut out tongues, but they did ban music and punish people for playing it, so she fled to Bamako.

Even those who wanted to stay found they had no means to live. With the town ransacked and the state workers gone, much of the city's infrastructure had shut down. The jihadists had saved the electricity plant, but it was low on fuel and there were frequent power shortages and blackouts. Few shops were open, and every bank had been smashed up, so there was no way of getting money. Diagayeté's main reason for being in Timbuktu was his job at the institute, but now the institute was closed. "I said to myself, when the little cash I have in my pockets is finished, what will happen next?" he remembered. "I can cope, but how about my little children? If my money runs out, how would I be able to get away, or even eat?" When he found a place on a truck heading south on the third day of the occupation, he didn't hesitate. He dropped some computers and hard drives with scans of manuscripts at the house of a colleague—it was just a small part of the collection, but he did what he could—then he left.

Alkadi and his wife, Fatouma, discussed leaving every day. Their house was in the Arab and Tuareg neighborhood of Abaraju, where many of the rebels and their sympathizers lived, and now they felt intimidated. They would see AQIM leaders in the street daily, and all their neighbors who had dark skin like them had gone or were preparing to go: whatever the jihadists said about all races being equal before God, Alkadi and Fatouma didn't believe it. Alkadi lived next to a shop that sold mobile phone credits, and one day a group of looters banged on his door, believing that he ran the shop. He told Fatouma to lock herself in after that.

He still went out daily, riding around town on his little motorbike, observing. Sometimes he stopped by the bus station in the middle of the Grand Marché, trying to gauge how easy it would be to leave, but it was always so busy with people that he couldn't even get in. His colleagues were all fleeing: each day he would discover that another one had left. Once a group of them asked him to go with them in a car they had rented, but he said no, there was still too much chaos. It was better to stay until things had settled down and then see what to do. He still believed the Malian army might come back and retake the town.

Alkadi and his colleagues kept in touch with Abba, the caretaker at the old Ahmad Baba building on the Rue de Chemnitz, where most of the manuscripts—around 24,000—were still held. Although gunmen had been sniffing around, the manuscripts were safe. It was the MNLA who had posed the gravest danger, and now that they had been chased out, the threat wasn't so great. "We didn't worry about the jihadists at the start, because the manuscripts spoke of Islam," he remembered. "They spoke of good things. Since these people were Muslims, they would never harm them."

Anyway, even if they had wanted to, they couldn't move the manuscripts. There were far too many.

OF THE MANY ACCOUNTS of flight from Timbuktu, none was more colorful than that of Ismael Diadié Haidara. It was, he said later, like a Malian *Schindler's List*.

With his manuscripts hidden, he decided to leave quietly on the first Saturday after the occupation, April 7, and hired a pickup to take him to the river, where the Fondo Kati had a boat. The vehicle arrived at dawn that day, and he gathered his children and his belongings. Opening the front door of his house, he found a crowd of more than fifty friends and neighbors standing in the street with their bags.

"What are you doing here?" he asked.

"We are coming with you," they said.

The quiet exit he had envisaged would be impossible with so many. Ansar Dine or the MNLA would be bound to hear the commotion and come to investigate, and anyway the truck he had hired wasn't nearly big enough to carry them. But they were desperate. He had to try. He told them to climb on—there were two women in their eighties, as well as children and even babies—and when the truck was completely over-loaded he told the others the driver would come back. Ismael then climbed in with his two children—the only members of his family who were with him in Timbuktu—as well as a computer and four of his most precious manuscripts, which he carried in a bag. The driver warned him that if the men at the first checkpoint saw the bag, it would be stolen, but he could hide it in the space under his seat, so that was where it was put.

As the truck started to move, the people left behind began to cry. Ismael told the driver to stop and went over to reassure them. "You are going to leave Timbuktu," he said. "Not a single person will stay here." Then he climbed back into the overburdened vehicle, which set off to-ward the river.

They were stopped at an MNLA checkpoint by the turnoff to the airport, where two rebel fighters covered them with guns while others climbed into the truck to search it, asking if they had weapons or were hiding soldiers. "No," Ismael told them, "there are no soldiers here. We are all civilians." After examining the bags thoroughly, the MNLA waved them on, and the truck continued toward the ferry at Koriume. There they were stopped again, and again everyone was asked to get out while the MNLA fighters searched the vehicle.

"Who is in charge here?" asked the commander.

Ismael came forward.

"If you want to leave," the commander said, "I will first have to explain who we are and why we have become the MNLA." He then launched into a political speech that lasted more than ten minutes, telling the refugees that they fought for everyone, not just the Tuareg but all the people of the north, whom they intended to free from the domination of the Malian government. He explained the origin and purpose of the movement, even down to the design of the MNLA flag, and when he had finished, he asked if everyone understood. The passengers nodded.

He took Ismael by the shoulder: "What do you say?"

"You ask me my opinion, so I will tell you what I think," Ismael said. "I think you have done a very bad thing. If you came here to liberate the population, instead of burning houses and shooting and making people afraid, you should explain this to the people in Timbuktu, then I am almost sure that a big part of them will follow you. You have to take the people into account. We have an opinion too. We can agree with you, or disagree."

The commander called over another man, whose desert turban was wrapped around his face so that only his eyes were visible. He asked Ismael to repeat what he had said, and a discussion began that ran on for almost thirty minutes. By the time they had finished, the driver of the pickup had returned to Timbuktu to collect the second group from the library and bring them to Koriume.

It was now after two p.m., and the political arguments were still being exchanged when the masked rebel said that if they wanted to leave, they must go immediately, since he and his men were about to be relieved and they couldn't guarantee the next group would let them out.

Ismael thanked him.

"One more thing," said the masked man. "At nightfall, wherever you are, stop there. They will shoot anything that moves."

The refugees went to the port, where they climbed aboard the Fondo Kati's *pinasse*. They had traveled only a short distance upriver by nightfall, but Ismael, heeding the rebel's advice, told the boat's captain to stop at the next village. They were welcomed with food and mattresses in the villagers' houses, and at five the following morning they continued toward Mopti. It took almost a week, but eventually all of Ismael's passengers reached government territory.

In Bamako, the librarian moved into an empty house that belonged to his brother. "I was with all my family then," he said. He was also with his four most precious manuscripts, which he had evacuated from Timbuktu.

As ISMAEL WAS SETTING OFF UPRIVER, Haidara left his house to look around the city. It was a week into the occupation, and the first time he had ventured out since his arrival the previous Sunday. He walked south toward the administrative quarter, passing the mairie and the governorate in the Place de l'Indépendance. The paper that was scattered about the streets alarmed him: it was precisely this sort of danger that had brought him back to Timbuktu. "Truly that made me feel bad," he said. "They had started with the government buildings and moved on to all the other administrative buildings. They were all ransacked." There was still some looting, and he understood that if it carried on, they would eventually come to the libraries, which were often housed in grand buildings and were obvious targets.

He returned to the house in a state of anxiety, determined to "do something." It was impossible to hold meetings at the time, so he spent the next days speaking on the phone to his colleagues and friends among the major library-owning families. "They asked me, 'What do you want to say? We see the paper in the streets, the damage, yes, but what do you suggest?'"

They should pack the manuscripts in chests and lockers, he said, and bring them into the family homes.

"They said, 'Okay, we agree, but we do not have the money to buy lockers. We can't do it.'"

Haidara didn't have any cash either, but he did have a $12,000 grant from the Ford Foundation that was meant to pay for him to learn English at Oxford University. He hadn't used it—nor, friends said, did he intend to—and now he sent a message to the foundation saying he wanted authorization to spend the money on the manuscripts. "They said, 'Sure, it's done, it's authorized,'" Haidara recalled.

His next difficulty was to get his hands on the money. The banks had been looted, but transportation was still working, so he wrote a check and sent it with a colleague 250 miles south to Mopti, which was still in government hands. It was too much money to take out all at once, so he did a deal with a trader there who agreed to hold it and pay out small amounts as needed. Now he had a pot of money—five or six million West African francs—with which he could purchase lockers. He bought them almost daily in the market after that, until the city had run out and more had to be ordered in. Eventually the supply in Mopti would run out too, and Haidara would have to have them made, buying empty oil drums in Timbuktu and sending them south to be worked into lockers and shipped north again.

Haidara was not alone in asking people to move their manuscripts into their houses; and many manuscript-owning families, including Ismael and the al-Wangaris, didn't need to be told. Sane Chirfi Alpha said that in those early days of occupation there was a "discreet meeting," which was aimed largely at the manuscripts belonging to the Ahmad Baba institute. "We met with the members of the High Islamic Council," he said. "They felt they had to do something to move the manuscripts." In the end it seemed too risky to try to move the state archive, but others were advised to try to move their manuscripts discreetly: "They passed the message among themselves that each one should smuggle his manuscripts and hide them where he could."

The operation progressed rapidly—in Haidara's case a little too rapidly. In the second week of occupation, a television crew from Al Jazeera visited Timbuktu. Mohamed Vall, the channel's North Africa correspondent, had been given permission by Ansar Dine to report on life in the occupied town, and he asked about the manuscript collections. The jihadists told him they were perfectly safe, and he should see for himself.

On Saturday, April 14, Vall went to see Haidara's nephew Mohamed Touré, who looked after the Mamma Haidara Memorial Library, and told him he wanted to do a tour of the building to see the famous manuscripts. Touré started to sweat: he knew the place was almost empty and he might be accused of stealing. The library wasn't worth seeing, he told Vall—really, there was nothing of interest there, it wouldn't make good TV, and anyway he wasn't free to show him around. Vall went back to tell the jihadists what had happened.

Shortly afterward, gunmen showed up at Touré's house with the television crew in tow. "They forced me to go to the library," said Touré. "I went, I opened it up, they filmed it all, they saw the places, the offices, everywhere." But there was nothing there: the camera zoomed in on empty shelves and cupboards. The only manuscripts they could find were several boxes Touré had hidden in a bathroom.

Where are the rest? Vall asked, as his escort of three jihadists waited by the library door. "I don't know," lied Touré. "You'll have to talk to the boss. I'm not in the loop."

Vall filed a somewhat confused report.

Abdoulaye Cissé meanwhile continued to visit the new building at Sankore to check that nothing more was being looted. In the second week, he found a new jihadist in charge whom he didn't recognize. The senior leaders had taken up residence in the building, Cissé was told, and he couldn't come in. A few days later, Cissé heard that the "senior leaders" included Abdelhamid Abou Zeid, who had moved in with several French hostages. The Ahmad Baba institute had become a jihadist barracks.

Cissé would not be allowed inside again.

PART TWO

DESTRUCTION

\\\\\\\\

And do you think that unto such as you,
A maggot-minded, starved, fanatic crew,
God gave the Secret, and denied it me?—
Well, well, what matters it! believe that too.

—Omar Khayyám, *Rubáiyát*

8

THE ARMCHAIR EXPLORER

1830–1849

Even by the standards of nineteenth-century portrait photography, William Desborough Cooley looks cantankerous. Caught in middle age, he stares into the future with a downturned mouth and skeptical, bag-laden eyes. Posterity was not going to be kind to Cooley. Nor, especially, were the explorers of his day: few "armchair geographers," as he was derided, were more hated than this one. Cooley did, however, possess a remarkable ability. While they tramped through the disease-ridden wetlands and forests of tropical Africa armed with maps and compasses, he was making equally groundbreaking discoveries by leafing through documents in the British Library. It was Cooley who pushed the search for Timbuktu and the Sudan beyond mere cartography, initiating European inquiry into early West African history.

He was born in Ireland, probably in 1795, the year Park first set out to find the Niger. The son of a barrister and grandson of a notable architect, Cooley was educated at Trinity College, Dublin, and as a young man moved to England, where he joined the London literary scene, becoming staff writer on *The Athenæum* magazine and a contributor to *The Edinburgh Review*. In 1830 he began an account of Europe's global exploration, *The History of Maritime and Inland Discovery*, which established his reputation as a geographer, and became one of the first fellows of a new exploration club that met in the rooms of the Horticultural Society in Regent Street. This organization, which soon absorbed the declining African Association, would be called the Royal Geographical Society.

Cooley's combative spirit was soon engaged in the business of setting straight the grandiose claims of some of his contemporaries. In 1832 he secured an early triumph against a rival of England by exposing the apparently fraudulent travels of the explorer Jean-Baptiste Douville, who claimed to have reached deep into the interior of Angola and for this achievement had been awarded a gold medal by the Société de Géographie. Cooley began his review of Douville's three-volume *Voyage au Congo et dans l'intérieur de l'Afrique équinoxiale* with trademark sarcasm: "Africa, distinguished in all ages as a land of prodigies and wonders, has never given birth to anything more extraordinary than the volumes now before us," he wrote, before establishing that the journey would have been impossible within the time Douville had claimed. The results were catastrophic for the Frenchman: his reputation was shattered and his ashamed fiancée committed suicide. Douville challenged to a duel anyone who repeated Cooley's remarks, but he eventually fled France for Brazil, where he was murdered on the banks of the Amazon in 1837.

This unhappy episode appears to have given Cooley a taste for the takedown. It certainly boosted his reputation: in 1832 he was elected to the RGS council, and three years later he became vice president, but his rise through the English establishment came to an abrupt halt when he picked a fight with the RGS secretary, Captain Alexander Maconochie, accusing him of financial misconduct. The incident, which may have been sparked by a matter as trivial as the mislaying of Cooley's sub-scription fee, escalated to offers of a duel, and Cooley was forced to step down from his official post. From then on, he devoted himself to searching for what the leading eminence of Victorian exploration, David Livingstone, called "theoretical discoveries," which, however, brought method and rigor to European ideas about Africa, chiefly the Western Sudan.

In 1834, Cooley interviewed an Arab merchant and his black slave in London about East African geography. He correlated their information with Portuguese and other sources and produced a groundbreaking work on the interior of the continent, in which he proposed the existence of an undiscovered inland sea in East Africa called Lake Nyassi, now known as Lake Tanganyika. This led him into a thorough exploration of another group of sources, which until then had been poorly used: the early Arab geographies. With these he believed he could correct the errors of his forebears, notably the brilliant eighteenth-century French mapmaker Jean-Baptiste Bourguignon d'Anville and the African As-sociation's own cartographer, James Rennell:

> The Arab geography of Africa lies, at present, a large but confused heap of materials, into which modern writers occasionally dip their hands, each selecting what appears to serve his purpose, and adapt-ing it to his views by an interpretation as narrow and partial as his mode of inquiry. Modern geographers—D'Anville and Rennell not excepted—have allowed fancied resemblances of sound to lead them far away from fact and the straight path of investigation. . . .

The disorder introduced into the early geography of Central Africa by this false method of proceeding has deprived it of all its value.

Cooley determined to "examine the Arab authors of greatest value" and develop the information found in them. In this task he would be helped by a friend, the Spanish Orientalist Pascual de Gayangos, who was charting the history of Islam in his country by returning to the manuscripts of the Arab chroniclers and comparing them with existing European accounts. Cooley used the same technique: cross-referencing the Arab sources with those of Europeans, such as the Portuguese historian João de Barros and the Spaniard Luis del Mármol Carvajal, as well as the more recent writings of Park and Caillié. In this way he could estimate the reliability of each source and establish the origin of the information. He would start from scratch, abandoning all previous hypotheses about the locations of the empires of Ghana and Mali. By this vigorous process, which he called "rectification of sources," the more fantastical reports and secondhand accounts were eliminated.

Cooley's use of Arab texts was indicative of his approach, which was broad-minded for his time. European geography in his view was parochial; his writing would emphasize the fact that black Africans had their own past, and was largely free of the racism that would come after him. He did not, for example, fail to note, when describing "barbarous" executions at the court of Mwata Yamvo in eastern Angola, that the penal codes in European countries were similarly draconian.

Two Arab geographers were especially useful to Cooley: the Andalusian Abu Ubayd al-Bakri, whose most important work, *Book of the Routes and Realms*, was written in 1068, and Ibn Khaldun, a scholar born in Tunis in 1332. These two authors had written extensively about the West African civilizations, Cooley realized. Al-Bakri was particularly useful on the empire of ancient Ghana, which, unlike the modern state of that name, lay three hundred miles due west of Timbuktu and was still in the ascendant when he was alive. Ibn Khaldun, meanwhile, was a key source for the Mali empire, which stretched from Gao to the Senegalese coast and subsumed Ghana in the thirteenth century.

The name Ghana, al-Bakri noted, meant various things. It was a title given to the rulers of the kingdom, but there was also a "city of Ghana" which

> consists of two towns situated on a plain. One of these towns, which is inhabited by Muslims, is large and possesses twelve mosques, in one of which they assemble for the Friday prayer. There are salaried imams and muezzins, as well as jurists and scholars. In the environs are wells with sweet water, from which they drink and with which they grow vegetables.

Six miles away from the city of Ghana was the "king's town," al-Ghaba. It had a court of justice, a mosque, and domed buildings, and around it were woods that contained prisons, as well as groves and thickets where the "sorcerers of these people, men in charge of the religious cult" lived. The king was pagan, adorning himself with necklaces and bracelets and a high cap decorated with gold, but he surrounded himself with Muslim interpreters and ministers. Around his pavilion stood ten horses covered with gold-embroidered materials, while behind him were the same number of pages, holding shields and swords decorated with gold, and on his right were the sons of vassal kings, dressed in splendid garments, their hair plaited with gold. At the door of the pavilion were guard dogs of excellent pedigree that wore collars of gold and silver, studded with a number of balls of the same precious metals.

The Ghanaian king, it was said, could put two hundred thousand men into the field, more than forty thousand of whom were archers. He financed this military might by taxing the raw materials that were mined in the kingdom, al-Bakri noted:

On every donkey-load of salt when it is brought into the country their king levies one golden dinar, and two dinars when it is sent out. From a load of copper the king's due is five mithqals, and from a load of other goods 10 mithqals. [A mithqal, the Sudanese equivalent of the dinar or ducat, was around 4.25 grams of gold.] The best gold found in this land comes from the town of Ghiyaru, which is 18 days travelling distant from the king's town over a country inhabited by tribes of the Sudan whose dwellings are continuous. . . . The nuggets found in all the mines of his country are reserved for the king, only this gold dust being left for the people. But for this, the people would accumulate gold until it lost its value. The nuggets may weigh from an ounce to a pound.

According to al-Bakri, the king owned a single golden nugget that was as big as a boulder.

Three hundred years later, in 1374, Ibn Khaldun, who had traveled widely in northern Africa and Spain, finding employment in the courts of Fez, Granada, Tlemcen, and Cairo, embarked on an epic, seven-volume history of the world. The last of his volumes, often known as *History of the Berbers*, contained valuable information on the Western Sudan, and on the rulers of the empire of Mali. By his era, he noted, the

Ghanaian empire had been annexed by the kingdom of Mali, which stretched as far as Gao, two hundred miles east of Timbuktu, and had become "extremely powerful." It was a Muslim empire: the earliest kings of Mali embraced Islam in the thirteenth century, and many of them had made the journey to Mecca. Ibn Khaldun lingered particularly over the 1324 pilgrimage of Mansa Musa, "an upright man and a great king." Tales of Musa's justice were still being told in North Africa fifty years later. Musa brought several Muslim scholars with him on his return from Mecca, including the Andalusian poet and man of letters Abu Ishaq al-Sahili. One of these companions told Ibn Khaldun:

> We used to keep the sultan company during this progress, I and [al-Sahili], to the exclusion of his viziers and chief men, and [would] converse to his enjoyment. At each halt he would regale us with rare foods and confectionery. His equipment and furnishings were carried by 12,000 private slave women wearing gowns of brocade and Yemeni silk.

Al-Sahili returned with the king to his capital, where he wished to have a house built with plaster, which was unfamiliar in his land, and the Andalusian rose to the task, erecting a square building with a dome. "He had a good knowledge of handicrafts and lavished all his skill on it," Ibn Khaldun was told. "He plastered it over and covered it with coloured patterns so that it turned out to be the most elegant of buildings. It caused the sultan great astonishment because of the ignorance of the art of building in their land and he rewarded Abu Ishaq [al-Sahili] for it with 12,000 mithqals [about 50 kilograms] of gold dust apart from the preference, favour and splendid gifts which he enjoyed."

Al-Sahili was also said to have built a palace for Musa in Timbuktu, and the first incarnation of the Jingere Ber mosque.

Musa's reign lasted for twenty-five years, according to Ibn Khaldun, and the Malian empire collapsed soon after, during the reign of his grandson, Mari Jata. Ibn Khaldun's source, a Moroccan *qadi*, or Islamic judge, who had worked at Gao, described Jata as "a most wicked ruler over them because of the tortures, tyrannies, and improprieties to which he subjected them." He squandered the empire's wealth by his "loose living" and even had to sell the boulder of gold that had been the prized possession of the Malian treasury. By the time of his death in 1373/1374, the monarchy was in crisis, and his successor, a far better ruler, was not able to keep power.

IN 1841, COOLEY PUBLISHED his groundbreaking work *The Negroland of the Arabs Examined and Explained*. It was the first reliable account of the historical geography of sub-Saharan Africa and represented the dawn of a new discipline, that of West African history. His identifications of place names from the medieval Arab geographers and historians have, for the greater part, gone unchallenged by later authorities, and *The Negroland* formed a basis for all succeeding investigation. Typically he relished the errors he had discovered in the work of others: Rennell had confused Kano, in modern Nigeria, with Ghana, and Cooley demonstrated that the two names were distinct in origin. He also understood that "Ghana" represented a kingdom as well as the monarch himself, and that the capital where the ruler resided had not always been the same city, but may have been a "wandering name" applied to different places at different times.

Cooley remained a controversial figure, however—a "stormy petrel," as one critic put it—and his contributions were little recognized during his lifetime. After his death in 1883, the official history of the Hakluyt Society, an organization he had founded to publish explorers' accounts of their voyages, described him as "a somewhat erratic genius." Other obituaries openly questioned his mental health on the grounds of his extraordinarily fixed views. Even though he had correctly deduced the existence of Mounts Kilimanjaro and Kenya, he maintained that they couldn't possibly be capped with snow long after European explorers had seen that they were, and he held that the two great African lakes of Malawi and Tanganyika were joined in a single giant stretch of water, contrary to the observations of Livingstone. He died in poverty in a house behind the railheads of King's Cross and Euston, in London, but his work on the Western Sudan would remain one of the few of the era to "measure up to the requirements of modern scholarship," as the historian John Ralph Willis would write.

Cooley was also the favorite reading of the one explorer with whom he appears to have struck up a relationship of mutual respect, a man who was not without misanthropic leanings of his own, and even shared Cooley's tendency toward bullheaded pedantry. "Previously to my journey into the region of the Niger," the explorer wrote, "scarcely any data were known with regard to the history of this wide and important tract, except a few isolated facts, elicited with great intelligence and research by Mr. Cooley."

This was the man who would go on to uncover the secrets of the largest kingdom in West African history, an empire whose heyday coincided with that of Timbuktu, and about which Europe was entirely ignorant. The kingdom was called Songhay, and the explorer's name was Heinrich Barth.

9

A HEADLESS HORSEMAN

APRIL–MAY 2012

Haidara returned to Bamako at the start of May to find the capital in chaos. Faced with harsh economic sanctions imposed by neighboring West African states, the officer who had led the coup in the capital, Captain Amadou "Bolly" Sanogo, had stood aside, and the government now consisted of an uneasy alliance between his supporters and an interim civilian president. In the space of a month the country had lost its elected leader and half its territory, the foreign aid on which it depended had been shut off, diplomats had been withdrawn and embassies closed or left with a skeleton staff. As Amnesty International put it, Mali was at the center of a "major international disaster."

On April 24, a new director had taken over at the Ahmad Baba institute. Abdoulkadri Idrissa Maiga was a bullish, powerfully built man, and he couldn't have begun his new job at a worse time. His predecessor had handed him a dog-eared document in a plastic ring binder that listed the organization's assets, but God only knew how many of them were left. His Timbuktu headquarters was being used as a barracks, its employees had fled, and he had no money, since one of the government's few substantive acts since the coup had been to shut off all spending for the north. There was also a tangible threat to the manuscripts it was his job to safeguard. What, then, could he do?

He started out by scraping together four hundred dollars a month to rent a couple of rooms above a rat-infested fish-and-chicken shop in the south Bamako district of Kalaban Coura. From here he would try to figure out how to pay his employees, and how to keep in touch with the few who remained in Timbuktu. He had been in regular contact with Haidara in the run-up to starting his new job—Haidara, in fact, had been the one to tell him he would be offered the position—and now the Timbuktien suggested they should hold a meeting.

"Who with?" asked Maiga.

"Ismael Diadié Haidara. I'll call him."

Since Maiga was the only one with an office in Bamako, the three men agreed to meet there. Soon, the directors of the most famous manuscript collections in Timbuktu, who among them could claim to control around 90,000 of the city's documents, were meeting almost daily. "We met, we spoke about the manuscripts, we talked about what we had to do to get help," recalled Abdel Kader Haidara.

The contrast among these three characters was pointed. Maiga, straight-talking and occasionally abrasive, was a former head of the Arabic department at Bamako University who had worked on a project to digitize and catalogue the manuscripts called MLI/015—"Mali Quinze"—so he knew the material, but he was a novice next to his manuscript-owning colleagues. Ismael, meanwhile, was effete, aristocratic, charming. He was descended, he said, from the sixteenth-century

Timbuktu scholar Mahmud Kati, after whom his Fondo Kati library was named, and he kept a home in Granada. Then there was Haidara himself, who also claimed to be the scion of a scholarly Timbuktu family. He could be capricious, distributing information as it suited him, but he liked to make people laugh, even in moments of deep stress. He and Ismael would jokingly address each other at these meetings as "my son," and even Maiga was occasionally caught up in this horseplay. "At first, it was really a strong team," he recalled. "We really trusted each other at the beginning. It was a really friendly atmosphere."

At these meetings, the librarians shared whatever information they could glean from their contacts in the north. The greatest risk to the manuscripts at this stage, they believed, was from bandits and MNLA looters.

For a month, UNESCO had been issuing regular statements about the threat the rebels posed to Timbuktu's heritage. In mid-April the organization had warned that the jihadists' move into the new Ahmad Baba building was cause for "great alarm," since it contained documents that dated back to Timbuktu's glory period between the twelfth and fifteenth centuries: "This heritage must be protected," said Director-General Irina Bokova. "The citizens of Timbuktu have rallied to protect these ancient documents, and I salute their courage and dedication. But they need our help." She appealed for concerted action from Mali's warring factions, neighboring governments, Interpol, customs organizations, the art market, and collectors to prevent the loss of these treasures, which were so important for the whole of humanity.

While UNESCO broadcast its concern, the librarians' instincts were to do the opposite, and the first decision they took was to try to keep the manuscripts out of the public eye. Haidara got his chance to try to silence the UN organization on May 18, when an emergency delegation landed in Bamako for the first major meeting with the Malian government since the start of the crisis. Haidara was invited to a conference in the culture ministry with the officials who worked on Malian heritage, and he went along with his own agenda. When he was asked to report on the state of the manuscripts, he told the politicians, officials, and journalists who were present that though he had just returned from Timbuktu he could not say anything about the collections. Why not? Because the manuscripts were the most fragile things in the cultural heritage of the city, he said, and they must not be mentioned on radio or television. The officials discussed the issue briefly, then the culture minister, Diallo Fadima Touré, stood up and asked the journalists not to publish or broadcast anything that was said about the manuscripts. "You must leave out everything you hear," she said.

Satisfied, Haidara went on to explain what had been done so far, telling them that many of the collections had been moved into people's homes, where they were safe enough for the moment. The only help he really needed at this point was for the manuscripts not to be mentioned in the media. "That is all," he said. The librarians' message had been delivered to his press and the most vocal world-heritage body, and would be passed to others. "In our many meetings we elaborated these strategies of communication," said Ismael. "We asked certain authorities not to speak too much about the manuscripts in the papers or on the television or the radio."

With the media blackout in place, the librarians moved on to discuss other contingencies. There was little prospect that the situation would improve; in fact, they had to assume it would get worse. What then? Maiga had been wondering how to get the institute's manuscripts to safety since he had taken up his new job, and now the three men openly discussed the idea.

Haidara didn't believe evacuation was the right answer at first. Shipping tens of thousands of fragile documents out from under the noses of the occupiers and across the dangerous desert carried huge risks, and not only for the documents. The tally of beatings and maimings in the north was growing daily, as were the rapes and killings committed by gunmen of various groups; by the end of April, Ansar Dine's sharia justice had led to summary executions, floggings, amputations, and even the cutting of the ear of a woman for wearing a short skirt. What would these people do to someone caught moving manuscripts? Then there was the issue of money: a one-way ticket on public transportation from Timbuktu to Bamako cost 25,000 West African francs, or around forty dollars. Given the number of shipments, and the extra sums that would be needed to spend on couriers and the essential bribes for police and customs men, a full evacuation would be expensive.

"We said, we must wait," Haidara recalled. "We didn't think the evacuation was a good idea at that time. There was a lot of tension, and if we started, we didn't think it would succeed. We said it was necessary to leave things for now, for the moment."

They did, however, begin the groundwork.

There was a fourth character in Bamako who occasionally met with Haidara, an American woman named Stephanie Diakité. Diakité was an attorney, she said later, and a trained book conservator who now ran a development consultancy called D Intl. She was in her fifties, gray-blonde, dynamic, international with a capital I. She had houses in Seattle and Bamako, and though her talent for language meant she could swear vigorously in both Bambara and English, she was most at home with the argot of consultancy, in which she could produce such phrases as "revolve hardware and software" and "investment facilitation" without breaking a sweat. She and Haidara had first met in the late 1990s, when she was traveling around the Timbuktu region assessing a girls' education project, and they struck up a lasting but tempestuous friendship over the manuscripts. (Their spouses—he had two wives; she, a Malian husband—liked to call them "the terrible twosome," she later said.) He was the owner of a major collection, while she had access to the world of international development, and was good at process to boot. Together they had turned Savama, the NGO that Haidara set up to safeguard the future of the city's written heritage, into an institution with which the international donor community could do business.

Diakité drafted an appeal and sent it to all the major international cultural institutions in her contacts book, while the librarians themselves toured the embassies to try to drum up financial support. At one point Haidara was convinced they had the backing of South Africa: they had only to prepare a letter requesting help and sign it jointly with the president of the High Islamic Council of Mali, he was told. "In the letter, we asked for our Muslim brothers of South Africa to come to our aid, or else to come with us to Timbuktu to see how we should do things," recalled Haidara. They sent the letter off, and every day expected good news, but no reply ever came, and gradually they realized the South African support wasn't going to materialize. "We were really discouraged," Haidara said. "It was the only hope we had, and it had gone."

They continued to approach others—embassies, foundations, NGOs—but no one wanted to take on such a bold and politically risky task. "UNESCO said smuggling did not fit into its remit," Maiga remembered. "They said they would not get into that game."

.   .   .

IN THE NORTH, the jihadists were consolidating their grip on Timbuktu. In the last week of April, the unemployed tourist guide Bastos
watched a flurry of activity at the empty Malian Solidarity Bank (BMS)
across the street from his house. From the vantage point of his roof terrace, he saw a group of jihadists arrive in a truck piled high with mattresses and bedding they had taken from the luxury La Palmeraie hotel,
which in different days had been a favorite of the pop stars who sometimes came to Timbuktu. They entered the looted bank, looked around,
cleaned it, then moved in with all their furnishings.

Bastos, who nowadays had little to do but tend his garden down
by the river, spent much of the next year watching the day-to-day activities of his neighbors in the building across the street. It was mostly
the foot soldiers who lived there, the policemen, customs officers, and
guards. The leaders chose accommodation elsewhere, but treated the
BMS building as an office. Abou Zeid, "the big chief," would arrive
each morning at eight, with his Kalashnikov slung over a shoulder and
a satellite phone in his pocket, in a vehicle driven by a young man Bastos was told was his son. Abou Zeid wore only three changes of clothes
during the whole occupation, Bastos said, but he carried huge amounts
of cash: "I saw the way he spent it. For them, money was nothing."
There was a canteen in the BMS building, and each morning Abou Zeid
would discuss the menu with the cook before doling out enough notes
for him to buy what he needed at the market. To Bastos's irritation, the
cook would often come to him and take condiments and utensils from
his kitchen. He couldn't refuse: "I saw their mentality," said Bastos. "If
you say no, they will think you are against them. If you once refuse
him, you become the enemy. So you say nothing."

Each day, Bastos observed Abou Zeid leaving the BMS at around three p.m., and each evening he watched the more junior fighters walk across the roof to a dormitory building next door. He came to recognize these men well, and knew from their accents that they came from all over the Muslim world. As word of Timbuktu's capture had spread, jihadists of all nationalities had come to the city. Many were Algerians, but there were also Pakistanis, Somalians, Moroccans, Tunisians, and even a Frenchman, Gilles Le Guen. Le Guen had spent thirty years in the merchant marine before moving to the desert, embracing Islam, and adopting the jihadist nom de guerre Abdel Jelil.

There were Malians among the jihadists too, many of whom had been converted by the extremist preachers who had been coming to Timbuktu for decades. According to Mohamed "Hamou" Dédéou, a modern-day Timbuktu scholar, the proselytizers had arrived in caravans up to forty strong, and stayed in the city's mosques. At first they were welcomed. People were even keen to listen to their philosophy and engage them in religious discussions. They were called Wahhabists, after the puritanical eighteenth-century cleric Muhammad ibn Abd al-Wahhab, or Salafists, after the Salaf, the first three generations of Muslims, of whom the Prophet said: "The people of my own generation are the best, then those who come after them, and then those of the next generation." The Salafist-Wahhabists believed that the pure faith of Islam's early days had been polluted by religious innovations and foreign influences, and these had to be purged so that Muslims could return to the blessed original state. In time, though, the Timbuktiens largely became sick of being harangued and patronized, and grew suspicious of the missionaries' means. Who was funding them? Who could afford to spend three months away from his wife and family, preaching in Africa? When they began to speak in the mosques, the congregations would stand up and file out. But the visitors did not give up.

Some Salafists were homegrown. Redbeard Hamaha was one of these, but the most extreme was Hamed Mossa. Mossa had been born into a Tuareg family not far from the city and lived for a time in Saudi Arabia before returning to Timbuktu, determined to convert the city to his way of thinking. He was deeply unpopular—"a dark soul," one neighbor recalled; a racist who believed black people should be slaves and who loved to humiliate—but he had access to large amounts of money for his radicalization project, and when his sermons were no longer welcome in the city's mosques, he built his own. Mossa's mosque became a haven for radicals and foreign preachers, and ordinary worshippers who lived nearby decided they would be safer praying at home. To lure them back, Mossa and his friends handed out food and money on the condition that they came to listen, and the keener acolytes were invited to attend weeklong radicalization camps in the bush.

Ag Alfousseyni Houka, known as "Houka Houka," was one Timbuktien who was radicalized in this way. He was an intelligent man, a teacher at the Franco-Arab school, whose faith was anchored by his older brother, Mohamed Issa, a serious soul with a deep knowledge of the Kuran. When the Salafist preachers spoke, Issa would tell Houka Houka and the younger men to be careful. "They are trying to deceive you," he would say. But Issa died young, and after his death, Houka Houka fell under the sway of Mossa. He started attending the camps in the bush, and soon he was preaching in Mossa's mosque. Ahmad al-Faqi al-Mahdi was another local man who became a Salafist convert. Al-Mahdi would later be the first man to be sentenced for cultural destruction by the International Criminal Court.

Mossa, Houka Houka, and al-Mahdi were quick to join the rebels in April 2012, and as the Islamic revolution in Mali needed high-profile Malians, all three were given prominent roles in the city's new administration. Houka Houka was made the sharia judge, while Mossa and al-Mahdi joined the Islamic Police, the latter as head of the "morality brigade," or Hizba. These men were tasked with enforcing the new penal code in accordance with a literal interpretation of the six *hadd* punishments prescribed in the Kuran and hadiths:

For theft: amputation of the hand

For illicit sexual relations: death by stoning or a hundred lashes

For making unproven accusations of illicit sex: eighty lashes

For drinking intoxicants: eighty lashes

For apostasy: death or banishment

For highway robbery: death

Several days after the jihadists' arrival at the bank opposite his house, Bastos saw they had put up a plaque that read "Islamic Police" in Arabic. A group of gunmen who wore blue tabards adorned with a badge of two crossed Kalashnikovs moved in and began patrols around the town, though at first they were careful not to enforce the new laws too harshly.

"They were very cunning," Bastos remembered.

THROUGH APRIL AND INTO MAY, the population of Timbuktu was tossed between the two fractious rebel groups. The MNLA still occupied the southern fringes of the town, and whenever they wanted something to be done, they went to the city's civic leaders, while the jihadists went to the religious authorities on the High Islamic Council, led by the grand imam, Abderrahmane Ben Essayouti. The town's administration was therefore chaotic and its people confused. Decisions were sometimes made twice or not at all, and when people were arrested under the new laws, no one knew whom to approach to plead their case. Issues of urgent civic importance began to stack up. Who would manage the shipments of charitable aid sent to Timbuktu from the south? Who would organize the irrigation of the fields, now that the rainy season was approaching?

The elders of Timbuktu—a democratic city if ever there was one—did what they always did in times of trouble: they held a meeting. The meeting resulted in the creation of a new civic body, the Crisis Committee, which consisted of the leaders of the eighteen Timbuktu neighborhoods, with Mayor Cissé as president and the former deputy mayor Diadié as vice president. It was decided that the Crisis Committee should meet at the mayor's office twice a week, and as a precaution the elders set out their purpose in writing and sent it to the jihadists for approval.

While awaiting a response, the elders decided to address the most urgent issue, that of organizing the irrigation of the fields. They put out a message on the community radio station calling all the farmers who worked in the major agricultural districts to the mairie the following morning. At nine a.m. the next day, just as people were starting to gather, the Islamic Police pulled up in front of the building in two vehicles and told them to disperse. Four members of the Crisis Committee, including Diadié, decided to remain in the courtyard, and thirty minutes later the jihadists returned. They cocked their weapons and climbed down from their truck.

"Didn't you hear us say everyone had to leave?"

"Yes," said Diadié. "You did tell the people to leave. They have left."

"What are you doing here?"

"We are the officials," said Diadié. "We told the people to come. Now we have to wait to tell people who arrive why there is nobody here and why there is no meeting. When we have finished telling them, we will go, but we can't leave before that. We are the representatives of the people."

Four days later, Diadié received a note summoning the Crisis Committee to appear before the jihadists. They went to the police station, and from there were driven to the former Land Registry office, where Abou Zeid was now staying, and shown into a spacious living area that had been fitted out with carpets and mattresses for the guests. Here they found the entire jihadist high command: baby-faced Ag Ghaly, diminutive Abou Zeid, the handsome, urbane spokesman Sanda Ould Bouamama, and a host of other officers of various nationalities, each of whom had a Kalashnikov close by. Over tea, the occupiers of the city explained that they had made inquiries, and they were happy to accept that the Crisis Committee did indeed represent the people of Timbuktu. They repeated the mantra that they had come simply to ensure that the holy city lived by the principles laid down by God. They would soon hold a congress in Gao that would found the Islamic Republic of Azawad, they said, and from that moment it must be understood that there was no state in northern Mali—no prefect, no governor appointed by Bamako, no mayor or Malian constitution—there was only the law of sharia. The committee should understand their aims and help guide the city to the right path, and it would be of no use for them to sulk or fight, because God had given them the means to make people do as they wished. Yet they preferred persuasion to force, which was why the elders had been invited today.

"From that time on we would work together," Diadié recalled. "If we felt things were not suitable, we should tell them, and vice versa. Collaboration had more or less begun."

There were some topics, though, that the committee and the jihadists would not be able to discuss. One of these was the issue of the manuscripts: "It was too dangerous," Mayor Cissé recalled. "That was a problem that was hidden."

Another was the fate of the city's World Heritage monuments. For the jihadists, that would be nonnegotiable.

AMADOU HAMPÂTÉ BÂ once described the Muslim empire of Ahmad Lobbo as having been erected on an "ancient substratum of local religions." This, according to Hampâté Bâ, established a social framework in which different peoples could live side by side while jealously preserving their various ethnicities and characteristics. At the start of the twenty-first century, this mixture of beliefs still existed along the Niger. Mali was a country filled with mosques, where people's lives were governed in the main by the principles of the Maliki school of Sunni Islam, but it was also a country where marabouts made *ju-ju* and *gris-gris* amulets for truck drivers and boat captains to ward off evil, and where journalists commissioned spells to help their interviewees open up. Some of these practices were evidence of the "ancient substratum" at work; others were manifestations of the Sufi mysticism that had long played a role in African Islam.

Sufis, broadly speaking, believe the living can find enlightenment through their inner dedication to God. The holiest Sufi leaders develop special intimacy with the divine, and are sometimes venerated as saints. The mausoleums around Timbuktu contained the bodies of hundreds of these saints, and people would pray to the more powerful and well-known of them to intercede in their lives. Sixteen of these mausoleums were inscribed in UNESCO's list of World Heritage monuments in 1988, along with the Jingere Ber, Sankore, and Sidi Yahya mosques, and the saints buried within—historic figures such as Ahmad Baba's great-uncle Shaykh Sidi Mahmud, the great sixteenth-century *qadi* of Timbuktu, and Shaykh Alfa Moy, who was killed by Moroccan troops in 1594—formed a spiritual rampart that miraculously protected the city. Air Mali explained how this worked in practice: "If you take the medina of Timbuktu, there are mausoleums at the four corners of the town, and each saint occupies a corner. That means nothing bad can enter there, so the town is safe. And even if you throw a bomb or a missile, remember that it will not fall in the interior of the town. It will rather fall outside." According to Sane Chirfi Alpha, the spiritual defense had saved the town from a shower of mortar shells that fell on it during the 1992 Tuareg rebellion, but didn't explode. "There was no scientific explanation for it," he said.

The jihadists considered many of these beliefs, including the veneration of the Timbuktu Saints, to be dangerous "innovations" on the practices of the Salaf, the first and purest of Muslims. In order to return the city and its religion to the pure state, these innovations would have to be eradicated.

When it came, the conflict did not erupt over a saint, however, but over a jinn.

In the second half of April, a ghostly figure was said to have appeared in the town, dressed all in white, with a length of cotton bound round his face in the Tuareg style, and riding a white horse. This was al-Farouk, the talismanic symbol of the city who for centuries had protected it from malicious spirits and bad behavior. Al-Farouk was said to crisscross the town after dark enforcing a three-strike curfew system: the first two times he caught young people out misbehaving he would send them home with a warning, but the third time he would make them disappear forever. Once, centuries before, he had foolishly attempted to dress down some holy visitors from Jenne who stayed late in the mosque, and the imam of Sankore was so angry he imprisoned al-Farouk for seven hundred years in the waters of the Bani River. The jinn had since returned, and had been restored to his rightful place at the heart of Timbuktu, with his own monument on a traffic island in the Place de l'Indépendance.

Mamadou Kassé, a young Malian whose father was said to be a muezzin in Bamako, thought al-Farouk was a false idol. When he arrived in Timbuktu in April 2012 to join the jihad and was told about the jinn, he decided the best thing for him to do was to destroy the monument. "I climbed up and I smashed it in front of everyone who told me that it is the jinn who protects the town," he said. He was unable to destroy the whole thing—the plinth was large and made of thick concrete—but he managed to knock off the horseman's head and feet and those of his steed. "Look, your genie is nothing!" he told the crowd who gathered to watch. "It is God who protects us!"

Instead of being convinced, the people were angered by his act of vandalism and demonstrated their fury by marching on the military camp. The jihadists dispersed the protesters by shooting over their heads.

The al-Farouk monument was neither old nor especially valuable, but it was a symbol of something the occupiers wanted to eradicate, and Kassé's vandalism was significant as an opening salvo in the battle with Timbuktu's spirits that lay ahead.

Two weeks after the jinn's monument was targeted, the jihadists attacked something far more precious: the mausoleum of Shaykh Sidi Mahmud. This saint, who died in 1548, had been a great Timbuktu scholar, recognized for his dignity. His tomb, made out of stones and raw earth, had been built on a low hill on the site of the vestibule of his house, to the north of the town. His followers had been buried around him, so that he now lay in the center of a substantial cemetery, and people regularly went to pray there.

On Friday, May 4, a group of jihadists who saw the worshippers told them that what they were doing was forbidden and that they should "seek help from God directly" rather than from the dead. They then began to attack the tomb, tearing off the door of the mausoleum and ripping out its windows, burning the white curtain separating the sepulcher from the place of prayer and smashing several stelae. An anonymous assistant mayor told a reporter the following day that the jihadists had promised to destroy other mausoleums, as well as some manuscripts. "Timbuktu is in shock," he said.

Cultural experts around Mali reacted with a mix of anger and sadness. "I suffer and everyone suffers in the same way with me," said Professor Baba Akib Haidara, a Timbuktien manuscripts expert. "They are going backward, backward, it is unacceptable. They attack our values, our spirits, that which is deepest in the soul of Timbuktu. UNESCO must mobilize international opinion. This is not Islam, and there will be a great catastrophe if nothing is done." For the filmmaker and former culture minister Cheikh Oumar Sissoko, the tomb was "part of the cultural and spiritual heritage of Timbuktu, and of humanity in general," and the intolerance the attack demonstrated was a "tragedy." The Malian government, meanwhile, condemned "with its last breath" a "contemptible act which tramples on the basic precepts of Islam, a religion of tolerance and respect."

On May 14, the city's cultural community—artists, intellectuals, and manuscript workers—launched a call for help from the UN secretary-general. "Total anarchy and lawlessness now reign here in Timbuktu," the declaration stated, adding that there was "serious risk of destruction of all its riches." If world heritage meant anything, the international community must act now, since "Timbuktu is about to lose its soul. Timbuktu is threatened with outrageous vandalism. Timbuktu has at its throat a sharp assassin's knife."

The jihadists were unmoved. They were doing God's work. "The height of a tomb must not exceed the level of the ankle," Redbeard Hamaha explained. "If a tomb is higher than that, you must knock it down."

FOR THE TRIUMVIRATE of librarians in Bamako, the desecration of Sidi Mahmud's tomb was a worrying new development. How far would these people go? What would it mean for the manuscripts? As anyone who had spent time with the documents knew, their contents were not restricted to subjects the jihadists would find acceptable. In particular, the idea of intercession—in which Muslims could ask a saint to make special requests to Allah on their behalf—was widely discussed in the manuscripts, but was anathema to the Salafists. As refugees from the city reported, the town's occupiers deemed some of the books in the Ahmad Baba institute to be "not consistent with Islam."

Reports also reached the librarians that the jihadists had begun to challenge Timbuktu's principal religious festival, Mawlid, the Prophet's birthday. Sunni Muslims all over the Islamic world had been celebrating Mawlid since the twelfth century, but the Salafists disapproved of it: in their view, it was an innovation that elevated the Prophet to the level of near divinity. This was a major concern for the librarians, since Mawlid celebrations in Timbuktu were based around the *Ishriniyyat*, or "The Twenties," an allegorical poem of twenty rhyming verses praising the Prophet's life. Written by Abd al-Rahman al-Fazazi in the thirteenth century in Córdoba, this devotional text had been introduced to Timbuktu from Morocco in the fifteenth century and copied extensively. In the buildup to the festival, the entire poem was read four times: first over a forty-day period, and then over a week, then over three days. Finally, it was read in the course of the single night before the holy day itself. Since this work was found among many manuscript collections, Haidara feared it would draw the attention of the occupiers of the town to certain documents they would not like.

"There were a lot of meetings in Timbuktu between the occupiers and the notables and marabouts about the organization of the Mawlid festival," Haidara remembered. "The occupiers said, 'No, no, no, Mawlid is something we forbid. And the manuscripts that speak of it really are not good manuscripts.' We heard that. That made us start to think. We said that that is perhaps a threat."

He also began to hear reports that the rebels had caught people with manuscripts in their luggage and destroyed them. "They found some manuscripts and they burned them," he recalled. "It was not a big deal, they were little manuscripts, but they burned them." These stories played on Haidara's imagination. If they had destroyed a few sheaves of manuscripts, what would they do to a library full of them?

"We said that is not good," said Haidara. "We knew that was how things begin, little by little."

According to Maiga, these pieces of information crystallized into a decision in the last week of May.

"One day," recalled Haidara, "I said to Maiga, I think we must find a solution to bring the manuscripts to Bamako. Now, I said, it is time."

10

THE POPE OF TIMBUKTU

1850–1854

A rare bank of fog drifted across western Libya on the morning of March 31, 1850, signaling the likelihood of rain. It had been a wet spring, and as Heinrich Barth and his Prussian colleague Adolf Overweg waited for their expedition leader at the rendezvous south of Tripoli, they were surprised by the greenery of the desert, which looked like a prairie; it was filled with cornfields, pasture, flocks of sheep, and a rich array of blue wildflowers. As the sky began to unburden itself, James Richardson's party arrived, and Barth looked on skeptically as his servants set about pitching a tent the size of a field hospital. It rained so heavily for the next twenty-four hours that their plans to depart were postponed, but if Barth was frustrated, he didn't confide it to his journal. He was finally on the brink of the journey that would define him, a five-year odyssey that would solve the conundrum of Africa's missing golden heart.

Few men were so suited to a task as Barth was to exploration. A lithograph depicting him as a young man reveals a skeptical, mustachioed figure with a ramrod-straight back. The ramrod was instilled by his parents, Johann and Charlotte Barth of Hamburg, Lutherans who raised their offspring according to strict principles of morality, duty, and industry. Heinrich was the third of four children, born in 1821, and was sent at the age of eleven to the elite Johanneum academy, where he had few friends and displayed what one contemporary described as an "aristocratic aloofness." He was a driven pupil, however, who filled his spare time reading classical history and geography in the original Greek and Latin. In his teens, believing himself to be physically weak, he adopted a routine of exercises and cold baths, even in winter, to toughen himself up.

Two weeks after leaving the Johanneum in 1839 he enrolled at Berlin University, one of the most vibrant educational institutions of the time, where fellow students included Karl Marx, Friedrich Engels, and Søren Kierkegaard. Barth was taught by two titans of nineteenth-century science: Carl Ritter, the father of modern geography, and Alexander von Humboldt, the naturalist whose epic five-year exploration of Latin America had hoovered up sixty thousand species of plants and thirty-five crates of insects, birds, rocks, and other specimens. This fine education alone would set Barth apart from the adventurers who had gone before. He carried Cooley's *Negroland* with him, and his journals reveal a detailed knowledge of the Arab geographers, as well as the findings of his predecessors Park, Caillié, and the Scottish naval officer Hugh Clapperton, who visited Central Africa in the 1820s. To the old hands at the Royal Geographic Society he must have seemed overeducated, but he could also point to hard experience in the field. A year after graduating from university he had embarked on a solo three-year expedition from Tangiers through Barbary and the Middle East. Between Tripoli and Egypt he was attacked in the night by Bedouin bandits, shot in both legs and knocked unconscious. By the time he returned home, he was, according to his brother-in-law and future biographer, Gustav von Schubert, "silent and withdrawn," a hard man to get to know:

> It took a long time before I was able to thaw the ice around his heart and experience the depths of his character. In his first letter to me, he wrote, "If you make my sister unhappy, I will shoot you dead," which was clear enough.

Beneath this carapace lay a man who needed to be needed: his only goal, he once wrote, was "to be *useful* to humanity, to encourage them toward common enlightenment, to feed their spirits and give them strength." Sadly for Barth, his account of his North African journey left humanity underwhelmed. *The Athenæum*'s anonymous reviewer wrote of *Wanderings Along the Punic and Cyrenaic Shores of the Mediterranean* that "a more perplexing specimen . . . of some of the worst faults of German prose has rarely fallen in our way," and plans for a second volume were scrapped. More hurtful even than the professional slights he received at this time was the rejection of a marriage proposal. "The experience was a great blow to Barth's self-esteem," Schubert wrote, without recording the woman's name. "His bitter fear of romantic relationships lasted for a long time after that, and even in later years he could not bring himself to enter in marriage."

No matter. Barth would deploy his passion in foreign parts, where he always seemed more comfortable.

In 1849, he found his opportunity, on James Richardson's British expedition to the African interior. The evangelical Richardson had joined the British and Foreign Anti-Slavery Society on its establishment in 1839 and developed a special interest in the part of the trade that crossed the Sahara. In 1845, his investigations led him as far as the oasis of Ghat, in Fezzan, and on his return he floated the idea of an expedition to Lake Chad to the foreign secretary, Lord Palmerston, with the aim of supplanting the slave trade with trade in British manufactured goods. Palmerston agreed. Since Richardson was no expert at geographical observations, he turned to his Prussian contacts for a scientist, and on Ritter's recommendation recruited Barth and Overweg. They would travel at Britain's expense on what Richardson called a "Journey of Discovery and Philanthropy to Central Africa via the Great Desert of the Sahara."

Unusually, and perhaps ominously, the three men drew up a contract before their departure to establish their roles. Richardson, as leader, would determine the choice of route and the method of advance, but he was also obliged to help them in their scientific work. If they reached Lake Chad alive, he would retire, leaving the Germans whatever instruments they needed to carry out their observations.

Tensions between Barth and his leader were evident from the start. "Mr. Richardson was waiting in Paris for dispatches when Mr. Overweg and I reached Tunis," was how Barth would choose, years later, to open his five-volume account of the journey; it would be a further six weeks before the dithering Richardson reached Tripoli. Barth used the time to take Overweg on a substantial tour of the coastal regions, a digression the Briton took as a sign of "European impetuosity." After Richardson's arrival, the delays only escalated as he waited for prodigious quantities of equipment to be shipped in from Malta. The biggest holdup was the boat. Although the first 1,500 miles of the expedition's route led them across the desert, they would carry a heavy rowing wherry in which they hoped one day to survey Lake Chad. They also needed a sailor to work it: Richardson had recruited a nephew to this task, but he was so difficult he would be sent home when they were halfway across the desert.

This sort of bungling was typical of Richardson, according to the British consul in Tripoli, G. W. Crowe, who expressed great surprise to the Foreign Office that such a man should have been chosen to lead an expedition into the interior: "I fear his wretched mismanagement will lower the reputation hitherto enjoyed by the English nation in Central Africa."

While Richardson organized the sawing of the boat into pieces that could be slung between eight large camels, the impatient Prussians rode south, promising to wait forty miles farther on at Wadi Mejenin. At last, on the morning of April 2, 1850, with the weather clear, the expedition was preparing to depart. The scene that greeted a visitor to the wadi would have been worthy of a Barnum & Bailey circus.

Sixty-two camels filled the dried-up riverbed, while tens of drivers, servants, and hangers-on fussed and argued around them. Richardson had employed an alcoholic dragoman named Yusuf Moknee, the son of a former governor of Fezzan, who had been forced to sign a sobriety contract, and two Arab janissaries who spent the first weeks threatening to kill each other. Next came a handful of freed slaves, returning with their families from Tunis to their homeland in sub-Saharan Africa, and a marabout from Fezzan. Most remarkable of all were two hangers-on Richardson described as "a couple of insane fellows," who he suspected were there solely to satirize the expedition. One of these men, who claimed the status of sharif, had "an unpleasant habit of threatening to cut everybody's throat." As soon as he arrived, he upset the caravan by starting fights and telling people he was going to stab or shoot them. "He fawned, however, on us Europeans," Richardson noted, "whilst he had a large knife concealed under his clothes ready to strike." A group of diplomats and expats had also come to the wadi to wave them off: the American consul, a Mr. Gaines; the British vice-consul, Mr. Reade; and Frederick Warrington, Alexander Gordon Laing's brother-in-law and Barth's friend, a man the Prussian described as "perhaps the most amiable possible specimen of an Arabized European."

Once the "insane fellows" had been sent back to Tripoli, the sharif under guard, the expedition set off. Warrington rode with them the first few days to the mountaintop town of Gharyan. They camped there among acacia bushes and looked out over the volcanic cone of Mount Tekut while Warrington had an immense bowl of couscous prepared. The following morning, April 5, he watched them ride away toward the southern horizon, much as his father had watched Alexander Gordon Laing depart twenty-five years before.

"We separated from Mr. Warrington," Barth wrote some years later, "and of the three travellers I was the only one whom he was ever to see again."

RICHARDSON PROVED to be as poor a leader as everyone had suspected, and their journey across the desert was almost as tortuous as Laing's. The caravan was milked by its own guides and stalked by Tuareg freebooters. By September 1850, when they reached the safety of Tintalous in the Air Mountains, Richardson was exhausted. While Barth set out on a side expedition to Agadez, where he heard of the existence of the great Sudanese empire of Songhay, Richardson rested in his tent. He couldn't stand the heat, and tried weakly to return to Tripoli but couldn't find a guide. He died in March the following year without the least struggle. Barth now took charge of the expedition, and together with his Prussian colleague made an extensive survey of Lake Chad, but repeated bouts of fever destroyed Overweg's health, and by late September 1852 he too was dead. Barth laid him in a grave on the shore of the lake, next to the boat.

Barth was deeply upset by Overweg's passing. "Thus died my sole friend and companion," he confided to his journal, "in the thirtieth year of his age, and in the prime of his youth." Lake Chad was now "intolerable" for him, and there was only one thing to do: move forward. Palmerston left the expedition's future direction entirely to his discretion, writing that he would be "perfectly satisfied" with a westerly course if Barth chose it, and that was what the explorer now did. "I determined to set out as soon as possible on my journey toward the Niger," he wrote, "to new countries and new people." On November 25, he embarked on the dangerous road to Timbuktu, adopting a Muslim disguise, as Caillié had done. He was "Abdel Karim," a Turkish-speaking Syrian who was traveling to the city with books for the shaykh of Timbuktu, a man Barth had heard about on his travels named Ahmad al-Bakkai.

The route west was an arduous journey, into "almost unknown regions, never trodden by European foot," which involved crossing many minor kingdoms as well as terrain made dangerous by rain. Yet long before he reached the city, Barth began to make momentous discoveries relating to the history of Songhay, a subject of growing fascination for the explorer.

In April 1853, almost halfway along his 1,500-mile journey to Timbuktu, he reached Wurno in Sokoto, where he met an educated man named Abdel Kader dan Taffa, who had much of the history of the Songhay dynasties "perfectly in his head," as Barth put it, information which was "of the greatest importance" in giving the explorer insight into the region's past. More exciting still, this man told him of the existence of a great chronicle of the Songhay empire, written, he said, by the scholar Ahmad Baba.

Barth began to seek manuscripts wherever he went. That month, he found at least two, the *Tazyin al-waraqat*, a chronicle written by Abdullahi dan Fodio, and Muhammad Bello's *Infaq al-maysur*, of which an extract had been brought back by Clapperton in 1825, but this had since been lost. Both works told of the early-nineteenth-century Fulani jihad, which resulted in the founding of the Sokoto caliphate, yet these were small reward compared with the document he would find farther west. In June, as violent rains set in, Barth reached Gando, on the border of the modern state of Niger, where he was loaned a copy of "that most valuable historical work of Ahmad Baba," the history of the Sudan that Abdel Kader dan Taffa had told him about. Barth sat with the "respectable quarto volume" of the chronicle for three or four days, using his fluent Arabic to extract the more important passages. These, he wrote,

> opened to me quite a new insight into the history of the regions on the middle course of the Niger, whither I was bending my steps, exciting in me a far more lively interest than I had previously felt in a kingdom the great power of which, in former times, I here found set forth in very clear and distinct outlines.

Barth copied out as much of the chronicle as time allowed, focusing on the historical data, but he couldn't properly digest what he was reading before he had to move on toward Timbuktu.

On June 20, at Say, he was elated to see the Niger for the first time, "a noble unbroken stream" about seven hundred yards across. The great river slid in a south-southwesterly direction with a moderate current of about three miles an hour. His little party crossed on two boats made of hollowed-out tree trunks sewn together, and Barth was "filled with delight when floating on the waters of this celebrated stream, the exploration of which had cost the sacrifice of so many noble lives." He was soon struggling west again, along tracks that had been turned into bog by rain, and across dangerously swollen rivers. Guinea worm infected one of his servants, and mosquitoes and biting flies penetrated their clothing and made him feverish, but in late August he reached Sareyamou, in the inland delta, where he was able to hire a riverboat to take him almost to his destination. As they worked, the boatmen sang about the deeds of a notable ruler of Songhay, Askiya the Great.

On September 5, Barth was at Kabara and riding now in the footsteps of that "very meritorious French traveller," René Caillié. He was alarmed to learn there that Shaykh al-Bakkai, the man on whom he was relying for protection, was not in Timbuktu. He sent his guide ahead to the city to ask the shaykh's brother, Sidi Alawate, for protection, and passed a tense day, harassed by Tuareg, awaiting a response. He had felt obliged to confidentially tell Alawate that he was a Christian, and say that he was under the protection of the sultan of Istanbul. At last, around midnight, Alawate arrived. He was suspicious and asked to see Barth's letter of protection from the Ottomans, a document the explorer had requested from the Foreign Office but had never received. Barth was embarrassed by the lack of written evidence for his claim, which left him in a dangerous position, but Alawate nevertheless agreed to protect him.

At ten o'clock on the morning of September 7, 1853, Barth and his party set out on the infamous eight-mile track north. Beyond the murderous halfway point, he saw a mass of people coming from the city to greet their important visitor, Abdel Karim. Realizing he must brazen out the situation or risk being killed, he galloped forward, gun in hand, to receive their many salaams. His fake identity was almost uncovered by a man who addressed him in Turkish, which Barth had forgotten, but he pushed past the throng to avoid further questions and get into the safety of the town. He walked through the narrow streets and lanes to the "populous and wealthy" quarter of Sane-gungu, where he was offered a house opposite that of Shaykh al-Bakkai.

There, he was seized by a severe attack of fever and collapsed.

TIMBUKTU WAS JUST AS DANGEROUS for a Christian in 1853 as it had been in the mid-1820s. It was still under the sway of the Fulani empire of Masina, now ruled by Lobbo's young grandson Ahmad III, though he was beginning to lose his grip on the city to the Tuareg. Shaykh al-Bakkai, the town's spiritual and political ruler, was performing a delicate balancing act, playing one group against another to maintain a degree of independence: he had arranged a system of two *qadi*s to adjudicate in disputes between the Fulani and the Tuareg, but it was an uneasy peace, and the city was filled with agents waiting for the right moment to strike and win Ahmad's favor. This febrile atmosphere would keep Barth in Timbuktu for almost a year.

Having shed his disguise, the explorer spent his first three weeks in the city barricaded inside the house, convinced Alawate was conspiring with his treacherous guide to rob him before his inevitable murder, but at three a.m. on September 26 he heard music strike up outside his window: a group of women were celebrating the arrival of al-Bakkai. Barth's excitement at the appearance of the man on whom his safety depended sent him into a new paroxysm of fever, and he was unable to pay his respects the next day, but the shaykh, demonstrating his famous good manners, sent a message begging the explorer to rest, while presenting him with a gift of two oxen, two sheep, two vessels of butter, a camel-load each of rice and corn, and a warning not to eat anything that did not come from his house. It was an auspicious beginning for the relationship between the explorer and the man he would call "my friend" and "my Protector," and whose influence he would compare to that of the pope. No other character in Barth's monumental account of his expedition—not Overweg, nor even the rulers of the Central African states he visited—received the adoration the explorer lavished on al-Bakkai, the first Timbuktu scholar to have prolonged, documented contact with a European.

The next morning—a blustery day, the anniversary of Overweg's death, as Barth reminded himself—the explorer had recovered enough to pay a courtesy visit to al-Bakkai's house. He found the shaykh in a small upper room that looked onto a roof terrace, in the company of two of his students and a young nephew. The man who rose to greet Barth was about fifty years old, tall and "full proportioned," with gray-flecked whiskers and dressed all in black. Barth immediately noted his cheerful, intelligent countenance and "straightforward and manly character": he had gambled his life on this man, and now, he was certain, he would be safe. After he had paid his compliments and presented al-Bakkai with the gift of a six-shooter, they fell into a long and deep exchange. Laing, the only Christian anyone in Timbuktu had knowingly encountered, was their first topic of conversation, and Barth learned that al-Bakkai was the son of Sidi Muhammad al-Kunti, the shaykh who had helped Laing before succumbing to an epidemic.

The pistol . . . with which I presented him, soon directed our conversation to the subject of the superiority of Europeans in manufacturing skill . . . and one of the first questions which my host put to me was whether it was true, as [Major Laing] had informed his father, Sidi [Muhammad], during his stay in Azawad, that the capital of the British empire contained twenty times 100,000 people.

Al-Bakkai expressed "admiration of the major's bodily strength, as well as his noble and chivalrous character," but when Barth inquired after Laing's papers, he was told they no longer existed, even though the shaykh was aware that Laing had drawn up a map of the whole northerly part of the desert while staying in Azawad.

After their meeting, Barth sent more presents across the street, but al-Bakkai begged him to stop, asking only that he should not forget him when he returned to England, and that he "request Her Majesty's Government to send him some good fire-arms and some Arabic books." Literature was highly esteemed by the Timbnktu elite. While he was in the city, Barth heard rumors of large, ancient libraries, some of which had been destroyed by the Fulani, others of which had been hidden, and although al-Bakkai did not show Barth a manuscript collection, he did reveal a small collection of treasured works, including a copy of Hippocrates in Arabic that Clapperton had given the sultan of Sokoto as a present, which the sultan had passed on to al-Bakkai. There was such great demand for the written word here and in the Western Sudan as a whole, Barth noted, that

I may assert, with full confidence, that those few books taken by the gallant Scotch captain [Clapperton] into Central Africa have had a greater effect in reconciling the men of authority in Africa to the character of Europeans than the most costly present ever made to them.

As Barth observed the shaykh over the following weeks and months, the Timbuktien's gentle, scholarly nature became ever more evident. Al-Bakkai was often attended by pupils, some of whom had come great distances to study with him. He had established a place of prayer in the small square in front of his house where the students could spend the night, and late in the evenings he would tell them stories with religious themes, or open theocratic discussions, demonstrating "unmistakable proofs of an enlightened and elevated mind." Among his favorite subjects were the lives of the prophets, each of whom, he said, possessed a character trait that set them apart: "He dwelt particularly on the distinguished qualities of Moses, or Musa, who was a great favourite with him," Barth noted. On one occasion the explorer was deeply moved by the way al-Bakkai led his students in recitations of the Islamic texts:

> Part of the day the sheikh read and recited to his pupils chapters from the hadith of Bokhari, while his young son repeated his lesson aloud from the Kuran, and in the evening several surat, or chapters, of the holy book were beautifully chanted by the pupils to a late hour of the night. There was nothing more charming to me than to hear these beautiful verses chanted by sonorous voices in this open desert country.

Al-Bakkai was not simply a scholar and holy man; he was a political force in the region who used his influence for the good of Timbuktu. Sometimes he would resolve conflicts between warring clans, try to reopen trading routes that had been closed by the tribes, or plot the liberation of the city from its oppressor, Ahmad III. Barth's presence was a huge political headache for al-Bakkai, but one the shaykh seemed to relish. For eight months he skillfully maneuvered the explorer in and out of the city, summoning his allies to protect Barth when necessary. He was no doubt motivated by regret at what had happened to Laing and the hope that Britain could be an ally against the French, who were already making aggressive military thrusts into the Sahara, but his main reason for protecting the Christian, according to Barth, was to show the Fulani who ruled Timbuktu.

In late 1853, after al-Bakkai had frustrated several attempts to seize Barth, Sultan Ahmad sent a message ordering that the Christian and his property be handed over. The shaykh was almost as enraged by the ignoble birth of the messenger as he was by the letter's content, and he penned an offensive poem in response, attacking the sultan for plotting to kill his friend, a man who was better versed in religion than the Fulani ruler himself. "My guest is my honour," he asserted, after producing a list of his long and noble ancestry. Had the slave really been sent by Ahmad to take Barth into custody, "that [Ahmad] might plunder him, and fetter him?" If the sultan persisted, al-Bakkai would be fully justified before God in calling on his followers in Masina to overthrow the sultan's rule:

I have among the tribe of the Fullan a body of men in the land who run and hasten to defend the religion of Allah. Dearer to them than their house, and family, and souls is the religion of Allah, who is mighty! Whenever they see infidelity and rebellion against their Lord, they resist, and go aside from every impious person. And I have some of the men of Allah in the land, and also of the angels, as an auxiliary and a scattering host. . . . He is God, who is great! He redoubles His aid against every oppressor who is violent and exorbitant.

Ahmad's courtiers sent numerous other emissaries to Timbuktu to try to capture Barth, but the Fulani were too weak there, and al-Bakkai was relentless in his defense. One evening, when the threat against Barth was especially great, the German went to al-Bakkai's house around midnight and "found the holy man himself, armed with a double-barreled gun." He spent the night with al-Bakkai and his men, waiting for an attack that never came. To pass the time, the shaykh, seated on the raised platform of clay that occupied a corner of the parlor, "entertained the sleepy assembly with stories of the prophets, especially Musa [Moses] and Mohammed, and the victories achieved by the latter, in the beginning of his career, over his numerous adversaries."

ALTHOUGH OFTEN CONFINED to his house, Barth was at times able to roam the city, and during his lengthy stay he was able to make the most extensive European observations yet of Timbuktu life. He didn't contradict the findings of Caillié, who had visited the city for just thirteen days and was hampered by his false identity, but with his much greater knowledge of the region, and with far better contacts and resources, the Prussian portrayed Timbuktu in a different light.

He drew a detailed ground plan, noting the separate quarters of town and describing the nature of each. The city's most significant buildings were its three large mosques, and the stately Jingere Ber made a lasting impression on him. Timbuktu's defenses—including a wall which "seems never to have been of great magnitude"—had been destroyed during the Fulani conquest in 1826, Barth wrote. He counted 980 clay houses and a couple hundred huts, which led him to estimate that the town had a permanent population at that time of about 13,000, but during the trading season, from November to January, it grew by 5,000 to 10,000, and it had probably at one time been twice as large, extending a thousand yards farther north to include the mausoleum of Sidi Mahmud, which was now in the desert.

Timbuktu's shrines had a special role to play in the spiritual lives of the people. When al-Bakkai's mother-in-law died, the shaykh went to pray for her soul at the sepulcher of Sidi al-Mukhtar, on the east side of town. This was an indication of the reverence in which women were held, Barth noted, adding, "There are . . . several women famed for the holiness of their life, and even authoresses of well-digested religious tracts, among the tribe of the Kunta." Later, he witnessed another role for the saint: as a peacemaker. Al-Bakkai, his brothers, and the sons of Barth's guard "attempted to bring about a friendly understanding among themselves," and the explorer was surprised to be told this would take place at "the venerated cemetery a few hundred yards east of the town, where Sidi Mukhtar lies buried." Barth inspected Sidi al-Mukhtar's mausoleum closely and found it to be "a spacious clay apartment, surrounded by several smaller tombs of people who were desirous of placing themselves under the protection of the spirit of this holy man, even in the other world."

Barth's portrait of the economic life of the historic city, meanwhile, would not be bettered. The richest area was the one in which he was staying, Sane-gungu, where the most expensive houses were owned by merchants. The only goods made in Timbuktu were leatherwork and the products of the blacksmith, he noted, and the city's wealth was based on foreign commerce, which found this "the most favoured spot for intercourse." Goods flowed into the city along three great trade routes: two led across the desert, one to Morocco and the other to Ghadames, in Libya; the third ran southwest on the river. On Christmas

Day 1853, Barth witnessed the Niger's inundations reach right up to Timbuktu, flooding the southern and southwestern part of the city, and noted that "small boats very nearly approached the town." Gold, produced in the famous mines of Bambuk, in what is now western Mali, was the principal traded material, although by this time it did not exceed £20,000 in value a year. It was brought to the town in rings, but must have been traded in dust form too. A mithqal of gold in Timbuktu weighed the same as twenty-four grains of the carob tree, and was worth three or four thousand cowrie shells.

Timbuktu's other main commodity was salt, brought from the mines at Taoudenni. The salt here formed in five layers, each of which carried a different value, and was dug out in slabs weighing up to sixty-five pounds. A midsize slab would be worth three to six thousand cowrie shells, the highest prices being paid toward spring, when the caravans became scarce because of the blood-sucking flies that infested the region. The salt was exchanged principally for cloth manufactured in Kano, the Sokoto caliphate. Kano was such a significant producer of textiles that Barth called it the "Manchester of Africa." The third most valuable commodity was the kola nut, a luxury item of which there were many different varieties. Slaves, as far as he could ascertain, were not exported in "any considerable amount." The chief agricultural products in the market were rice, sorghum, and millet, as well as vegetable butter, which was used for cooking and lighting. As Caillié had, he also found European merchandise, including cloth, looking-glasses, cutlery, tobacco, and swords of German manufacture, imported across the desert. Barth saw calico printed with the name of a Manchester firm in Arabic letters, and noted that "all the cutlery in Timbuktu is of English workmanship."

Recognizing that the city was no longer what it had been, he concluded that there was an immense opportunity for Europe to revive the trade that had formerly animated this quarter of the globe. After all, the situation in Timbuktu was still "of the highest commercial importance," lying as it did between the great river of West Africa and the north.

During his prolonged stay, Barth also returned to his study of the manuscript of the *Tarikh al-sudan* he had found in Gando. On December 15, 1853, he sent his notes, via caravan, to Professor Emil Rödiger at the German Oriental Society in Leipzig. The chronicle, he wrote, had apparently been completed by the scholar Ahmad Baba in 1653/1654, and it threw a "completely unsuspected light" on the history of a region that had been totally neglected, while his account of the Songhay emperor made Leo Africanus's description look "hollow and empty." Time pressure meant he had been forced to leave out an infinite number of details—"naturally a traveler in these regions does not have the peace of a scholar in his study," Barth noted—but he had little doubt that someone would bring an entire copy of the book to Europe in the near future.

"You will have heard about my circumstances in this peculiar city from other sources," he told Rödiger. "They are not entirely pleasant, but God the Merciful will protect my life and lead me home, happy and unharmed, to develop to his glory what I began here."

Barth was finally able to leave Timbuktu in the spring of 1854. Al-Bakkai accompanied him to Gao, the once splendid capital of the Songhay empire, which Barth found was now a disappointment. There, on July 8, they parted company. "Although I felt sincerely attached to my protector," Barth wrote, "I could not but feel greatly satisfied at being at length enabled to retrace my steps homeward."

.   .   .

ON LEARNING OF THE DEATH of Richardson, the British government had appointed a new assistant for Barth, a young German named Eduard Vogel, who had set out from Tripoli in the summer of 1853 with instructions to find the explorer. A year later, Vogel was told that Barth had died one hundred miles from Sokoto, and he wrote to the consul in Tripoli to relay the bad news. The letter was forwarded to the Foreign Office, and Barth's siblings and parents in Hamburg were informed. They were "thrown into the deepest grief," Barth wrote, and held a funeral during which, lacking a body, they buried all the explorer's possessions.

On December 1, 1854, Barth was traveling through an inhospitable stretch of forest toward Kukawa, the capital of Bornu, when he met the source of the false report. He saw a small group advancing toward him, led by a man of "strange aspect—a young man of very fair complexion, dressed in a tobe [a simple cloth garment] like the one I wore myself, and with a white turban wound thickly round his head." Barth recognized one of the travelers as his servant, Madi, whom he had left to guard a house he had taken in Kukawa two years before. Madi told the pale young man it was "Abdel Karim," at which point the stranger rushed forward.

Seventeen years later, Henry Morton Stanley would greet another lost African explorer on the banks of Lake Tanganyika with the premeditated line "Dr. Livingstone, I presume?" and create one of the most celebrated encounters in history. The chance meeting of the two Prussians is rather less famous. Where Stanley wrote a book, Barth devoted less than two pages of his published journal to this, his first contact with a European in two years. They were both surprised, he noted. They gave each other a hearty greeting, then dismounted and sat down. Barth had some coffee boiled, "so that we were quite at home," whereupon Vogel told Barth—to the older man's "great amazement"—that he had used all the expedition's supplies, including the stores that had been carefully placed at Kukawa and Zinder. If this was not grievous enough, Vogel had also failed to bring any alcohol:

> The news of the want of pecuniary supplies did not cause me so much surprise as the report which I received from him that he did not possess a single bottle of wine; for, having now been for more than three years without a drop of any stimulant except coffee . . . I had an insuperable longing for the juice of the grape, of which former experience had taught me the benefit.

It had taken Vogel eighteen months to find Barth. After two hours, the pair decided to separate, Vogel to continue to Zinder, and Barth to Kukawa.

"I hastened," Barth wrote, "to overtake my people."

11.

SECRET AGENTS

JUNE–SEPTEMBER 2012

heikh Diouara remembered exactly where he was when the jihadists began their wholesale destruction of Timbuktu's tombs. It was early on the morning of Saturday, June 30, and the video journalist was traveling to a meeting of the UNESCO World Heritage Committee in Saint Petersburg. He had been in Timbuktu filming the profaned tomb of Sidi Mahmud, and UNESCO had invited him to show the committee his footage as evidence of what had happened. There had been a mix-up with his baggage, however, and he'd missed his connecting flight, so he was stuck in Casablanca. At seven a.m. his cellphone rang.

The voice at the other end belonged to a young al-Qaeda fighter Diouara knew from Timbuktu. They had become friends after the journalist took a few photos of him posing with his gun.

"I think they are going to smash the mausoleums," the mujahid told him. "They've just been talking about it." A group of jihadists had gone to the hardware store in Timbuktu's market to buy the pickaxes and hoes they needed, he said, "then they're going to go and do it."

Diouara was stuck. His instincts told him to hurry back to Mali, but the next flight he could get to Bamako was four days away. He wrote a quick story for Reuters, then called his young fighter friend back. The destruction hadn't yet begun.

"When we're over there near the tombs, I won't be able to talk to you," said the fighter. What about just sending a text? No, he didn't know how to write. That didn't matter, Diouara persisted; it could be empty, as long as they both knew it was the signal that the attacks on the mausoleums had started. The jihadist agreed.

A short time later, Diouara received a blank message.

It wasn't entirely a coincidence that the destruction began in the week the thirty-sixth session of the World Heritage Committee was meeting in Saint Petersburg. Tension between the MNLA and AQIM had been simmering for months, and on Wednesday, June 27, at Gao, it finally broke out into an open firefight. It ended with the MNLA's secretary-general, Bilal Ag Cherif, fleeing his own headquarters, while the body of a senior MNLA commander, a Malian army defector, Colonel Bouna Ag Teyib, was dragged through the streets behind a pickup. Al-Qaeda followed this victory by ordering the MNLA to leave their base at Timbuktu airport by five p.m. the following afternoon. The MNLA meekly complied, leaving the jihadists the sole authority in northern Mali. "From that moment it was their kingdom," the city elder Jansky recalled.

The delegates at the UNESCO meeting gathered at the Tauride Palace, an opulent eighteenth-century mansion created for Catherine the Great's lover Prince Grigory Potemkin, with views over the Neva

River. Their business was essentially to manage two lists. The first of these, the World Heritage List, consisted of a thousand of the world's most precious treasures: monuments, archaeological sites, and natural phenomena that were deemed of "outstanding universal value." The second, the List of World Heritage in Danger, was a subset of the first, and comprised those locations threatened by deterioration, natural disaster, or war. The UN body deemed that "major operations" were necessary to protect these sites, and assistance was requested.

After a late Malian government submission, the committee that week debated whether to move the mausoleums of Timbuktu onto the Danger list. Giving its formal response, recorded in the minutes as Decision 36 COM 7B.106, the committee congratulated the Malian government for having expressed its concern, appealed to the African Union and the Economic Community of West African States to ensure that the cultural heritage of north Mali was protected, and—the fateful decision—agreed to inscribe the monuments in question on the list of threatened world sites. UNESCO director-general Irina Bokova would later try to explain this move. It was not her decision, but that of the committee. It was also a no-win situation. "I know there is this thinking that we don't have to tease [the jihadists]; we have to appease them, which I understand in some cases," she said. "But there are others, especially now when everything is so globalized, everything is so visible and so connected, where UNESCO is more criticized for not doing enough than for provoking destruction."

What was most unfortunate was the committee's timing: the decision was made on Thursday, June 28, the day the jihadists, still pumped up after their victory at Gao, forced the MNLA to retreat from Timbuktu. The next morning, on the Muslim holy day, they went to the city's mosques to speak against the cult of Timbuktu's saints. The morning after that, Diouara received his phone call in Casablanca.

Ahmad al-Faqi al-Mahdi, the Islamic Police leader from a nearby village, was ordered to carry out the destruction. He began on the northern edge of the city, in Abaraju, with the mausoleum of Sidi Mahmud. They had already attacked the tomb of this powerful saint, and now they finished it off. The tomb was a boxlike construction made of rammed earth and stones, which stood on a hill by a tree, encircled by the graves of the saint's disciples, who were said to number 167. It was a quiet spot, a place where people came daily to pray, pay their respects, and ask for the saint's help. At eight a.m., around a hundred jihadists, shouting *"Allahu Akbar!"* and carrying the hoes, pickaxes, crowbars, and hammers they had bought in the hardware store, surrounded the tomb and started to attack it. Bystanders were kept away by machine guns pointed in their direction. "Nobody was allowed to approach," Jansky recalled.

The tomb was not built to withstand any kind of assault. The men were soon able to pry away one of the walls with a crowbar and hack it into rubble. A black-bearded jihadist explained to camera his reasons for desecrating the mausoleum. "There is a Kuranic law that says a tomb must be only a few centimeters above the ground," he said. "And that no one must be venerated but God. It is for that reason that we are destroying the tomb." By the time they had finished, the building was a heap of earth, stones, and timber spars. The demolition team then moved on to the tomb of Shaykh Muhammad Mahmud al-Arawani, in the same cemetery.

"We are all Muslims," said the jihadist spokesman Sanda Ould Bouamama. "UNESCO is what?" This was just the start of their cleansing of the city: "Today, Ansar Dine is going to destroy all the mausoleums in the town. All of them, without exception." Redbeard Hamaha described those who had worshipped at the shrines as being "driven by Satan": "It is forbidden by Islam to pray on tombs and ask for blessings," he told a reporter. "Ansar Dine is showing the rest of the world, especially Western countries, that whether they want it or not, we will not let the younger generation believe in shrines . . . regardless of what the UN, UNESCO, the International Criminal Court, or ECOWAS [the Economic Community of West African States] have to say. We do not recognize these organizations. The only thing we recognize is the court of God, sharia. Sharia is a divine obligation. People don't get to choose whether they like it or not."

At around ten a.m., the men with the hoes and pickaxes moved east, to the cemetery of Sidi al-Mukhtar al-Kunti, where Barth had witnessed al-Bakkai negotiate with his brothers 158 years before. They destroyed more mausoleums here, including that of the shaykh himself, and al-Mahdi declared: "We are going to wipe out from our landscape all that does not belong there." In the afternoon, al-Mahdi's gang moved south to the cemetery of Alfa Moy, where they worked until sunset.

Some residents cried as they watched their holiest sites being smashed; others were mute, uncomprehending. That night, the town went to bed at dusk. "Everyone was exhausted," Air Mali recalled. "It felt as if the days of Timbuktu were finished."

The rampage continued the next day, with three more mausoleums demolished in Jingere Ber. Air Mali sensed a method in their assault: they were attacking the tombs at the edges of the town, the cornerstones of its spiritual defense. On the third day, the jihadists chose a new target. In a wall on the west side of the Sidi Yahya mosque, beneath a triangular lintel, was an elegant wooden door embossed in traditional Timbuktu style with decorative metalwork. According to local belief, it was to remain shut until the end of days. "The symbolism of the Sidi Yahya door was quite simply there are people who said when you open the door, it is the end of the world," Grand Imam Abderrahmane Ben Essayouti explained. It wasn't magic or idolatry—just a myth that had been invented for a pragmatic purpose. "The ancients told the story to the little children to stop them from approaching the door, because behind it the wall was not very solid and there was a risk it would collapse on people. The people thought that you had to leave it. It was a way of keeping people safe."

The Salafists saw it as heresy. "Their mentality was to defy that," said Ben Essayouti. "They wanted to demonstrate that it was not true, although of course everyone knew it was not true. It was simply something we told the children to make them afraid."

On Monday morning, a group of gunmen in turbans approached the mosque. They dragged out the wooden lintel first, which came away easily. The doors posed more of a problem: the men had to put their backs into that, ripping them out of the sunbaked earth that held them in place. A black-turbaned jihadist, aware of the video camera filming him, came away from the task rubbing his neck. "God is great," he said, adding with sarcasm: "And now is the time of the end of the world."

People among the small crowd of Timbuktiens who had gathered to watch began to cry.

Even two years later, this moment was raw for the grand imam. "When the mausoleums were destroyed, that was the moment when morale dropped," he said, his voice weary. "For them it is perhaps Islam. The hadiths say that near the end of times Islam will be divided into seventy-three sects, and a single sect will be the real truth. We are witnessing that. Every day you hear a new sect that manifests itself, declaring itself. For them, in their spirit, these things are the truth. People now are so confused."

Many blamed the World Heritage Committee. "If UNESCO had not said what they did, the jihadists would not have touched the cultural heritage," said Air Mali. "Given what UNESCO decreed, they had to attack that which they had forgotten to attack."

The Crisis Committee wrote to their contacts in Bamako afterward, asking them to stop denouncing the jihadists' behavior, while the librarians in Bamako took it as a further spur to try to keep people quiet. "Every time UNESCO spoke about the manuscripts, I phoned them and said, no, you must not speak about the manuscripts," Haidara said.

The day after the destruction of the mausoleums, Haidara took a call from a senior UNESCO official in Paris. The organization's job was to work for global heritage, the official said, and when it was in danger, they were obliged to act. So why did Haidara call them every time they spoke up and tell them to keep quiet?

"I told him we are in the middle of something very important, and if you continue to speak to the media about the manuscripts, the people there will become aware of what we are doing," said Haidara. "The next day he called again and told me, 'Okay, we are going to have a deal between you and me. Every day I am going to call you, you are going to tell us what is happening.' I said okay."

From that moment, the official would call every morning, and Haidara would give him an update. "We had a lot of conversations afterwards," he remembered. "They understood."

Diouara understood something too: the jihadists' rampage meant they had stopped trying to win over the people of the city. They had given up the pretense and now revealed themselves as they really were. "They had entered into a new phase of the occupation, a decisive phase," he said. "I understood then that there would be mutilations, whipping, and everything else that was to come."

THE OUTPOURING of fury that rained down on the jihadists came from all quarters and all corners of the globe. The prosecutor for the International Criminal Court (ICC) declared the destruction of the mausoleums a war crime, which her office had authority to investigate. Six West African leaders issued a statement encouraging the ICC to take action and called on Mali to ask the UN to intervene militarily against the groups in northern Mali. The U.S. State Department "strongly condemned" the destruction, while Russia described it as a "barbarian" act that could "only arouse indignation." For France it was "intolerable," a "systematic violation of places of reverence and prayer," which for centuries had been part of the soul of the famed sub-Saharan city. At Paris's request, the UN Security Council unanimously passed Resolution 2056, which called for sanctions on the jihadists responsible and condemned "the desecration, damage and destruction of sites of holy, historic and cultural significance" in the city.

In southern Mali the reaction was equally hostile. On July 4, Muslim leaders in Bamako marched against the Islamists in the north. "No to imported Islam, yes to the Islam of our parents," read one slogan, while a protester explained that "Timbuktu was founded on a pure Islam, respectful of men, of all men." The culture minister, Diallo Fadima Touré, called on the UN to "take concrete steps to stop these crimes against the cultural heritage of my people." Even the MNLA, without irony, called for international intervention, asking for "the USA, France and all other countries who want to stand against Ansar Dine, Boko Haram and al-Qaeda who are now holding Timbuktu, Gao and Kidal to help us kill them and help the people in those cities."

The most unlikely outburst, however, came from the hideout, probably in the Kabylie mountains east of Algiers, of the AQIM leader, Abdelmalek Droukdel.

To mark the start of the holy month of Ramadan on July 20, the emir and his advisers put the finishing touches to an eighty-page memo titled "General Guidelines Concerning the Islamic Jihadist Project in Azawad" and fired it off to his commanders in Mali. Pages of this internal document would not be seen by the wider world until the following year, when it was found by reporters digging through the rubble and paperwork Timbuktu's occupiers had left behind. The document was carefully structured, with criticism bracketed fore and aft by positive remarks about the great opportunity of the "new baby" of the Islamic Azawad project. In parts it included the sort of business-speak one might find in a company report: there were several mentions of "external stakeholders" and warnings against "high visibility on the current political and military stage," as well as concerns about the al-Qaeda brand. The gist of the memo was clear: AQIM's Saharan branch was in danger of screwing up this whole jihadist project.

The great powers might not be in a position to use force because of the exhaustion of their armies and the ongoing global financial crisis, Droukdel wrote, but they would nevertheless try to hinder the creation of an Islamic state of Azawad. It was probable—even certain—that they would undertake some sort of military intervention or exert pressure through a complete economic, political, and military embargo, at which point AQIM's brigades would be forced to retire to their bases in the desert. Bearing in mind that al-Qaeda was a red rag to the West, it was vital that they disguise themselves. "Be silent and make it look as if you are a 'domestic' movement that has its own causes and concerns," Droukdel advised. "Foreign intervention will be imminent and rapid if we [AQIM] have a hand in government and our influence is clearly asserted."

They must also avoid taking risks. The speed with which AQIM's local commanders were moving against the Islam of the region was a huge mistake. "Among your foolish policies," Droukdel noted in one scathing paragraph, was "the rush to apply sharia without taking into account the principle of progressive application in an environment where the populations have not known religious precepts for centuries." Previous experience had proved that applying sharia in this way "will lead to people's rejecting the religion, and engender hatred toward the mujahideen." It would, consequently, lead to the failure of "our experiment."

Specific examples of this hastiness, which he and AQIM's ruling council ordered them not to repeat, included the destruction of the mausoleums and the imposition of the *hadd* punishments. Of the decision to smash the mausoleums, he wrote: "We are not powerful enough today, foreign intervention is imminent and the people have known the Islamic conquest for only a short time. . . . The side effects of this action are not trivial and we will not be forgiven if we carry on in this way." But their "gravest error" was the falling-out with the MNLA, who were necessary partners in the struggle to achieve al-Qaeda's aims, even if they did not appear natural friends. Droukdel despaired at the breakdown of agreements with them and with the Arab rebel movement. These groups, he wrote, should be used to build the state and defend against foreign intervention. In his eyes, the agreement that had been drawn up between the MNLA and al-Qaeda was a great "conquest" that surpassed all AQIM's hopes for a movement that supposedly had secular tendencies.

In sum, while al-Qaeda should lend its resources to the state of Azawad, it was in neither its interest nor its capacity to govern the territory when its overriding objective was global jihad. It should therefore keep to the background, supporting a government of Azawad led by Iyad Ag Ghaly and Ansar Dine, but which included representatives of all communities in the north—the MNLA, the Arabs, the Songhay, and the Fulani—and focus its energies on the big picture.

"Finally," he concluded, "we consider these directives and this general vision as the best way of avoiding the errors of the past, which we hope not to make again."

At whom was Droukdel's memo aimed? Surely not Abou Zeid, a Droukdel protégé whose kidnappings had dramatically raised the organization's profile and its cash reserves. More likely it was Mokhtar Belmokhtar, the one-eyed commander who led the fighting against the MNLA in Gao. Belmokhtar would soon split with AQIM altogether to set up the rival Signers in Blood brigade, and would write to the global leader of al-Qaeda, Ayman al-Zawahiri, telling him that Droukdel was deeply out of touch. Given that jihadists had already dragged the body of Colonel Bouna Ag Teyib through the streets of Gao and forced the MNLA's secretary-general to flee his headquarters, he had a point: the moment for patching up relations with the MNLA was surely long gone.

Whatever AQIM's Saharan commanders thought of the emir's words, they had little effect. Locked on their path, administering a territory where it was a struggle to keep the lights on, Timbuktu's new leaders moved even more quickly than before.

. . .

FOR THE LIBRARIANS IN BAMAKO, the evacuation was growing urgent. Haidara spent his days in a cycle of fruitless fund-raising meetings. He toured the embassies again, contacting "friends of Mali" ("Mali," said Haidara, "has many friends") to see if anything had changed, but these contacts gave the same response over and over: "It was 'No, no, no, we cannot do anything like that,'" he recalled. "That's the national heritage of Mali, we are friends of Mali, and if our country starts to help you do that, Mali will start accusing us. We cannot get mixed up in that." It seemed to him that his contacts were no longer talking to him in the same respectful tone they had once used. Finally, one "friend" explained to him that the international partners had no confidence in what was being done in the country, so they would not spend money there. Haidara felt he had been duped.

"I understood many things," he said. "It reminded me of many meetings that I had had with other people. They were not open with us."

The librarians tried a new tack after that, making appointments with the senior figures in the Malian government in charge of heritage. They began with the Ministry of Higher Education and Scientific Research, the government department responsible for the Ahmad Baba institute. The Timbuktu manuscripts were threatened, Haidara told them, but the librarians did not have the means to save them. "What are you going to do to help?"

"The way I see you today, I know you are serious," the secretary-general of the department told him. "But I am going to tell you something. We cannot help you politically, or materially, in any way. The only thing I can tell you is that all you are able to do in this business, you must do it. We are behind you."

Next they went to the Ministry of Culture, which oversaw the private manuscript collections. Haidara gave the same speech and got the same answer. You need to do it, he recalled being told, we are behind you. "I told them I would try," Haidara said, "but I wanted them to be aware of it, because if there were problems they had to help me." The officials agreed.

With the backing of the ministries, Haidara now called his contacts abroad. He had a friend in Geneva who told him to come to Switzerland, and even paid for his plane ticket. Haidara spent several days there, meeting people who dealt with world heritage, including some who had worked to save manuscripts in Iraq and Afghanistan. They told him he should start the operation soon, but take it slowly and carefully. Even if he managed to smuggle only a single manuscript out of the city each day, it would be worthwhile. One woman gave him a piece of advice that would stick with him. "She said you must never lose someone who starts to work with you," he recalled. "You must always keep them happy, even if it is not in your interest, even if they make wrong calculations. She said it to me three times."

He returned from Switzerland with a lot to think about, but he still had no money.

Ismael at that time also wanted to travel. For a man who liked to spend an hour every morning and evening walking in the open desert around Timbuktu, Bamako was claustrophobic. The village Mungo Park had passed through in 1796 was now a city of more than two million, and thousands more were arriving from the north every week. Its cinder-block homes stretched for twenty miles; its streets and bridges were crowded with honking vehicles that coughed brown smog into the humid air. Ismael's sense of being choked was compounded by the political tension that occasionally spilled over into gunfights in the streets, including an attempted countercoup by the deposed president's guard that left fourteen people dead.

"I was not good in Bamako," he said.

Exiled from Timbuktu, with the manuscripts of his Fondo Kati library hidden, he had little to tie him to Mali and its crisis. He decided to return to his second home, in Andalusia.

The other librarians understood. "It happened that our friend Ismael was tired," said Haidara. "He said, 'Good. I am going to let you carry on.'"

"The truth was that when we were looking for solutions, Ismael had no problem," Maiga said. "He was with us to give us ideas. By the time we made the decision to intervene, he was already in Spain. He had secured his manuscripts before going, and he left."

He did not come back.

BY JULY, Alkadi was also in Bamako. The Ahmad Baba researcher with the easy smile and the sleepy eyes had left Timbuktu with his family in late April. After a nightmarish bus journey that lasted almost a week, they reached Segu, where he found a cheap house to rent. But there was nothing for him to do there, and with no money coming in, he and Fatouma decided in June that he should go to Bamako. Every day Alkadi went to offer himself for employment in the small first-floor offices in Kalaban Coura that the director, Maiga, had hired. Even here, there wasn't much work: the only materials the institute had were a few digitized documents that had been brought south on hard drives, plus several hundred manuscripts Maiga had acquired in Bamako.

On July 23, however, Maiga called Alkadi in. There was something very difficult that he needed to ask him, but he had to be very discreet.

"No problem," said Alkadi. "If I can do it, it's not a problem. I will try."

The director related some of what Haidara had learned on his Swiss trip: how manuscript libraries suffered catastrophic losses during the Iraq War, and how others had been destroyed in Sudan and Libya. The institute's manuscripts were also now at risk of being destroyed, Maiga said: if the Islamists didn't do it, there was a strong chance the MNLA might.

"What I want you to do," he concluded, "is bring the manuscripts out of the libraries in Timbuktu."

"No problem," said Alkadi.

It was typical of Alkadi to respond in a calm, even cool, manner, which was why Maiga had asked him. The director was still new in his job, but he had taken soundings among senior staff in Timbuktu as to who could be trusted with a special and sensitive mission, and Alkadi's name had been the first on the list. Two other agents would accompany him. One was Abdoulaye Sadidi, who also had the reputation of being levelheaded. The third was someone whom neither of them knew well, but who would be invaluable since he was the manager of the Ahmad Baba library: Bouya Haidara.

Maiga asked Alkadi to call in the other two; then he laid out the plan.

The "agents" should make their way to Timbuktu, where they would contact Abba Traoré, the caretaker at the old building on the

Rue de Chemnitz, and tell him to let them into the depository at the back. There they would pack up a few hundred manuscripts—they would have to make their own decisions about which, but he would prefer them to pick the less valuable ones, or those for which there were multiple copies, in case they were lost—and bring them to Bamako. They should avoid traveling back together, since if one of them was caught, they could lose everything. Each agent should also have a cover story in case he was challenged. (Alkadi's was that he had asked for a leave of absence from the institute to visit his brother, who was still living in Timbuktu.) Finally, Maiga said, they must not tell anyone, not even their closest relations, where they were going or what they were planning to do there.

"I know that the people of Timbuktu and Gao have a mouth," he said, "but I want you to close yours."

The director had no money for the mission since his funding was still blocked, so he paid for their journey from his own resources. He drove them to the bank up the road and withdrew a substantial sum, handing 100,000 West African francs ($170) to each agent. Then he told them to go home and pack.

At three p.m. the following day, the agents carried their bags to the Sogolon roundabout, with its giant sculpture of a water buffalo, and boarded a bus bound for Mopti.

TRAVELING IN MALI was hard in the calmest of times. The vehicles were slow, their springs broken, the seats uncomfortable and the tires dangerously bald, and even though bush mechanics worked miracles, breakdowns dogged almost every journey. There were only 3,400 miles of tarmac in a country twice the size of France, and trucks and vans competed on them with speeding cars, overladen donkey carts, pedestrians, and cyclists, dodging broken-down buses and the corpses of animals. Despite the country's lack of roads, a Malian was almost seven times as likely to die in a car accident as a Briton, and a little over twice as likely as an American.

The stress of the journey was made worse by the agents' mission. To enter jihadist territory was risky enough; how much worse it was to be traveling with illicit intent, no matter how noble, that could lead to imprisonment, amputation, or death. On the way north, the men examined the checkpoints they would have to cross with their cargo on the way south. At Douentza, where their route left the tarmac, they saw their first jihadists. "They were everywhere," Alkadi recalled. There were additional checkpoints a hundred miles north, at Bambara Maounde, and just south of the river. At each stop they had to show their ID cards and answer the jihadists' questions. Who are you? Where are you going? What's your business?

By the time they reached the Niger ferry crossing opposite Koriume, they had been traveling for thirty-six hours. It was dusk, and they were not allowed to enter Timbuktu after dark, so they prepared to bed down in the open, on the south bank of the great silvery river. They weren't alone: Bouya, a nervy character with a high-pitched laugh, recognized a friend and, despite what Maiga had said, couldn't stop himself from revealing the secret that had been weighing him down. They were on a mission, he told the friend, and perhaps they would even try to get into one of the Ahmad Baba buildings. The friend was astonished. It would be suicidal to attempt such a thing. Before anyone could stop him, he was making a phone call to discuss it with his brother, who agreed that they must not try to get inside the institute under any circumstances: "If you enter the building, the Islamists are going to kill you," he warned them.

It wasn't the advice that worried Alkadi and Sadidi so much as the fact that word of the mission was now out.

The agents pressed on. In the morning they crossed the river and passed through the final checkpoints, at Koriume and at the Total gas station at the entrance to town. Sadidi and Alkadi then went to rest at Alkadi's house in Abaraju, where his brother was still living, and the next day they went to see a colleague, Aboubacrine Maiga, who lived with his family close to the Sidi Yahya mosque, to tell him they had been sent to bring some manuscripts out of Timbuktu.

It was agreed that Bouya, as the senior man, should now go to see the old caretaker Abba and his grandson Hassini and tell them about the task. Soon after leaving, Bouya called to say he had spoken with them and there was no problem, so Alkadi and Sadidi walked through the sandy alleys to the Rue de Chemnitz. Abba led them to the small yard planted with trees at the back of the building and opened the door to the depository, a white-walled room where the manuscripts, each carefully placed in its own acid-free box, were stored in wooden cabinets. The agents had come prepared with a number of empty ten-kilo rice sacks, and they took the manuscripts out of the boxes and carefully packed them into the bags.

They were all nervous, especially Bouya: "The first day we were enormously afraid because it was our first time," he recalled. "We were really scared, but what can we do? It was not without risk!" Sadidi had an extra problem: he was allergic to dust, which was everywhere, and he kept breaking out in uncontrollable coughing fits.

They hurried to fill the sacks, then one of them went out into the road to call a porter with a *push-push* to carry the manuscripts to Abou-bacrine Maiga's house opposite the Sidi Yahya mosque. There they made a list of what they had taken. By Alkadi's estimate they had around eight hundred documents. They managed to find one steel locker, but that was soon filled—some of the leather-bound volumes were huge, with five hundred or even six hundred pages—so they put the rest in two large rucksacks, then divided up the luggage among themselves. Bouya and Sadidi had a backpack each, while Alkadi took the locker plus two huge manuscripts he could not fit inside.

The plan had been for each agent to travel south separately, but now Alkadi and Sadidi preferred not to let Bouya go alone. "When they saw that Bouya began to give information about the mission, they said if they left him alone, he might give away too much and the mission would fail," recalled Maiga. Sadidi volunteered to leave first. He would phone when he had made it successfully through the checkpoints; then Alkadi and Bouya could leave together.

Alkadi passed an anxious day waiting for Sadidi's call. When it finally came, Sadidi said he was in Sevare and that there had been no problem. The only people who wanted to look in his backpack were the Malian gendarmes, but he'd told them he was carrying manuscripts that belonged to the state and they had let him pass. Now Alkadi and Bouya set out. Unlike the MNLA, the jihadists weren't interested in the baggage, and the two passed through the checkpoints without prob-lems. It was only after Sevare, in government territory, that the pas-sengers were ordered to open all their bags.

"The police were searching the bus everywhere," recalled Alkadi. "They got everything down and looked through all the material." He watched as a soldier worked his way toward his luggage, coming at last to the locker full of manuscripts. Before he could open it Alkadi stepped forward with a letter Maiga had written explaining that he was traveling on state business.

"I'm not here to look at your mission," said the soldier. "I'm here to check the luggage."

Alkadi had no choice but to show him the locker's contents. The soldier's eyes widened. "Ah," he exclaimed, "it's manuscripts!"

There was an awkward moment, but Alkadi remained calm, and since he wasn't carrying anything illegal, the soldier simply closed the steel box. It was okay, he said, they could get back on the bus.

They reached Bamako in the early evening, and Alkadi called Maiga to let him know. The following day he brought the manuscripts to the office above the fish-and-chicken shop and told the director what had happened.

When Haidara heard about the rumors circulating in Timbuktu, he wasn't happy. "I said, 'Okay, we are going to change the strategy,'" he recalled. "I told them again how it would work."

BARELY A WEEK after he had returned from Timbuktu, Alkadi was once again heading north, this time on his own. Sadidi had been ruled out of this second evacuation attempt because of his allergy, while Bouya was a security risk. Maiga had reminded Alkadi not to speak of his mission to anyone else, especially not his family. All the researcher could tell his wife in Segu was that he had to go away again for a few days.

In Mopti he found a 4x4 bound for Timbuktu, which he shared with an assistant mayor and several others. They reached the south bank of the river just before nightfall, but the ferry had stopped for the evening, so they hailed a fishing pirogue, which carried them to the other side, then talked the driver of a Land Rover into taking them the last nine miles to Timbuktu. At the checkpoint by the Total gas station, a young mujahid with a gun, a waistcoat, and a turban in the Afghan style approached the vehicle. Alkadi thought he was a Pakistani.

The assistant mayor was fidgety—what if they found out who he was?—but the young jihadist didn't even ask for their IDs. His only concern was the elderly woman who was sitting with the men in the back seats.

Alkadi, an educated and devout Muslim, was caught by surprise. She was an old woman, he said. Her son was accompanying her. There was no ban on men and women traveling together in Islam.

"You are lying!" yelled the young fighter. "You deliberately put the woman between you! You have to get out. Get out!"

The passengers hurried to do as the gunman said, and the driver quickly arranged for the woman to swap with a man in the front seat. She was still sitting next to a man—the driver—but the jihadist was satisfied that Salafist protocols had been restored, and the Land Rover was waved on its way.

It was dark by the time Alkadi reached his house in Abaraju. He phoned Aboubacrine to tell him he was back, then went to rest, and the following day they went together to the old building, where they met Abba and Hassini again. They called Maiga from there: the director wanted to explain the new mission personally to the caretaker. That afternoon, they set to the task, which soon became a routine.

Alkadi would leave his house at midday for the *duha* prayer at a mosque in the market. Then, as the temperature climbed and people went home to eat and rest, he made his way to the Rue de Chemnitz, bringing a dozen or so rice sacks with him. Hassini would let him into the depository. There they worked together, Alkadi taking the boxes off the shelves and passing them one by one to Hassini, who placed them on the table and opened them while Alkadi noted each manuscript's catalogue number. On the first mission they had noted the titles too, but since Hassini couldn't read Arabic, they now just took the numbers. They removed the manuscripts from the boxes to save space in the lockers, and Hassini held open each sack while Alkadi carefully filled it. Apart from a few scientific documents he recognized, Alkadi didn't know exactly what the manuscripts were; he just grabbed what he could.

They worked until four p.m., breaking off as the city began to re-awaken, and then Alkadi stayed with Hassini and Abba in their house in the library compound till dusk. When night had fallen, one of them went into the street to hail a *push-push*, which was brought around to the back entrance and loaded with the sacks. When they were ready to move, Abba would walk up to the main road to check if the coast was clear. On his signal, the men would set off, Hassini walking in front of the porter with the cart, Alkadi behind, as they escorted the documents the half mile to Aboubacrine's house. They were careful to choose a different *push-push* every night so that no one became too suspicious, and they took the back lanes as much as possible to avoid jihadist patrols.

On the second day they added an evening shift. It was harder working at night—there were frequent power outages, and Abba had to hold a flashlight—so they couldn't stick at it too long, but the manuscript were soon piling up in the house opposite the Sidi Yahya mosque.

Aboubacrine then contacted Maiga, who gave them the number of a trader Haidara knew who would bring the manuscripts south. The trader dropped off ten lockers, telling them to fill them and take them to a particular building in the nearby neighborhood of Bellafarandi. Alkadi and Aboubacrine then transferred the documents to the lockers. When each one was full, they fastened it with a padlock at either end and Alkadi pocketed the keys. They wheeled these, one by one, to the trader's house, no more than two or three a day and at different times, to avoid being noticed. From there the lockers were shipped south on the vehicles that still plied the desert, working the trade route from Timbuktu to Bamako. Even in wartime, the transporters continued to work, since the jihadists wanted the city's commerce and needed the food imports. According to Maiga, the occupiers trusted the merchant: "He had the confidence of the Islamists, and took the opportunity to get things out without people bothering him," he said.

The manuscripts made their way south under piles of Timbuktu produce, as well as Coca-Cola and Fanta and other imported goods shipped from Algeria and Mauritania. "Sometimes the trucks took two lockers, sometimes four," said Haidara. "Sometimes there were two cars and in each car there were five lockers, or three cars with three lockers. That's how we carried on." Sometimes one of Haidara's people would accompany the shipments, but at other times they were on their own, "under God's protection," as Alkadi put it.

When the manuscripts reached the Poste de Nyamana, the giant customs checkpoint at the edge of Bamako, the driver or courier would call to tell the librarians they had arrived, and Maiga or Haidara would go to meet them and, if necessary, ease their passage through the bureaucracy. "I took my car to meet them there at the entry to Bamako," recalled Haidara. "There was often a blockage there and I paid a lot of money. That was a big problem." The lockers were then taken to the Ahmad Baba office in Kalaban Coura. Sometimes Maiga drove them personally, but if there was a large number coming in, he would hire one of the green-painted Sotrama minibus-taxis that carry commuters all over Bamako.

As the operation progressed, the strain began to get to Alkadi. He became paranoid about the children who played around his house. What if they told someone about his movements? He started to leave before dawn, before the kids were out, waiting in the trader's house in Bellafarandi until two p.m. before starting the job. He also worried that Aboubacrine lived too close to the market: the road by his house was always busy with traffic and people and patrols. It was impossible to hide the lockers when they moved them to the trader's house, and people stared. If he was asked, Alkadi told them they just contained market goods, but he worried that the cover story was wearing thin. What if someone asked him to open a locker? "Perhaps they knew we were up to something," he thought. "Perhaps they would check inside Aboubacrine's house, then there would be a big problem."

He told Maiga he believed people were becoming suspicious. The director thought he had a point. "People saw too much back-and-forth, they wondered what was happening," he recalled. So when they had placed ten full lockers in the trader's house, Maiga told him he had done enough. Alkadi traveled back in mid-August, reaching Bamako on the 23rd, fifteen days after setting out.

On the first trip the three agents had moved almost a thousand manuscripts. After working hard for a week, with the help of Hassini, Abba, and Aboubacrine, Alkadi had now shifted around eight thousand more. Roughly two-thirds of the collection that had been stored in the old building still remained.

A short time after Alkadi had settled back in Bamako, Maiga called him in again. "Now you have to go and bring them all," he said.

HAIDARA CAME TO THE OFFICE to see Maiga and Alkadi before the third evacuation. He wanted to speak to Alkadi, to reassure him that he was doing the right thing. "He told me that I shouldn't be afraid and said it was a job that would be good for us in the long run, but it had to be done as if it was no big deal," Alkadi remembered. "He encouraged me and calmed me."

Alkadi's paranoia was such that he didn't even tell Aboubacrine about this final trip. He worked only at night, with Abba and Hassini, and faster than ever. The ten-kilogram sacks were too small, he decided, so he brought around twenty hundred-kilo sacks. They loaded these in bulk, sewing them closed when they were full. There was no attempt even to count the manuscripts now; such was the rush, it was all they could do to try to stop the loose pages from getting mixed up. They worked long into the night, until they were exhausted, then brought the sacks by *push-push* and donkey cart straight to the house in Bellafarandi. There they closed the door, unloaded the manuscripts, and returned with the empty sacks to the depository. In the mornings, Alkadi worked alone at packing the documents into lockers. When one of the steel chests was full, he moved it to another room in the house: the trader would take it from there and place it on the transports. At midday Alkadi went home to rest, heading back to the institute at nightfall to start a new shift.

After ten grueling days, the archive at the institute was empty, and Alkadi felt a world of trouble lifting from his shoulders. Leaving the building for the last time, he bumped into Sadidi, the colleague who had accompanied him on the first trip. His friend was surprised to see him back, unannounced, in Timbuktu. "What are you up to? I thought you were in Bamako!"

Even now, speaking to a friend and fellow agent, Alkadi didn't drop his guard. He had been sent to Gourma Rharous, he told Sadidi, the next major town downriver, and had gone into the institute to give his regards to Abba. "I'm just passing through," he said.

Alkadi left Timbuktu in mid-September, having moved the entire collection of around 24,000 documents from the old building.

THE OPERATION had been conducted in great secrecy, but Maiga felt he now had to tell some of his colleagues what had been done. One of these people was the most senior employee left in Timbuktu, Abdoulaye Cissé. When he had taken up his new job, Maiga had entrusted the manuscripts to Cissé, telling him to make sure nothing moved. Two days after the evacuation was complete, Maiga called to say the entire collection from the Rue du Chemnitz had been transferred to Bamako. "We had evacuated all the manuscripts in the old building from under his nose," Maiga recalled, "and he wasn't even aware of it!"

Maiga also had to inform the civil servants in the Ministry of Higher Education, which had responsibility for the Ahmad Baba institute. He had been in the job only five months, after all, and now he and Haidara had covertly moved the bulk of the state collection six hundred miles southwest to his new office in Kalaban Coura.

He decided to host a surprise reception, what Haidara described as a "little cocktail," and invited a select group from the ministry, including the technical adviser with special responsibility for the Ahmad Baba institute, Drissa Diakité, and a handful of his own staff. He left out the minister, as he didn't want it to be too high-profile an event; they still needed to keep their operations secret.

The men from the ministry were shown into a room filled with the sorts of steel lockers that were used for shipping items all around Mali. "It was clear that they had no idea we had begun something," recalled Haidara. When Maiga opened the boxes, the men recoiled. "They said, 'Ah! What is that?'" recalled Maiga. "They were very surprised, very surprised."

Since the jihadist assault on the tombs of the Timbuktu saints, the ministers had been dreading that something similar would happen to the city's written heritage. "We were preoccupied with an attack on the manuscripts," Diakité said, so when the lockers were opened and he saw what they had done, he thought it was "marvelous," something "salutary." Questions tumbled out. How had they managed to get them through all the checkpoints? How had they even formed the idea of smuggling them south? Diakité did not question the decision to keep the operation hidden. "It was necessary that this was secret, so they did not inform the authorities," he said. At the same time, he found the thought of the manuscripts in transit in lockers "frightening," and knew a lot of work remained to be done. "We had to find the means to stop them from being all concentrated in the same locale, because that was also dangerous for the manuscripts." The humid climate of Bamako was also a threat. "We had to improve the conditions in which they were being held. There were a lot of question marks."

Overall, though, the men from the ministry were overjoyed. They spoke of giving medals to Maiga and Haidara. "No, no, no," said Haidara. What else, then, could they do for him?

"You have the manuscripts," Haidara said, "but what I ask is that you must not speak about it, because our manuscripts are still there."

He was referring to the private collections, which, he said, made up 85 percent of the total number of documents in the city. Those were still in danger. "Soon we are going to start evacuating them," he said. "It is not over. So the best present you could give me would be to not talk about it."

The men from the government agreed.

THERE WERE TWO STRANGE POSTSCRIPTS to the operation to smuggle the Ahmad Baba institute's manuscripts south. The first was that Maiga was called in by the minister of higher education and berated for what he had done. "Who gave you the order to move the manuscripts?" the minister asked. Maiga explained that in the times they were living through he had decided not to wait for approval, whereupon the minister brusquely told him he must be informed of anything that was done and dismissed him.

"People always think the worst," said Maiga.

The second consequence was that relations between the librarians began to deteriorate.

At the start of September, Haidara had traveled to Dubai to set out his problems to Juma al-Majid, a veteran Arab philanthropist who ran a center for the preservation of Arabic manuscripts and had funded previous projects in Timbuktu. Haidara explained how they had been forced to move the documents into people's houses, where they were now kept in poor conditions in wooden or steel trunks, and that the jihadists' behavior was increasingly threatening. Al-Majid told him not to delay but to shift them from Timbuktu in any way he could. "I will help you immediately," he said. "You must start working on it from today." He would send Haidara $30,000 to get him started.

Maiga felt cut out of this transaction. "He told me, 'Once the money is there, I'll give you a part that you will use to take out the manuscripts,'" the Ahmad Baba director recalled. "But—these are things that are not good to say—I knew he already had the money. And he had already contacted merchants and traders who had already bought lockers and trunks for manuscripts in Timbuktu. He knew that I had just arrived [in the job], and I had no means, and he played on that."

Maiga expected to get a financial breakdown of how much Haidara had raised and how much they could spend, and to have a discussion with him about how large a share would be allocated to the Ahmad Baba manuscripts. But Haidara didn't provide any of this information. "I was shocked for two reasons," said Maiga. "First, when we started the meetings in my office, we said we were going to manage it together, to the end. But when he had the money, this was not the case. Second, if I had known he had the money, I would not have paid for things out of my own pocket."

Later, Haidara maintained that he had never promised Maiga any of the money he raised—"We never spoke about it," he said—and that anyway it was he, not Maiga, whom the government had authorized to evacuate the manuscripts.

By September, the alliance of three powerful librarians who had begun meeting in May had collapsed. Haidara would pursue his evacuation of the privately owned manuscripts without Maiga's help.

"He pushed me away," said Maiga.

PART THREE

LIBERATION

///////////

Somewhere . . . someone had to do the saving and keeping, one way or another, in books, in records, in people's heads, any way at all so long as it was safe, free from moths, silverfish, rust and dry-rot, and men with matches.

—RAY BRADBURY, *Fahrenheit 451*

12.

LIVES OF THE SCHOLARS

1854–1865

The extracts of the *Tarikh al-sudan* Heinrich Barth had copied in Gando didn't reach Europe till late the following year, after a tortuous journey across the desert. The task of reconstructing parts of the manuscript from Barth's notes fell to the German Arabist Christian Ralfs, who spent much of the winter of 1854–1855 trying to make sense of the fragments he had been given. Whole sections were missing from the text, and the Arabic itself was wooden and occasionally ungrammatical. Nevertheless, by the spring Ralfs believed he had managed to produce a faithful German translation of the main points of Barth's extracts, which were published in the journal of the German Oriental Society of Leipzig later that year. The explorer himself had not yet returned from Africa.

These new "Contributions to the History and Geography of Sudan" filled seventy-six pages, thirty-nine of which were devoted to the pair's copious footnotes. In Ralfs's opinion, the text showed the extreme poverty of all previous contributions to the knowledge of West Africa, including those of Ibn Battuta and Leo Africanus. Leo had made brief mention of a Songhay king, but the newly uncovered chronicle revealed a powerful empire ruled by a dynasty called the askiyas, including the "mighty conqueror" Askiya al-hajj Muhammad. This was but one example of the wealth of new historical information, which now enabled the Europeans to unlock the story of an "entirely unknown and now destroyed world."

Barth had been told the chronicle was composed by Ahmad Baba, and indeed part of it was, since it included lengthy extracts of his biographical dictionary of Maliki scholars, the *Kifayat al-muhtaj.* In his haste, however, the explorer had missed key evidence pointing to the identity of its real author, Abd al-Rahman Abd Allah al-Sadi. Al-Sadi had been born into a Timbuktu family on May 28, 1594, and in 1626/1627 was made imam of the Sankore mosque in Jenne. A decade later he returned home, becoming an imam and administrator in Timbuktu. His chronicle was written in the seventeenth century in Arabic and ran to thirty-eight chapters, some of which were based on earlier histories, and some on the author's own observations and interviews. Its grammar was imperfect enough to make later historians believe Songhay, rather than Arabic, was the author's first language, and its style at times recalled the folk stories of the brothers Grimm or the tales of *The Thousand and One Nights.*

Barth, short of time and desperate to fill in the immense gaps in European knowledge, had extracted as much data as he could, focusing on the parts of the chronicle devoted to kings, identifiable dates, and empires. The broad sweep, in other words, of history.

The *tarikh* began with a list of ancient Songhay rulers, the Zuwa dynasty, and went on to relate the founding myth of their kingdom. The first of these princes was Zuwa Alayaman. This person, it was said, had left Yemen with his brother to travel the world, and destiny had brought them, starving and dressed in ragged animal skins, to the town of Kukiya, an "ancient city" on the Niger that had existed, according to the chronicle, since the time of the ancient Egyptians: it was even from Kukiya that the pharaoh had brought the troupe of magicians he had used in his argument with Moses. When the people of the city asked the strangers their names, one of the brothers misunderstood the question and said that they were from Yemen—*jaa min al-yaman*—so the Kukiyans, who had difficulty pronouncing the Arabic words, called him Zuwa Alayaman.

Zuwa Alayaman found that the people in this country worshipped a demon that appeared in the river in the form of a fish with a ring in its nose. At these times a crowd gathered to hear the demon's instructions, which everyone would obey. After witnessing this ceremony and recognizing that the people were on a false path, Zuwa Alayaman determined to put an end to the creature. He threw a harpoon at the fish and killed it, and soon afterward the people took an oath to the slayer of the fish-god and made him king. "Zuwa" became the title of all the princes who ruled after him. "They bred and multiplied to such an extent that only God Most High knows their number," al-Sadi recorded. "They were distinguished by their strength, intrepidness, and bravery, and by their great height and heavy build."

Later in its history, the country of Songhay was subjugated by Mali, the empire that supplanted ancient Ghana in the Western Sudan, but the kingdom won its independence thanks to two princes of Songhay, the half brothers Ali Kulun and Silman Nari. It was tradition that princes of vassal states such as Songhay were sent to serve the Malian emperor and that they would disappear from time to time to pursue their fortunes. Ali Kulun, an "extremely intelligent and clever" prince, had another project in mind: the liberation of his kingdom. He prepared the ground artfully, traveling ever farther from the sultan's court and closer to his Songhay homeland, building up caches of weapons and provisions along the way. One day, the brothers gave their horses a special strengthening food, and then they made their escape. The sultan of Mali sent many men to stop the fugitives and there were many skirmishes, but the princes always routed their opponents and safely reached their homeland. Afterward, according to the chronicle, Ali Kulun became the Songhay king. He took the title "Sunni" and delivered his people from the yoke of Malian rule.

Al-Sadi devoted a full chapter to the establishment of Timbuktu. The settlement was founded at the start of the twelfth century by Tuareg people who came to the region to graze their flocks, he wrote. In the summer they camped on the banks of the Niger, and in the rainy season migrated to the desert wells of Arawan, 150 miles north. Eventually some of them chose to settle on this route, a short distance from the river:

> Thus did they choose the location of this virtuous, pure, undefiled, and proud city, blessed with divine favour, a healthy climate, and [commercial] activity which is my birthplace and my heart's desire. It is a city unsullied by the worship of idols, where none has prostrated save to God the Compassionate, a refuge of scholarly and righteous folk, a haunt of saints and ascetics, and a meeting place of caravans and boats.

The travelers who came to this crossroads soon began to use it for storage. The traders entrusted their utensils and grain to the supervision of a slave woman called Tinbuktu—a word, al-Sadi reports, that signifies someone with a "lump" or perhaps a protuberant navel—

and it was from her that the blessed place took its name. Settlers arrived in great numbers from neighboring regions—from Walata, the emporium of ancient Ghana, in modern Mauritania, and also from Egypt, Fezzan, Ghadames, Tuat, Fez, Sus, and Bitu—and little by little Timbuktu became a commercial hub for the region. It was filled with caravans from all countries, and scholars and pious people of every race flocked to it. The prosperity of Timbuktu sucked all the caravan trade from Walata, and brought about that city's ruin. Meanwhile, in Timbuktu, straw huts enclosed with fences were gradually replaced by clay houses, which were surrounded by a low wall, of the sort that from the outside one could see what was happening inside.

The town's development accelerated after Mansa Musa returned from his pilgrimage in 1325. On his way back from Mecca, Musa—"a just and pious man, whom none of the other sultans of Mali equalled in such qualities"—ordered the construction of a mosque wherever Friday found him. He built one of these at Gao, and then moved west to Timbuktu, becoming the first ruler to take possession of it. He installed a representative there and ordered the construction of a royal palace. He was also said to have built the tower-minaret of the Jingere Ber mosque, al-Sadi recorded. Musa and his successors ruled Timbuktu for a hundred years.

Malian power faded in the fifteenth century, according to al-Sadi, and the Tuareg leader Sultan Akil dominated Timbuktu from 1433/1434 until the rise of the Songhay king Sunni Ali, who reigned for twenty-four years, from 1468/1469. Sunni Ali was a great tyrant and an oppressor of the scholars of Timbuktu, al-Sadi wrote, but a man with tremendous physical strength and energy who turned his Songhay kingdom into a great empire. After his death, his son was deposed by one of Sunni Ali's regional governors, Muhammad ibn Abi Bakr al-Turi, who took the throne in 1493 and was the first to assume the name "askiya." Al-Sadi had nothing but praise for Askiya al-hajj Muhammad, or Askiya the Great, as he became known. He founded a dynasty of askiyas and built on his predecessor's conquests to establish Songhay as the largest empire West Africa had ever seen, stretching from the Senegal River in the west to Agadez in the east, and from the salt mines at Taghaza in the north to Borgu in the south, an area the size of Western Europe. The reign of the askiyas would last 101 years, until the sultan of Marrakesh sent an army across the desert to seize the Songhay lands.

In Barth's eyes, the *Tarikh al-sudan* was immensely significant. "I have no hesitation in asserting that the [chronicle] will be one of the most important additions which the present age has made to the history of mankind, in a branch which was formerly almost unknown," he would write. The extracts demonstrated that Timbuktu was home to a rich and sophisticated society capable of recording its own account of the past, and it at last gave Europe access to more than the few isolated facts recorded by foreign visitors to the empire such as al-Bakri, Ibn Khaldun, and Leo Africanus. It also overthrew many of the ideas Europe had about this part of Africa: the kingdoms of the region were much older than anyone had believed, their geographical locations were at last adequately defined, and the chronology of the empires of ancient Ghana, Mali, and Songhay at last seemed complete.

Of course, the chronicle included embellishments and accounts that were based on oral histories and legends—perhaps the fish-god was based on a manatee, a real creature of the Niger? Or was it a representation of the holy river itself?—but it was unquestionably a work of history, and its discoverer would become the founding father of the discipline of Songhay studies.

Ralfs finished his translation with an entreaty to Barth to return safely so that he could enjoy the "reverence and admiration" he richly deserved.

The explorer reached London on September 6, 1855, in the company of two slaves Overweg had bought and freed, Dorugu and Abbega, whom Barth had promised to look after. They were amazed by England, a country that had grand houses but not even the least amount of sand. The Prussian, who had been away for nearly five and a half years and traveled more than ten thousand miles, logging every village, tribe, and geographical feature along the way, was "most kindly received" by Palmerston, who was now prime minister, and Lord Clarendon, now secretary of state for foreign affairs. Clarendon congratulated him on his "fortitude, perseverance and sound judgement" during the expedition.

The London *Times*, which had noted the false report of Barth's death, made no reference to his safe return. In the decades to come, this newspaper and others would heap praise on successive African explorers, such men as Livingstone, Burton, John Hanning Speke, James Grant, and Samuel Baker. For Barth, though, there was no interest. It was an ominous indication of the way in which the public would treat him.

On October 1 he left England to see his family in Hamburg, with Dorugu and Abbega in tow.

WHILE BARTH WAS IN GERMANY, extracts from a second major text by a Timbuktu scholar appeared in Europe. These were taken from Ahmad Baba's biographical dictionary of the scholars of Maliki Islam, the *Kifayat al-muhtaj*, the same work whose partial inclusion in the

Tarikh al-sudan had fed confusion over the chronicle's authorship. Barth had read this material but, in his haste to record the historical data, had not copied it out. Now two versions had been sent to the eminent French Orientalist Auguste Cherbonneau, who published translated sections of it in the *Annuaire de la Societé Archéologique de Constantine*, along with an introductory essay on the Arab literature of the Sudan.

Cherbonneau was as excited about Baba's dictionary as Barth had been about the chronicle: it was "a singular and unexpected revelation of a literary movement in the heart of Africa, in Timbuktu!" he wrote, which opened up "new horizons" whose existence Europeans had never even suspected. The book contained numerous short biographies of the eminent scholars of the Maliki sect, who had been born in Timbuktu or had come there to teach. It revealed the existence of an education system in Timbuktu that was on a par with those in the great Islamic cities of Córdoba, Tunis, and Cairo, with schools run by learned men and attended by large numbers of students. It showed that considerable libraries containing hundreds of books had been kept in the city and explained how the scholars were eagerly supported by the princes of the country. Baba's work did nothing less, wrote Cherbonneau, than demonstrate the participation of the black races in intellectual life, and reveal the almost infinite number of connections that existed between the Western Sudan and the Arab world.

Reading the extracts of Baba's dictionary in conjunction with those from al-Sadi's chronicle, Europeans now had a clear picture of the working lives of Timbuktu's scholarly elite.

By the mid–fourteenth century, the city was a substantial commercial center and more and more scholars came to settle there. At its peak, there were an estimated two to three hundred scholars at the top of society, drawn from the leading families of the town. The most powerful citizens in the elite were the *qadi*s, who dispensed justice based on their knowledge of Islamic law. Then came all manner of other holy men, including imams, jurists, and counselors, drawn mostly from the wealthy merchant class, as well as schoolteachers, mosque workers, and scribes, plus a large number of *alfa*s, scholars of lower birth who earned a living from their Islamic education. The Sankore quarter was the center of scholarly activity in the city, and it was here that the influential descendants of Muhammad Aqit, the great-great-grandfather of Ahmad Baba, settled. The Timbuktu scholars were in regular contact with North Africa and Egypt, and some traveled there, while others came south to study in Timbuktu. They were therefore familiar with a wide range of secular sciences, including mathematics, astronomy, and history, although all such knowledge was taught in an Islamic context.

The preeminent Timbuktu scholars were not simply religious leaders and teachers; they were also believed to possess divine grace, or *baraka*, which enabled them to perform acts that would be impossible for lesser mortals. One of the earliest holy men mentioned by Baba was known simply as al-Hajj; he came to Timbuktu from Walata and held the post of *qadi* in the early fifteenth century, during the last days of Malian rule. One day, a group of people were sitting down to eat when they heard that the army of the neighboring kingdom of Mossi was approaching Timbuktu. Al-Hajj murmured something over the shared plate and instructed them to eat, then told them: "Go off and fight. Their arrows will do you no harm." The Mossi army was driven off, and all the men returned except one: al-Hajj's son-in-law had not eaten, as it would have been a sign of disrespect to share food with his wife's father.

In the mid–fifteenth century, when the Tuareg chieftain Akil ruled over the town, the influx of Islamic scholars to Timbuktu reached new heights. Akil and his people continued to pursue their semi-nomadic lifestyle outside the city, leaving the town in the care of a governor who worked to promote its scholarly activities. One of the prominent men to arrive at this time was Modibbo Muhammad al-Kabari. According to Ahmad Baba, al-Kabari "attained the very pinnacle of scholarship and righteousness," instructing a great number of students, and was also the source of many miracles. On one occasion, an influential Moroccan scholar started to slander him, punning that he was not so much al-Kabari as "al-Kafiri," the Unbeliever. God afflicted this man with leprosy as punishment, Baba relates. Doctors were brought from far and wide to try to treat him, and one recommended that the only cure would be for him to eat the heart of a young boy. Many boys were slaughtered, but the man died "in a most pitiable condition" for disrespecting the great *qadi*.

Al-Kabari was even said to be able to walk on water. One year, on the feast day of Tabaski, he needed to cross the river to collect a sacrificial ram, so he simply marched across its surface. A pupil chose to follow him, but he sank, and when the shaykh reached the far side and saw his student struggling in the river, he went to rescue him. "What made you do that?" he shouted.

"When I saw what you did, I did the same."

The shaykh was unsympathetic. "How can you compare your foot to one that has never walked in disobedience to God?" he asked.

A virtuous scholarly life was not only filled with divine grace; it could also be healthy and extremely long. The *qadi* Katib Musa was blessed with such an extraordinary constitution, it was said, that he never had to delegate a single prayer in the mosque. He attributed his great well-being to four simple rules: he never slept outdoors, always oiled his body before going to bed, took a hot bath every morning, and made sure he had breakfast.

Perhaps the most famous immigrant to Timbuktu in the fifteenth century was Sidi Yahya al-Tadallisi. Sidi Yahya was invited to Timbuktu by its governor, Muhammad-n-Allah, who built the mosque that still carries his name. In Baba's description, Sidi Yahya "became famous in every land, his *baraka* manifesting itself to high and low. He was the locus of manifestations of divine grace, and was clairvoyant." On the day al-Kabari died and his body was placed in a mausoleum, Sidi Yahya pronounced an elegy for him, which is one of the earliest examples of Timbuktu poetry. It included the following lines:

> Muhammad Modibbo the professor, possessed of a fine
>   intelligence, long suffering, and fortified with continuous
>   patience.
> I wonder if after him there will be one who makes things clear.
>   O Arabs, is there any champion after him?

It was said of Sidi Yahya that "no foot more virtuous . . . ever trod the soil of Timbuktu." He was a sought-after teacher, and one day he was giving a lesson at the foot of the minaret when dark clouds gathered overhead and a peal of thunder was heard. His students hurried to collect their things and get inside, but Sidi Yahya told them to stay where they were. "Take your time!" he said. "[Rain] will not fall here while the angel is directing it to fall on such and such a locality." The rain passed them by. Weather forecasting wasn't Sidi Yahya's only talent: on another occasion, his servant girls spent all day trying to cook a fish, but the fire had no effect on its flesh. "This morning," he told them, "when I went out for the early-morning worship, my foot brushed against something damp in the entrance hall; perhaps it was that fish. Whatever my body touches cannot be burned by fire."

Of all the virtues that were valued in fifteenth-century Timbuktu, modesty does not seem to have been one of them.

Toward the end of his life, governor Muhammad-n-Allah had a dream in which he saw the sun setting and the moon disappear immediately after. He recounted it to his friend Sidi Yahya, who told him that as long as he promised not to become afraid, he would explain the dream.

Muhammad-n-Allah declared that he would not be afraid.

Very well, said Sidi Yahya. "It means I will die and you will die shortly afterwards."

Muhammad-n-Allah became deeply upset.

"Did you not tell me that you would not be afraid?" said Sidi Yahya.

"My distress comes not from the fear of death," the governor said, "but rather from concern for my young children."

"Place them under the care of God Most High," Sidi Yahya responded.

The holy man died soon afterward, and Muhammad-n-Allah followed him to the grave. The friends were buried close to each other in the same mosque.

The scholar for whom Baba reserves the greatest affection, and whose life he recounts in greatest detail, is his own teacher, Muhammad Baghayogho. A gentle and considerate soul, Baghayogho was "given by nature to . . . benign intent." He was "guileless, and naturally disposed to goodness, believing in people to such an extent that all men were virtually equal in his sight, so well did he think of them and absolve them of wrongdoing." He had great reserves of patience: he could teach all day without growing bored or tired, and took particular attention with the dull-witted, to the extent that Baba once heard a colleague say that he thought Baghayogho "must have drunk [holy] Zamzam water so that he would not get fed up during teaching."

Baba gives a detailed account of the hardworking Baghayogho's day. He would begin his lessons after the predawn prayers, breaking off only to perform the mid-morning worship, after which he would sometimes go to the *qadi* to plead on behalf of people who had asked for his help. Noon would find him teaching again, then taking the midday worship, and after that he would alternate teaching and prayers until the evening, when he would return home. Even then his day was not over, since he would spend the last part of the night in devotions.

Baghayogho's saintliness was especially evident when it came to his books, some of which were the most rare and precious "in all fields." He was so generous with these works that he would loan them out and not even ask for them back, wrote Baba:

> Sometimes a student would come to his door asking for a book, and he would give it to him without even knowing who the student was. In this matter he was truly astonishing, doing this for the sake of God Most High, despite his love for books and [his zeal in] acquiring them, whether by purchase or copying.

In this way, Baba recorded, Baghayogho gave away a large portion of his library of books.

. . .

IT IS A CLICHÉ that the traveler makes unexpected friends abroad and finds unexpected hostility at home, but this was precisely the situation in which Barth now found himself. Yes, he had twice navigated the great Sahara; he had talked his way out of a dozen lethal scrapes and even come back from the dead, but he would prove poor at plotting a course through the smoke-filled rooms of nineteenth-century European society. In a just world, his heroic voyage would immediately have sealed his reputation as a great scientist-explorer, his name ranked with that of Humboldt. In this, as in so many ways, he would be disappointed. The prickly twenty-eight-year-old who had left for Africa had returned with a proud, almost haughty demeanor, and his native mistrust now reached alarming levels. "Everywhere he went," his brother-in-law Schubert wrote, "he sensed deliberate and calculated attempts being made to exploit him."

He was initially well received in Germany. He was lauded by Humboldt and dined with the king of Prussia. He was given a gold medal by the city of Hamburg, offered honorary doctorates and decorations, and invited to speak at the Geographical Society in Berlin. Even in England, his achievements were recognized: the RGS awarded him its prestigious Patron's Gold Medal, and he was nominated for the Companion of the Order of the Bath. But Britain liked its heroes British, and as Hanmer Warrington had demonstrated three decades before, the doings of foreign gentlemen such as Barth were subject to a skepticism that bordered on paranoia. Even when he was traveling, officials in London had harbored suspicions about his loyalty. Why, the Foreign Office wondered, had he sent his infrequent dispatches to the Prussian ambassador in London and not to the government that was paying for the expedition? Why did his reports end up in German journals before they reached the RGS?

At the end of October, Barth received a poorly phrased letter from the RGS secretary, Norton Shaw, asking him to dine with some of the society's members before the speech he would give there. Shaw's presumption angered Barth, who fired back a letter saying that he had no such engagement and—forgetting his lecture to the Geographical Society in Berlin—would not address any scientific institution until he was ready to publish the narrative of his journey. Shaw became openly hostile after that, and an embarrassing feud ensued that lasted into the new year, when the explorer had returned to London. This was not Barth's only problem: despite the fact that his expedition had for years been short of money, several British newspapers ran stories about his alleged excessive spending. The impression of financial irregularity was made worse by the British consul in Murzuk, in Fezzan, who accused him of pursuing German commercial interests ahead of British ones, and he found himself being investigated by the Foreign Office.

He began to wish he had never come back. "How I long for the freedom of a bivouac in the desert," he told Schubert, "in that unfathomable expanse where, free of ambitions, free from the thousands of little things that torture people here, I would savor my freedom as I rolled out my bed at the end of a long day's march, my possessions, my camels, and my horse around me. I almost regret having put myself in these chains."

As a distraction, Barth threw himself into writing up the narrative of his journeys. The first three volumes of his *Travels and Discoveries in North and Central Africa* appeared in April 1857, beautifully published by Longman, with color illustrations based on Barth's sketches. There would be five volumes in all, 3,500 pages of densely packed information, a magnum opus of Humboldtian proportions. In the eyes of a later geographer, Lord Rennell of Rodd, the work would raise Barth to the status of "perhaps the greatest traveller there has ever been in Africa," but reviews at the time were less generous. No general reader could be expected to sustain an interest in the region over such an epic scale, critics said. This response pointed up the schism between Barth and the public: he believed his role was to deliver voluminous quantities of new data about Africa, much as his mentor, Humboldt, had compiled twenty-three volumes of scientific observations from his tour of the Spanish Americas. But the British audience was accustomed to more lightweight adventure stories of the sort Mungo Park had produced. They had devoured edition after edition of Park's account of his first journey in Africa, while David Livingstone's *Missionary Travels and Researches in South Africa* would sell more than fifty thousand copies. By contrast, the first three volumes of Barth's account sold poorly, and Longman printed only one thousand copies each of the last two.

None of that would have mattered if it had won Barth the academic acclaim he craved, but no British university offered him a position, and even Cooley was dismissive of his discoveries, failing completely to mention the new sources Barth had unearthed in his appraisal of the explorer's work for *The Edinburgh Review*:

A splendid and powerful empire in Negroland, extending its sway even northwards over the desert, would be remarkable enough, were there any proof of its existence. But no ingenuity of conjecture, no nice adaptation of dry and scanty traditions, can convert these hypothetical glories into history.

Further dishonor for Barth could be found in the government's treatment of his friend Shaykh Ahmad al-Bakkai. Barth had encouraged the Timbuktu holy man to establish diplomatic contact with the British government, believing it would be to the advantage of both: Britain would get a commercial partner in the heart of Africa; al-Bakkai would get the protection of a Great Power to stand with Timbuktu against the increasingly predatory French. The shaykh acted on Barth's advice, sending emissaries to Tripoli in 1857 to open talks. But Britain and France were now allies, and when the emissaries asked for permission to proceed to London, the Foreign Office said that since it was October it would be rather chilly for such warm-blooded men, and would they wait for spring? Reading this brush-off for what it was, the delegation retired south while al-Bakkai wrote a letter to Queen Victoria complaining about their treatment.

The following year, fed up with England, Barth returned to Berlin, hopeful of finding the recognition that Britain had failed to give. Instead he ran into the mirror image of the problem he had encountered in London: the Prussians derided him for working for the country that was now blocking German unification. His evidence for the depth and breadth of culture and history in central and western Sudan and his positive attitude toward Islam were not, meanwhile, what the German intelligentsia wanted to hear. In 1859 his nomination for full membership in the Royal Academy of Sciences, one of the highest accolades in European academia, was rejected. He had been opposed by the historian Leopold von Ranke, who argued that while Barth was no doubt a bold adventurer, he was not a serious scholar.

Barth continued to travel, to Spain, the Balkans, and the Alps. In 1865, he returned from one of his journeys to learn that al-Bakkai had died in battle, fighting for Timbuktu. Later that year, on November 23, the explorer was poleaxed by a massive pain in his abdomen: his stomach had burst, most likely as the result of an intestinal disease picked up on his travels. He lived for two more agonizing days before dying on November 25. He was forty-four.

Almost a century later, in 1958, the RGS's *Geographical Journal* commissioned a young lecturer from Liverpool University, Ralph Mansell Prothero, to write an appraisal of Barth's contributions to African exploration. Prothero, who would later be an eminent geography professor, described Barth's *Travels and Discoveries* as "without doubt the greatest single contribution to knowledge of the Western Sudan" and commented that it was odd that he had subsequently been so overlooked. One fact in particular struck Prothero: he had searched the RGS catalogue for all the papers published in Britain that had picked up on Barth's work. To his great surprise, he had found only one.

13.

THE TERRIBLE TWOSOME

SEPTEMBER 2012–JANUARY 2013

Haidara did not yet have an office in Bamako—"We wanted to be hidden," he said, "we didn't want people to know what we were doing. If we had had an office, it would have been official"—but Stephanie Diakité did, and in a much nicer part of town than Maiga's rat-infested premises. ACI 2000 was a newly zoned quarter on the north bank of the river, and Diakité's house was a modern building within it, almost pretty in a city of cinder-block monstrosities and slums. It was arranged around a small courtyard, which was planted with trees and flowers that struggled to survive at the hands of a bungling gardener, and consisted of a couple of bedrooms, a lounge with an exotic carpet, a kitchen, and a large office. The office was equipped with the fastest Internet connection Diakité could buy and a handful of phones, to supplement the ones Haidara kept in his voluminous robes. One wall of this room would become increasingly populated with the schedules and spreadsheets Diakité produced to model the evacuation.

Haidara and Diakité were now a team, as were their organizations: in future months they would describe themselves as a "consortium," consisting of Haidara's NGO Savama and Diakité's development organization D Intl. They met seven days a week and worked from morning until ten or eleven at night, according to one source. Haidara would sit in an easy chair by the coffee table, often with a cup of Lipton, while Diakité sat at the desk working on Excel spreadsheets. She liked to start early in the morning, while Haidara lived on desert time: he didn't reach the office till around nine or ten a.m. and did his best thinking at night. At noon they ate: Diakité was fond of her kitchen; she made sure they had good food—couscous, bulgur—at least twice a day, which Haidara avidly consumed. If he came to the house and nothing was offered, he would ask, "Where's the food?"

In between times, "the terrible twosome" worked on the plan for the evacuation of the private libraries. How many people did they need? How many SIM cards? How much would it all cost? What if the couriers were stopped? It took four days on average to get shipments from Timbuktu to Bamako. Each courier should be responsible for no more than three lockers per trip—an amount that would not be crippling if lost, and which could be carried on a single *push-push*. The number of lockers divided by three was the number of runs needed; that number divided by the number of trips each courier could make was the number of couriers required.

"There were plenty of details, a lot of organization," Haidara said.

One of the first concerns was where to put the manuscripts: they needed safe houses in Bamako. An unexpected benefit of the crisis was that the capital was now brimming with families who had fled the north, and Haidara called on them personally to find out if he could rely on them to take in his lockers. He wanted households that were calm, quiet, and free of inquisitive acquaintances. After a month of looking he had identified a string of twenty-seven families across the capital. "Most of them were people we had known very well for a long time," he said.

For the Ahmad Baba manuscripts, it had been good politics to include state employees in the operation, many of whom were not from Timbuktu, in case there was a catastrophic loss: "If there are crises, problems, the state is the state, so we made sure that the agents of the state were with us," he said. Now, with the private libraries, he was among his own people: "We had a trust between us. We knew our manuscripts. The families had no need of protocols."

Fund-raising was central to the operation. Haidara had good relationships with the Ford Foundation and the Juma al-Majid Center, but the money they had given him didn't last long. Diakité had meanwhile been working her contacts among the foreign governments and foundations she knew from her career in development. It was these organizations that would end up donating the largest quantities of cash.

One of them was an Amsterdam-based foundation, the Prince Claus Fund, named for the husband of Queen Beatrix of the Netherlands. The fund, which was supported by the Dutch government and the Dutch national lottery, specialized in cultural development. It even had a "Cultural Emergency Response" program, set up in the wake of the Taliban's destruction of the Bamiyan Buddhas in Afghanistan in 2001. The point of this program, according to its coordinator, Deborah Stolk, was "to make an international fist against the deliberate destruction of heritage," and in pursuit of this goal she had followed the crisis in Mali from the early days, attempting to identify people who could warn her about potential threats. The researchers at the University of Cape Town's Tombouctou Manuscripts Project had put her in touch with

Savama, and now she was in daily e-mail contact with Haidara and Diakité. She had never met them, but she felt Haidara "seemed to have a good track record," especially since he had already worked with the Ford Foundation. What was more, the Dutch embassy in Bamako confirmed that the applicant was a trustworthy and knowledgeable partner in this field, although several years after the crisis she appeared to mistakenly believe that he had once been director of the Ahmad Baba institute.

At the start of October, the information Stolk was receiving from Bamako via e-mail, phone, and Skype was increasingly alarming. In Haidara's view, the need to take action to save the manuscripts was becoming urgent, Diakité told her, because of two recent developments. The first, a "good change," as Diakité described it, was that since the MNLA had left Timbuktu, vehicles heading south were no longer being searched. This was "enabling," according to Haidara. The "bad change," on the other hand, was that the city's occupiers had implemented a "search and seize" policy in private homes and businesses, and Haidara was growing more concerned that the manuscripts would become the target. In fact, the MNLA had left Timbuktu after the battle of Gao at the end of June, so the "good change" Diakité spoke of was now at least three months old. A search-and-seize policy, meanwhile, appeared inconsistent with the jihadists' behavior since the start of the occupation. Still, Stolk and her Amsterdam-based team had little reason to question firsthand information from Mali, and after the destruction of the mausoleums, it fit the overall picture of jihadist vandalism.

There was a further worrying development in Timbuktu at this time. The jihadist Vice and Virtue Squad had begun a crackdown on the city's women and girls in mid-September, announcing an eleven p.m. curfew and a strict new dress code. No longer could they wear the light, transparent veils that were favored by the Songhay. Their hair, ears, necks, wrists, and ankles had to be covered by an Arab-style *toungou*, an opaque piece of cloth a dozen yards long, and they had to wear gloves. Women with manual jobs found it almost impossible to work dressed like this, but anyone who broke these rules could be punished by being locked in the new women's jail at the BMS, now branded the Center for the Recommendation of Propriety and the Prevention of Evil. This "jail" was actually the tiny kiosk where the bank's ATM had been kept. It wasn't large enough for even one person to lie down comfortably, and had no water or toilet. Even so, more than a dozen women at a time might be packed inside.

The man behind this morality mission was the "dark soul" who had invited so many Salafists to Timbuktu, Hamed Mossa. Mossa had just been appointed head of the Vice and Virtue Squad, and he and his men now went around Timbuktu beating and harassing those who weren't conforming to the code. Within days, Mossa had become the "most famous and cursed man in the city," as a local woman put it, and stories of his outrages abounded. When a teenage girl Mossa was chasing in his pickup eluded him, he locked up her father instead. On another occasion he ordered his men to grab a woman and throw her in the road "so that a vehicle crushes her head" because "she's a bitch!" He would lift women's clothes with the barrel of his rifle to check what type of undergarments they had on. Arrests he made became so frequent that when the children who played in the street around the BMS saw him returning without a new victim, they broke into a chant of "Hamed Mossa hasn't had his breakfast."

On Saturday, October 6, the women's fury at this new tyranny boiled over. That morning, a group of women who worked in the Petit

Marché decided spontaneously to march on Mossa's headquarters. As they approached the BMS building, the Islamic Police opened fire, shooting over their heads, and all but seven of the women ran for cover. These seven were brought before a group of senior jihadists, including Mossa, who warned them: "If you march again, you will see what will happen to you."

On October 8, Stolk received an e-mail from Savama describing this incident. The protest had been provoked by militia entering private homes to take unveiled girls into custody, the e-mail said. Against this alarming backdrop, Stolk was informed, the manuscript-owning families had indicated to Savama that they wanted to evacuate their collections. The lack of checks on the road south meant it was the perfect moment: there was a "window of opportunity" to get the manuscripts out.

Diakité gave details of how it would work. The manuscripts would be taken to Bamako in lockers, each of which would contain 250 to 300 documents, via two routes: one would take the main track south to Douentza and then Mopti; the other would go west, via Lere and Niono. Each shipment would be accompanied by couriers recruited from the manuscript-owning families, and there would be "supervisory and security personnel" camped out all along both routes, ready to give "indirect support services" and help in case of emergency. For extra security, each courier would check in eight times a day over a "quick turnaround secure (revolve hardware and software) cellphone communication network," Stolk was told. Once in Bamako, the manuscripts would be hidden in the safe houses Haidara had identified. All that was now missing was funding. When that was in place, the operation could begin.

Stolk was convinced. She knew that there was a risk involved in evacuating the manuscripts, and that it was not known for certain it would succeed, but since there was clearly an imminent threat, this seemed the best option.

On October 17, the Prince Claus Fund signed a contract with Haidara and Diakité for the evacuation of two hundred lockers of manuscripts, which had already been collected and prepared for evacuation by Savama. Stolk was told these were exactly half of the four hundred lockers, containing approximately 160,000 manuscripts, that needed to be moved in total, and the cost to the Dutch fund would be 100,000 euros, or roughly 500 euros a locker. This was a high price, given that a refugee at this time could travel with luggage from Timbuktu to Bamako for around forty euros, but running such an elaborate operation was expensive. (Haidara later said more than a hundred people worked on the evacuation, while Diakité put the number of couriers alone at three hundred.) The money wasn't just for transportation either, but for "overall coordination, transportation costs, couriers, cell phones to be used during evacuation, stipendium for families/safe houses," and so on, according to Stolk. Phones were a notable expense, said Haidara: "We bought lots of telephones, for everyone, and I sent credit every day to each person. . . . We had a trader here who gave credit, 5,000 francs [8 euros] for each person. And each week we paid him. We organised that because every morning they called me . . . all my colleagues."

According to a later report of the evacuation in *The New Republic* that was fact-checked by Diakité, the first shipments started to leave Timbuktu the day after the Prince Claus contract was signed:

On October 18, the first team of couriers loaded 35 lockers onto pushcarts and donkey-drawn carriages, and moved them to a depot on the outskirts of Timbuktu where couriers bought space on buses and trucks making the long drive south to Bamako.

That trip would be repeated daily for the next several months, *The New Republic*'s correspondent noted, sometimes many times a day, as the teams of smugglers passed hundreds of lockers along the same well-worn route to Bamako.

STOLK KNEW THAT the first Prince Claus–funded shipments had arrived safely because she received a photograph taken that day by Savama officials. The image showed a large number of stacked steel boxes, with the disembodied arms of a man—apparently the eminent librarian himself—holding up a copy of the day's newspaper, an authentication technique borrowed from the movies, as one of Haidara's aides put it. She received further photos as the weeks went by.

The manuscripts' journey south was fraught, however, and barely a day went by without a courier ringing in with what Haidara described later as *"petits problèmes,"* which ranged from mundane breakdowns to ransom demands and dangerous run-ins with the jihadists.

One of these *petits problèmes* concerned the Timbuktu office of Savama itself, which was on the Kabara Road, half a mile south of the town center. Savama had attracted the attention of the jihadists from the earliest weeks of the occupation, when the Islamic Police had called the organization's administrative secretary, Sane Chirfi Alpha, to tell him they were about to requisition the organization's assets. Alpha called Diadié, the vice president of the Crisis Committee, who also happened to be Savama's treasurer, and together they hurried to see the jihadist police commissioner. It was true, the commissioner said; they had decided that since Savama was supported by UNESCO and had American funding via the Ford Foundation, it was a collaborator with Western interests, so they had decided to take it over.

Diadié thought quickly. "I told him, you are right to bring me here," he recalled. If the commissioner did not understand the purpose of Savama, Diadié was more than happy to explain it to him. In fact, it was an association of people who held manuscripts, and its purpose was to safeguard their collections and create a framework for their development and exploitation. Since the families had no means, they had asked UNESCO and other organizations for support, but that didn't mean it belonged to the state or to UNESCO, not at all. Savama was the property of the people.

"Here are the statutes," Diadié concluded, showing the organization's founding documents.

The commissioner relented. He had been told Savama was part of UNESCO, but if it was a private organization, he would not take action. In fact, he would instruct his men to protect it.

Two months later, Savama's workers in Timbuktu had a more serious run-in with the police. Haidara's nephew Mohamed Touré had a shipment to send to Bamako, and the trucks generally loaded their cargo close to the BMS bank in the Grand Marché. As the area was now crawling with jihadists, he arranged for the trucks to come instead to the Savama office at night. He planned to load several lockers there before the vehicles were driven back to the Grand Marché to be filled with other goods. He left the center of town with two ten-ton vehicles, pulled up next to the Savama building, and let himself in. Working by flashlight, he took four heavy lockers and carried them outside. It wasn't exactly a covert operation—the large trucks standing by the building while flashlights flickered within—and soon they attracted the attention of one of the jihadists who had moved into the house next door. It was the Frenchman Gilles Le Guen, also known as Abdel Jelil.

"I was in the process of getting the lockers out," recalled Touré, "when Abdel Jelil came directly. He called to me, stopped me, and asked me what I was doing. I said I was in the middle of getting my books out because it was the moment to put them away for the rainy season. I was worried that the water would damage them."

Le Guen didn't buy Touré's story for a moment. "No," he said, "you would not be doing that at this time of night. You are a thief." He immediately called the Islamic Police, and soon a group of armed jihadists arrived. Among them was the commissioner himself.

"I am not a thief," the desperate Touré told the commissioner. "These things belong to me. Everything here is mine."

"Why didn't you tell us you were doing something like this?"

"I didn't know that every time you moved your own belongings you had to tell the police."

The commissioner ordered that the trucks be taken with the lockers to the police station, where they were parked in a yard, and Touré was told to call witnesses for the following day who could testify that the manuscripts belonged to him, and to bring his papers. Touré quickly phoned Haidara to explain the problem, and he in turn began calling his contacts in Timbuktu.

It wasn't Haidara who called Diadié, but rather the commissioner. Diadié was asked if he was aware that two trucks had been loaded with Savama manuscripts and were on the point of leaving town. "Trucks?" said Diadié. "How?" Come see for yourself, said the commissioner. Diadié said he would, but before doing so he went to find Touré.

Yes, Touré told him: as part of Haidara's efforts to protect the manuscripts, they had taken "a certain number of measures" and had started to dispatch them to Bamako. They had been caught.

Diadié was astonished. "When there were problems before, whose door do you knock on?" he asked. "Yet when you decided to take these manuscripts out, you didn't even feel able to tell us you were doing it. If you want to do these things you have to tell us!"

Still, he would come to Touré's aid. He went to see the commissioner and told him that he had indeed known about the movement of lockers. Savama had an operation to make conservation boxes in Bamako, and it was as part of this program that the manuscripts were being shipped south. "I did not know they were leaving yesterday, otherwise I would have informed you," he said.

Touré also went to the police with his papers. The commissioner gave the young man a rap on the knuckles. "If you want to do things like this, you must come to the Islamic Police to get authorization. You must not take things like that, when no one knows what you are doing, otherwise people will say you are stealing." The punishment for theft was severe, he warned.

Touré agreed to ask before he moved manuscripts in the future, and the trucks and lockers were released. They stopped the operation for a while at that time, Haidara said, and the trucks went south without the lockers. When Touré started to move them again, he did it in the daytime.

Le Guen, meanwhile, still seemed convinced he had caught a thief.

It wasn't only in the north that the manuscript smugglers ran into trouble. Later in October, Diakité told Stolk that government territory had become just as difficult, since numerous unofficial checkpoints had sprung up, manned by racketeers in uniform.

There were a host of legal infringements on which Malian travelers could be picked up—vehicle licenses not being carried; ID cards that were out of date—while others were dreamed up on the spot. Each problem could paralyze a bus for hours until the individual passengers had talked their way through it or paid a bribe. Between Sevare and Bamako there were nine government checkpoints, and Haidara had to make sure the couriers could pay their way through all of them. "We always had problems," he said. "The transport was expensive. But it is normal [in a war situation]. And the couriers were expensive. But what can you do? All the money we spent on transport we can justify, all that we spent on the couriers we can justify. But the amount that went into bribes—how can you justify that?"

Corruption made the tedious journeys south even more exhausting. Touré's worst trip, carrying six or seven heavy but "very beautiful, very important" lockers, lasted more than a week and involved five types of transportation. It began well: after sweet-talking his way through a jihadist search at Douentza by speaking Arabic and pretending to be ill, he reached government territory on the first evening. After that, the journey grew more and more difficult.

Whenever his manuscripts were found at a checkpoint, the uniformed officers made a big commotion. "They cried out when they saw the manuscripts," recalled Touré, "saying, 'Here we have a problem!'" Gendarmes were called. Touré would not say whether he paid them off, only that he "made them understand," and that they gave him permission to continue.

One bus broke down. Another went the wrong way and took him closer to Côte d'Ivoire than Bamako. Days later, exhausted, when he found what he hoped was the last minibus and negotiated a fare for Bamako, another set of gendarmes stopped him and took him to their barracks. He was kept there for a day as they looked over his papers, asked him questions, and opened the lockers. As soon as they did that, they knew they were on to something.

A commanding officer was called. "Look," he was told, "there is a young man who has brought the manuscripts of Timbuktu. They are everywhere!"

Touré called Haidara, who phoned a contact in Segu who could negotiate with the gendarmes, and finally they agreed Touré should be taken to Bamako under escort for further questioning. At one a.m. he arrived at the notorious Camp 1 gendarme base in the old colonial quarter of the capital, where the questions continued. He answered the best he could, and in the morning Haidara arrived to tell them that he was on legitimate business.

"I negotiated," Haidara remembered.

As soon as he was free, Touré set off again for the north.

The most dangerous moments the smugglers described were when couriers and their lockers were held for ransom.

The main route from Timbuktu to Bamako ran along the right, or southern, bank of the river, through the population centers of central Mali: Douentza, Sevare, Mopti, and Segu. There was another route, though, along the river's left bank. Instead of heading south from Timbuktu to Koriume and the ferry, 4x4s could take the track west through the sparsely populated desert to Niafounke and Lere before crossing the river to Segu. It was a long and wild drive of many hundreds of miles, through deep sand and around lakes that filled and emptied with the rhythm of the Niger's inundations. If it was safe, however, the couriers could avoid the checkpoints and save a great deal of hassle and money. Haidara was told by many people that there were no problems with the Lere route, so they decided to try it.

It happened that the vehicle chosen for this first run was an ancient 4x4, a "carcass," as Haidara described it, which kept breaking down: "You know, at the time, all the cars that you rented were carcasses. The cars that arrived from Sevare, for example, were exhausted, and they didn't even have the right paperwork. You were always obliged to take another car." They had scarcely traveled a hundred miles when Haidara's phone rang with alarming news: the couriers had been stopped at gunpoint by a group of men and were now being held hostage. Haidara had no idea who the gunmen were or how dangerous they might be—they could have been jihadists or the MNLA, but it was more likely they were one of the many groups of bandits who roamed the desert. "They took the car and threatened the people who were in it," said Haidara. "They said that they would not let the vehicle go and that we had to pay something."

For him, one dead courier would ruin the whole enterprise: "If something bad happened to these men, then all our work would be like nothing. It would be a big problem." So he tried to negotiate with the kidnappers to have the men and the lockers released. But conducting such a delicate conversation over the intermittent mobile phone network was impossible: "I was not able to reach an understanding with them. They wanted to take the couriers away. I didn't know what they would do to them. I didn't know what was going to happen! They got very afraid. We also got very afraid."

He knew Niafounke well, though, and called a friend, who in turn called a respected imam who lived in the village where the men were being held. The imam went to talk to the kidnappers on Haidara's behalf. "He spoke to them, negotiated a sum of money, and they were given their car back and allowed to pass," Haidara said. It helped that the car was such a wreck the kidnappers didn't want it.

Burned manuscripts in the Ahmad Baba institute's Sankore building, January 2013.

Joseph Banks, a founder of the African Association,
as painted by Sir Joshua Reynolds, soon after his return from
James Cook's first circumnavigation in 1771.

JOHN LEDYARD

BORN AT GROTON, CONNECTICUT, 1751. MEMBER OF THE FIRST CLASS IN DARTMOUTH COLLEGE. WHILE A FRESHMAN, ABSENTS HIMSELF WITHOUT PER-
MISSION FOR THREE MONTHS IN RAMBLES AMONG THE INDIANS OF CANADA AND THE SIX NATIONS. LEAVES THE COLLEGE IN A CANOE MADE WITH HIS
OWN HANDS AND DESCENDS THE CONNECTICUT ALONE TO HARTFORD. A SAILOR BEFORE THE MAST, GOES TO GIBRALTAR AND THE BARBARY COAST
RETURNING BY THE WEST INDIES. APPEARS IN LONDON AND THERE   MEETS CAPTAIN COOK, THEN ABOUT TO SAIL ON HIS LAST VOYAGE
ROUND THE WORLD, WHO APPOINTS HIM CORPORAL OF MARINES.   ON THIS EXPEDITION IS ABSENT FOUR YEARS, VISITING THE SOUTH
SEA ISLANDS, CHINA, SIBERIA, THE WESTERN COAST OF NORTH   AMERICA, TWICE ENTERING THE ARCTIC SEAS IN THE QUEST FOR
THE NORTHWEST PASSAGE. RETURNS TO AMERICA, PUBLISHES   HIS TRAVELS AND ENDEAVORS TO ENLIST MERCHANTS IN COM-
MERCE WITH THE EAST. IS NEXT SEEN IN SPAIN AND IN PARIS   THERE MEETING THOMAS JEFFERSON, AMERICAN MINISTER AT THE
COURT OF FRANCE, WHOM HE IMPRESSES WITH HIS PROJECT FOR   THE EXPLORATION OF THE TERRITORY BETWEEN THE PACIFIC
AND THE MISSISSIPPI, WHICH TWENTY YEARS LATER WAS TRA-   VERSED BY LEWIS AND CLARK, UNDER THE AUSPICES OF MR. JEF-
FERSON, THEN PRESIDENT. UNITES WITH JOHN PAUL JONES IN AN   UNDERTAKING TO ESTABLISH TRADING-POSTS ON THE NORTH-
WEST COAST AND TO TRAFFIC IN FURS, WHICH FAILS FOR WANT OF   ADEQUATE CAPITAL. DETERMINED TO EXPLORE WESTERN NORTH
AMERICA, PRESENTS HIMSELF AT ST. PETERSBURG AND FROM EMPRESS CATHERINE SECURES A PASSPORT ACROSS HER DOMINION TO BERING STRAIT
REACHES YAKUTSK ON THE LENA, WHEN HE IS RECALLED BECAUSE OF THE JEALOUSY OF RUSSIAN FUR-TRADERS, AND UNDER GUARD SENT BACK TO THE
CONFINES OF POLAND WHERE HE IS DISMISSED WITH THE COMMAND NEVER AGAIN TO ENTER THE EMPIRE. RESOLVES TO EXPLORE AFRICA, AND WHILE
FITTING OUT HIS CARAVAN DIES AT CAIRO, 1788, AT THE AGE OF THIRTY-SEVEN. IN COLLEGE HE WAS A FAVORITE WITH HIS FELLOW STUDENTS, NOT
UNDULY DILIGENT IN STUDY, FACILE IN ACQUISITION, IMPATIENT OF DISCIPLINE. ELSEWHERE MEN PAID TRIBUTE TO HIS KIND AND LOVABLE DISPO-
SITION, HIS UNSELFISHNESS AND PHILANTHROPY. HE FORESAW AND FORETOLD THE COMMERCIAL FUTURE OF WESTERN NORTH AMERICA AND THE FAR
EAST. HIS WAS THE DARTMOUTH SPIRIT. THIS IMPRINT IS NO. 10 OF A SERIES OF TWENTY, AND IS GIVEN BY JOHN ADAMS AIKEN, DARTMOUTH, '74, YO

An "extraordinary man": Connecticut-born John Ledyard,
the African Association's first explorer, who died in Cairo in 1789.

Mungo Park, a Scottish doctor, reached the Niger on July 21, 1796.
The account of his travels created a new archetype
for the adventurer in Africa.

Alexander Gordon Laing, who became the first modern European
to reach Timbuktu, wrote of the "abundant" records in the town.
He was murdered soon after leaving it.

René Caillié, who returned alive from Timbuktu,
was awarded the Société de Géographie's 10,000 franc prize,
which provoked a furious response in Britain.

Caillié's expedition to Timbuktu was low-cost and low-key: he learned Arabic and traveled in the guise of a Muslim.

Colonial troops raising the French flag over Timbuktu in 1894, as envisaged by the artist Frédéric Lix.

Heinrich Barth, perhaps the greatest explorer
of West Africa, found a copy of the
Tarikh al-sudan in June 1853 in Gando.

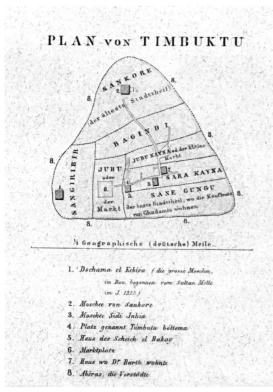

PLAN von TIMBUKTU

SANKORE
der älteste Stadttheil

BAGINDI

JUBU KAYNA od der kleine Markt

JUBU oder der Markt

SARA KAYNA

SANE GUNGU
der beste Stadttheil, wo die Kaufleute von Ghadamis wohnen

SANGIRIBIR

¼ Geographische (deutsche) Meile.

1. Dschama el Kebira (die grosse Moschee, im Bau begonnen vom Sultan Melle im J. 1325)
2. Moschee von Sankore
3. Moschee Sidi Jahia
4. Platz genannt Tumbutu bottema
5. Haus des Scheich el Bakay
6. Marktplatz
7. Haus wo Dr Barth wohnte
8. Abiras, die Vorstädte

A map of Timbuktu, drawn by Heinrich Barth, identifies six districts surrounding the market. The great mosque, Jingere Ber, is in the bottom left corner.

Barth arriving at Timbuktu on September 7, 1853.
Seeing a mass of people coming to welcome him,
he galloped forward, gun in hand, to receive their salaams.

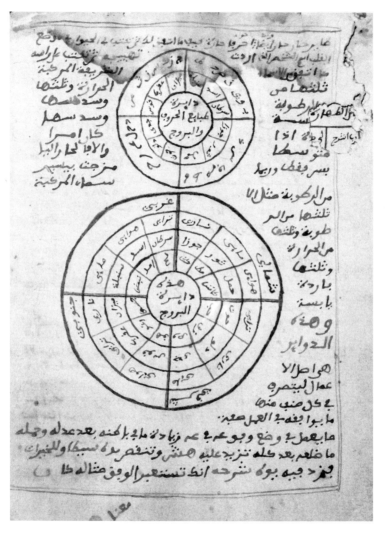

A manuscript on astrology, from the Mamma Haidara collection,
which depicts the signs of the zodiac and the points of the compass.

An illustrated manuscript with a famous collection of Muslim prayers,
the *Dalail al-khayrat*, in the Ahmad Baba institute.

Abdel Kader Haidara with some of his more precious manuscripts, on display in Savama's new Bamako office.

Haidara showing steel lockers filled with manuscripts to Dutch diplomats in Bamako in early 2013.

Ismael Diadié Haidara, the proprietor of the Fondo Kati library, who took four of his most precious manuscripts to Bamako after the first week of occupation.

Mukhtar bin Yahya al-Wangari outside his family library in central Timbuktu. The al-Wangari collection was one of many that remained in the city throughout the occupation.

Abou Zeid, the "Little Emir," was the al-Qaeda governor of Timbuktu in 2012.
He was killed by French forces in northern Mali in February 2013.

The Sankore mosque, in the north of the city.
The area around the mosque was home to many of Timbuktu's
Islamic scholars in the fifteenth and sixteenth centuries.

الحركة الوطنية لتحرير أزواد
تمثل رؤيتنا وصوتنا

Pro-MNLA demonstrators marching against jihadist rule in October 2012,
after a crackdown on Timbuktu's women by the Islamic Police.

A locker filled with manuscripts that were shown to
Dutch diplomats in a storage room in Bamako in early 2013.

They had been held hostage for twenty-four hours, and it took the couriers eight days to reach Bamako. "Eight days because the car was not good and they spent a day as hostages!"

It was the only time they tried the route via Lere. "We did not do that again," Haidara said.

NEAR THE END OF 2012, Savama informed the German embassy in Bamako that between 80,000 and 120,000 manuscripts had been successfully evacuated from Timbuktu. At this time, though, the Malian crisis was entering a far more dangerous phase. In the second week of December, Iyad Ag Ghaly called a congress of tribal elders and jihadist groups at Essakane, a two-hour drive west of Timbuktu. This place of rolling white dunes was hugely symbolic for Ansar Dine and its allies: it was here that the Festival in the Desert had been held each year since 2003, with Western musicians such as Robert Plant and Damon Albarn playing alongside Malian stars such as Salif Keita and Ali Farka Touré. The Irish superstar Bono had sung there with the Tuareg band Tinariwen only that January.

There would be no Festival in the Desert in 2013. Concerts were banned in the Islamic Republic of Azawad, and in place of musicians the dunes on those days were populated with jihadist fighters. At the summit's end, eyewitnesses reported seeing more than three hundred pickups race toward Timbuktu, with mujahideen clinging on in back, shouting *"Allahu Akbar!"* It was not yet clear what it all meant, but a rumor went around Timbuktu that a strategic decision had been made.

The cogs of international diplomacy were meanwhile grinding toward intervention. On December 20 the UN Security Council authorized the deployment of an African-led force in Mali, and three days later, the jihadists embarked on a new attack on the Timbuktu mausoleums in an act of defiance against the international community. Fighters drove through the streets and markets telling people that these places of idolatry had to be demolished. Then, as one eyewitness recalled, "using picks and shovels, the Islamic Police carried out the destruction of five mausoleums." Once again, they pledged that not a single one would be left standing.

If that were not traumatizing enough, negotiations in Timbuktu over Mawlid were also reaching a crisis point. In 2013 the celebration of the Prophet's birthday would fall on Thursday, January 24. The city had been largely resigned to canceling the event when Abou Zeid dropped in on Grand Imam Abderrahmane Ben Essayouti. The imam took the opportunity to ask the al-Qaeda emir about the festival. "He told Abou Zeid he wanted to speak about the celebration of Mawlid," recalled Sane Chirfi Alpha, who was given details of this meeting. Abou Zeid responded that he would defer on such matters to his Islamic legal experts, the *ulama*. "They will decide," he said. "When you are ready, you bring your *ulama* and we will bring ours and they can discuss it. If you can convince them, there won't be a problem."

As Mawlid approached, the two sides gathered and debated the matter all morning. "We met here at my house," the grand imam recalled. "They told us to bring arguments and supporting documents if we had them which would authorize Mawlid." The meeting lasted from nine a.m. to two p.m., as the Timbuktu *ulama* put forward their case, based on the Islamic texts, for the festival they had been celebrating for centuries. "We do not contradict anything you have advanced in your thesis," said the jihadists' experts, according to Alpha, "but there is one thing that happens during Mawlid we do not like: there is too much deviation, too much perversion. We cannot accept that."

"Those who perform the perversion and the deviation do not wait for Mawlid," replied the representatives of the town. "That is their life before, during, and after Mawlid. It is not Mawlid that causes this, and that is not a reason to stop us from celebrating it."

When the discussion was finished, the Timbuktiens were told that they would soon receive the resolution, on the basis of the work they had done together.

By the start of the new year, it was becoming clear what the Essakane meeting had been about. On January 1, Ag Ghaly sent two extravagant demands to the Malian government: it must recognize the autonomy of Azawad and proclaim the "Islamic character of the state of Mali" in the constitution. The government refused. The next day, around fifteen hundred jihadists began massing at Bambara Maounde, the truck-stop village halfway between Timbuktu and Douentza. On Tuesday, January 8, gunfire was exchanged across the front line, and that night hundreds of jihadist vehicles advanced toward Konna, forty miles inside government territory. At eight-thirty the following morning they attacked the town from three sides, and by late afternoon it had fallen. "We are in Konna for jihad," a rebel spokesman told Agence France-Presse on Thursday afternoon. "We have almost complete control of the town. After this we will continue to advance south."

Mopti was less than an hour's drive away. If the jihadists took that, there would be little to stop them from going all the way to Bamako.

The next morning, Friday, January 11, French president François Hollande announced that his country was going to war. "I have decided that France will respond, at the sides of our African partners, to the request of the Malian authorities," he said, standing in front of his nation's tricolor flag in the Élysée Palace. Operation Serval, the French offensive to retake the north of Mali, was about to begin.

. . .

HAIDARA HAD BEEN WARNED by heritage experts that the end of the occupation would be the most dangerous period for the manuscripts: "Before starting all this, people told me that the day they leave they are going to burn everything. They are going to sabotage it all. Everything that is important. That was part of the advice they gave me. But I did not know how it would happen." The prospect of renewed fighting also alarmed Shamil Jeppie, director of the Tombouctou Manuscripts Project at the University of Cape Town. "Wherever you see military intervention, things are bound to get destroyed," he said. "My initial fear was of neglect. The fear now is outright war and military engagement." The director-general of UNESCO sent out a plea to all military units in the country not to further damage the Timbuktu monuments: "I ask all armed forces to make every effort to protect the cultural heritage of the country," Irina Bokova said. "Mali's cultural heritage is a jewel whose protection is important for the whole of humanity. This is our common heritage, nothing can justify damaging it. It carries the identity and values of a people."

Against the backdrop of the pending conflict, Haidara and Diakité renewed their energetic fund-raising. On January 4, they went to the heavily fortified German embassy compound on the south bank of the river in Bamako. The ambassador was away on long-term sick leave, but a newly arrived chargé d'affaires, Thomas Strieder, agreed to meet them. Strieder remembered that Haidara seemed anxious. "He was searching for a few allies in the international community to help him to finance these [evacuation] actions," he said. "He needed money."

The librarian told Strieder that Savama had been authorized by the various families in Timbuktu to care for the manuscripts, which had been hidden among the people of Timbuktu in their homes. Now, however, the risk had become too great for them to remain in the city, since the rebel forces had been actively searching for the manuscripts and destroying them:

> He told me that there was an immediate danger, that they had been destroyed, burned, and it had been done . . . during these weeks again and again. I remember that some of the books were found then by the rebel forces and destroyed. Burned, or . . . I think burned, yes.

Strieder was told the manuscripts had to be brought out by any means. He was convinced the threat was genuine—"I had no reason to doubt it," he recalled—but he wanted more detail about how the evacuation would work. Was it even possible still to travel by road from Timbuktu to Bamako? Yes, said Haidara, but there were a lot of checkpoints to cross. How would the manuscripts be moved? By pickup trucks, in the night, hidden under fruit and vegetables that were grown in Timbuktu and shipped to the rest of Mali, Strieder was told.

There was no question that Germany would try to support the evacuation, the diplomat said, but he would need detailed costings as well as some sort of written agreement. He promised to talk to the German foreign ministry, and he and Diakité arranged subsequent meetings, including one at the bar in Bamako's Radisson Hotel, to formalize the details.

On January 7, Strieder wrote to Berlin, setting out the case for aid. He had been in touch with the people who were carrying out a rescue of the manuscript libraries of Timbuktu, he told them. The manuscripts were in acute danger, and the Islamists had already destroyed the offices of the libraries, including PCs and furniture. Now, given the likelihood of military intervention, the documents needed to be moved out "as fast as possible and as completely as possible": it was a question of saving these stocks "from the fire." Everything should be kept highly confidential, since if the occupiers got wind of what was going on, it would be impossible to proceed further; Haidara and Diakité had turned to the embassy because they "especially trust the Germans." They were looking for 500,000 euros over the next two years to relocate all the manuscripts and keep them safely in Bamako, but a quick donation of 10,000 euros right now would ensure the rescue of around twenty full lockers.

The money from Berlin came "astonishingly quickly," compared with the foreign ministry's normal procedures, Strieder said, since "they realized the urgency of the project at the top level." A contract was signed for the transport of four thousand manuscripts "under adverse conditions" in exchange for 10,000 euros, and just eight days after their first meeting with Strieder, Diakité and Haidara returned to the embassy to pick up the money. The large bundle of euro notes was handed over covertly in a plastic bag bearing the name of a Bamako bakery. The manuscript smugglers were not allowed a receipt.

WHEN THE VERDICT ON MAWLID came at last, it was in the form of a note: "Abou Zeid wrote a letter," recalled Sane Chirfi Alpha, "to say, truly, the arguments that you advance on Mawlid are just, but while we are here, we will not do it."

"It showed us clearly that in reality they did not want Mawlid," recalled the grand imam. The Timbuktiens decided not to force the issue, and the city's imams asked the inhabitants not to celebrate the festival.

At no point in the discussion were the manuscripts referred to, the grand imam said: "We did not speak of the manuscripts."

If the recollections of the grand imam and Alpha were correct, the jihadists did not appear hell-bent on destroying all copies of the *Ishriniyyat* and the collections that contained it. Abou Zeid had organized a legal discussion, then waited until the last moment before calling off the festival. Yet this was not the impression Stolk was given. Savama told her that Ansar Dine had warned the town on January 13 that Mawlid was *haram*—forbidden—and its celebration would have "repercussions." This was evidence that the manuscripts' situation "had indeed been that dangerous," and that the evacuation was justified.

The fighting in central Mali at this time meant the land route to Bamako had become too dangerous for most truckers to operate. Since there were still large numbers of manuscripts in Timbuktu, Haidara now decided to move them into the villages surrounding the city. "At that time, they took everything out," said Haidara. "They brought everything there was into the little villages near the river at Kabara, Iloa, Hondoubongo, Toya." Diakité would give an account of this move two months later, at a fund-raising lecture at the University of Oregon. It was a time, she said, when Malians from all walks of life helped bring the manuscripts to safety, spontaneously and at great personal risk:

> Housewives offered meals and shelter to our couriers along the route. Merchants transported couriers and footlockers of books without charge, when they saw our people pushing them in push-carts or carrying them on their backs to get them to the safety of the river. . . . Whole villages created diversions at checkpoints, so our couriers could get them through with the books. In all cases, in

the north but also in the south, the community came forward in the name of safeguarding the manuscripts. . . . They called [them] *our* heritage, *our* manuscripts.

By mid-January, tens of thousands of manuscripts were in the villages waiting to be shipped south, and with the desert crossing closed, there was only one way to move them: on the river. This carried significant new risks, however, and became a major source of disagreement between the librarian and his partner. "Abdel Kader [Haidara] and I argued about using the water," Diakité told her audience at the University of Oregon. "He was for it—he's the courageous one in our terrible twosome—and I was strongly against. A wet manuscript is just a pile of old rags. Most of the manuscripts are made of rag paper, with ink floating on top. None of the inks on these manuscripts has any kind of fixative. They are completely volatile." In the end they had no option, since the roads would only get more dangerous as French and Malian forces advanced. "The water became inevitable," Diakité recalled. "I stopped sleeping altogether at that point. Abdel Kader told me that he did too."

Transporting manuscripts by boat was not only risky, but also expensive. On Tuesday, January 15, Diakité set out once again to try to raise more funds, pitching up that day at the Dutch embassy in the Hippodrome quarter of eastern Bamako for a meeting with the embassy's head of development aid, To Tjoelker. Diakité had been given Tjoelker's name, as well as that of a charitable organization based in the Netherlands, the DOEN Foundation, by a contact in the Dutch development finance department. Tjoelker would at least listen, the contact had said. If anyone could make things happen, she could.

Diakité told Tjoelker the problem. "They said we would like you to help us because there are still 180,000 manuscripts left in Timbuktu and we can't get them out without extra money," the diplomat recalled. The jihadists' reaction to Mawlid presented a genuine threat, Tjoelker was informed, particularly since the French forces were now pushing the jihadists back. "After the battle of Konna, the AQIM fighters who were occupying Timbuktu became very angry and said, 'Okay, we will show you. We will do a big auto-da-fé on the day of Mawlid, the day of the birthday of Muhammad.'"

Auto-da-fé—meaning "act of faith" in Portuguese—was the term that had been used to describe the burning of heretics and heretical literature by the Inquisition in medieval Europe. But its modern resonance came from its use to describe Nazi book-burnings. Supervised by the SA and the SS, student societies in Nazi Germany destroyed blacklisted literature in pyres, including books written by Jewish authors, while reciting execration formulas. Josef Goebbels described these rituals as powerful and symbolic actions that would represent the dawning of the new age and the end of the old. Tjoelker was persuaded that this was what the jihadists now intended to do. "Mawlid is *haram* in the jihadists' minds, as are the manuscripts," Tjoelker recalled. "That's why they said on the 24th [of January] we will do a big auto-da-fé of all the manuscripts."

The "consortium" of Savama and D Intl spelled out the immediate nature of the Mawlid threat in a follow-up letter to the embassy, signed by Haidara. There were 454 lockers that needed to be evacuated immediately and in secret, the Dutch diplomats were told, since the jihadists had said they would destroy them. Failure to move them would mean that Timbuktu's cultural heritage, "which carries the hopes and pride of an entire people," would be "definitively lost." There was not much time, since the festival was only a week away.

Tjoelker had no budget for saving culture, but Diakité had come knocking at an opportune moment: the Dutch foreign minister, Lilianne Ploumen, had just sent a note to the embassy asking what the government could do to help Mali, and Tjoelker was convinced this was it. She told Diakité that she would try to make a case to the foreign ministry for funding the evacuation, and wrote that day to her superior in The Hague. The response that came back overnight was unhelpful. "It was, you know, 'It's a bit complicated,'" Tjoelker said. She was so angry she called her ambassador, Maarten Brouwer, who told her to go straight to Ploumen.

"I said, 'Okay, send [the request] directly to the minister and call the secretary to the minister,'" Brouwer recalled, "'tell her this is something that should be on her desk or in her bag because we really need a quick response.'" Tjoelker did as Brouwer suggested, bypassing the usual ministry hierarchy. The next morning, January 17, Ploumen gave her blessing to the operation. "She said, 'Okay, let's do it,'" Tjoelker said.

The project had to remain highly confidential: "I said to [Ploumen], 'You can't tell anyone about it, it has to be kept really secret, because if it becomes public AQIM will react and hinder Savama's saving action. . . . It is top secret and you can only get the publicity after four or five months but not now, you have to keep quiet.'" Ploumen took Tjoelker's entreaty for silence so seriously she relayed it to her ambassador. "Let's not talk about it until it's done," she told Brouwer. The embassy even marked down the money in its own accounts as being for school exercise books in order to hide the real purpose of the donation.

The Dutch foreign ministry allocated 323,475 euros to Savama.

Combined with the DOEN Foundation's 75,000 and the Prince Claus Fund's 100,000, the total donated by the Dutch public now stood at close to half a million euros. Tjoelker's reluctant manager at the Africa desk e-mailed to say he had been ordered to help, and that afternoon she began to make arrangements. She went to the finance department and told them, "Okay, I have a top-secret mission. How do we do it?" and worked late into the night to get the paperwork done. If she could produce a contract quickly, Savama had told her, it could be used to borrow money to finance the operation. "In two days we had fixed the contract, all the paperwork, and we could sign the contract with Abdel Kader so that in one week he would get the money," Tjoelker recalled. "He was working to a deadline, because there were so many manuscripts to move."

That Saturday, January 19, Tjoelker took the contract to the librarian for him to sign. She met him in the Bamako lockup where the manuscripts were being received and dispatched to the safe houses. He looked unwashed, she remembered, and "so tired," and to cheer him up she told him the work he was doing was "important for all humanity." The contract stipulated that he would evacuate 454 lockers, containing roughly 136,200 manuscripts, which made the cost of transporting each locker a whopping 660 euros, though this included storage in Bamako for a year, the making of an inventory, at 212 euros per locker, and a 10 percent "management fee" for Savama and for D Intl. The 454 lockers were part of 709 that the Dutch were told had to be evacuated in all.

"That weekend a large numbers of boats—around twenty—were already starting to leave Timbuktu," Tjoelker said. They could have loaded all the manuscripts at once on one of the larger Niger River *pinasses*, but instead they put only twenty or so lockers on each vessel, to reduce the risk of a catastrophic loss. The boats then set out on the 250-mile journey upriver, across the inland delta and Lake Debo, to Mopti, where they turned south up the Bani River for a further seventy miles to Jenne. There they were transferred to bush taxis that took the manuscripts the last 350 miles to Bamako by road. "In Jenne there were more than fifty pickups—even one hundred—that would take the manuscript boxes," said Tjoelker. These were typically Toyotas, and they carried two or three of the heavy boxes in the back each time, covered with other goods—hay, potatoes, grain—to hide them.

"There were a lot of pickups," said Tjoelker. "That's why it was so expensive."

IT WAS DURING THIS RIVERINE PHASE of the operation that, according to Haidara and Diakité, the incident with the helicopter occurred.

The Niger boatmen were terrified of French aircraft at this time. Captains such as Hassim Traoré of the Number One Transportation Company remembered seeing the helicopters flying over the river at night and even being approached by them. Their lights appeared "like a star, but flashing on and off," Traoré recalled. "We got very, very afraid. Many panicked, because people were saying that if the French didn't know who we were, they might bomb us, so we were really scared." According to Tjoelker, Diakité and Haidara went to see the commander of Operation Serval to ask that boats that were carrying manuscripts not be targeted; if this is true, the message does not seem to have reached the pilots. Colonel Frédéric Gout, commander of the French helicopter regiment deployed in Operation Serval, was unaware of any special dispensation for the Niger boats, although, he said, they needn't have worried: without positive identification of weapons on board, his men were not allowed to engage. Of course, the people traveling in the fragile vessels didn't know that.

One night, according to Haidara, ten manuscript-carrying boats were traveling together "in a big convoy" and had reached the middle of Lake Debo when a helicopter came to investigate, fixing a spotlight on them. "The people who were in the boats were frightened they would be turned into mincemeat," Haidara said. The whirring machine hovered over them for thirty seconds, scanning the vessels for weapons, before the pilot banked away. A terrified courier called Haidara at one in the morning to tell him they had almost been killed. "There is a helicopter that passed and was going to bomb us," the courier told him. Haidara ordered that from now on they must stop at five p.m. wherever they were, and no longer travel at night.

"I knew that in the helicopters there were detectors, and if they did not detect something serious they could not do harm," Haidara recalled. "But if they detected weapons or something like that, they could attack. They found that there were no weapons, so they left. But if they had been carrying weapons, they would have hit them, that is sure."

Diakité related a version of this story to her audience in Oregon. In her account, the pilot of the French helicopter "demanded that the couriers open their boxes or be sunk on suspicion of harboring weapons," but the pilot had a change of heart when he "saw the ship was carrying nothing but old piles of paper":

Boats full of manuscripts and couriers were in danger of being sunk by French combat helicopters, [which] pulled away and saluted our couriers when they risked their lives to stay on the water, open a footlocker and show the pilots we had manuscripts, not guns.

Diakité told *The New Republic* of a further incident on the river around this time, which occurred after the jihadists declared that the "city's elders had to turn over all the manuscripts so they could be burned before the [Mawlid] holiday began." The threat put the smugglers in a panic, and they began calling all the couriers and ordering them to get the lockers on the river as quickly as possible. They had soon loaded a fleet of forty-seven boats, which then began to make their way south. As they approached the southern edge of Lake Debo, according to *The New Republic*, disaster struck:

> Twenty of the boats entered a narrow strait of water. Suddenly, groups of men, their heads covered with turbans, materialized on both sides of the river, waving automatic weapons and ordering the boats to stop. The couriers had no choice but to pull their pirogues up to the shore, where the gunmen said they would burn their cargo unless they could deliver an astronomical sum of money. The teenage couriers pooled their cash, watches, and jewelry, but it wasn't enough.

The young men were eventually allowed to call Haidara, who launched negotiations. "He basically gave them an IOU," Diakité told *The New Republic*. "It was like Abdel Kader was using a credit card." The manuscripts and couriers were released. A few days later, Haidara sent the money.

Tjoelker was given brief updates on these types of incidents via text message. "They would text and say, 'They are at the Debo,' 'We have encountered a problem,' 'Problem solved,' 'We go on to Jenne,'" she said. "It was very short: 'Boats are at this place,' 'Problem of this night solved,' 'Still going on.'" She also remembered hearing a story about people stopping the couriers, and said they had to give them money to go on: "It was a sort of holdup near Lake Debo. . . . There were a lot of boats."

Once or twice during the operation Ambassador Brouwer asked how things were going, and he recalled being told of difficulties on the route: "We got some stories about [lockers] full of manuscripts that were transported by pirogues and that it was done during the night and they had a lot of problems on the way because there was the police, there were rebels, and so on," he said. He had heard that boats had been kidnapped or that people had threatened to set manuscripts on fire. "It was the people on the ground that solved those issues."

As the lockers reached Bamako, Haidara took Tjoelker to see them. "He really made me part of the reception of all those boxes. He showed me their way of accounting—which parts have been financed by the Ford Foundation, what has been financed by Prince Claus, by DOEN. Every box had a number and the name of the funder on it so they knew who had paid for what." She met some of the young couriers who accompanied the lockers. "Especially in Timbuktu I think they did really marvelous things to distract the AQIM guys, to get the manuscripts out of the city."

Ambassador Brouwer accompanied Tjoelker on one of these visits. He counted roughly five to six hundred containers in the room, easily enough for Savama to have fulfilled its contract with the Dutch government, and was told there were more elsewhere.

"I looked at To [Tjoelker] and I said, 'This is a lot. Are these all full?' They said, 'Yes, they are all full.'"

To be doubly sure, he even singled out one chest-deep in a stack at the back of the stockroom and said, "Okay, show me that one."

"It was foolish," he remembered, "but we actually did it."

When the locker was opened, he saw it was piled to the brim with manuscripts.

14.

KING LEOPOLD'S
PAPERWEIGHT

1865–1905

T hough Barth and Cherbonneau had discovered clear evidence that the people across the desert had produced literate civiliza- tions, they were swimming against the tide of late-nineteenth- century thought. They would soon be drowned out.

At the end of his seventeen-page report of recommendations for the International Society for the Suppression of Savage Customs, Mr. Kurtz, the ivory-trading antagonist at the center of Joseph Conrad's novella *Heart of Darkness*, reveals his underlying animus, scrawling in a crazed, unsteady hand: "Exterminate all the brutes!" Kurtz's logic for killing the people of Africa and stealing their resources is that whites, who are so highly developed,

must necessarily appear to them [savages] in the nature of super- natural beings—we approach them with the might of a deity. . . . By the simple exercise of our will we can exert a power for good practically unbounded.

Heart of Darkness was based on what Conrad had seen as acting skipper of the steamboat *Roi des Belges* in 1890 in the Congo Free State, the territory with which Leopold II of Belgium had fulfilled his long-held fantasy of ruling a colony. In Leopold's Congo, a private army known as the Force Publique would make the people strip the natural wealth of their own land, principally rubber and ivory, for the enrichment of Brussels. If quotas were not met, men would be killed, women raped, children mutilated, and villages torched. The number who died in the territory as a result of Leopold's reign has been estimated at ten million, or roughly half the population.

Joseph Banks would doubtless have been horrified to learn of the scale of the Belgian king's brutalizing of central Africa, but it was in many ways an inevitable extension of the process the African Association had begun, an extreme example of a pattern that was being repeated in discovered lands everywhere from the Americas to Australasia to the Arctic. The era of exploration was over; now came the exploitation. First, however, the great powers had to acquire the African territories, and in the late nineteenth century that was just what they did. In 1870 roughly 10 percent of the continent was under the control of a colonizing power. By 1914 only 10 percent was not.

The driving force of the new imperialism was partly financial. In the 1870s the growth of many Western nations stalled; their economies would remain sluggish for more than two decades. New markets and raw materials were needed, and Africa had both. This imperative coincided with a peak of European racism, fueled by the greatest technology gap between the industrialized world and Africa that history had ever seen, and promoted by a willing intelligentsia who built on hierarchies of ethnicity developed during the Enlightenment. For the few who had actually been to parts of the continent or studied it, attempting to resist this intellectual shift was impossible. Superficially Barth had been rejected by the Royal Academy of Sciences in Berlin for being an "adventurer" rather than a scholar; but how much of the academy's decision lay in its rejection of his account of the Western Sudan? The German establishment's view of Africa was still dominated by the thinking of Georg Hegel, who had announced early in the century that it "is no historical part of the World; it has no movement or development to exhibit." Obvious evidence of civilizations there, such as those at Carthage or in Egypt, were dismissed as not properly African—they did not "belong to the African Spirit." The result was that "what we properly understand by Africa, is the Unhistorical, Undeveloped Spirit, still involved in the conditions of mere nature . . . on the threshold of the World's History."

Hegel was neither the first nor the last European intellectual to write off the continent and its people. In the 1850s, the French ethnologist Joseph-Arthur Gobineau wrote the seminal work of the so-called science of racism, *The Moral and Intellectual Diversity of the Races*, which included a complete racial hierarchy with white people of European origin at the top and dark-skinned people at the bottom. Explorers such as Park may have "given to some negro a certificate of superior intelligence," wrote Gobineau, but it was improper to draw scientific conclusions from anecdotal encounters with a few intelligent individuals. The very physiognomy of the black races was evidence of inferiority: their pelvises had "a character of animalism" which seemed "to portend their destiny," while their foreheads were "narrow and receding," a sign that they were "inferior in reasoning capacity."

Racist theory began to reach into almost every aspect of European thinking about Africa, including exploration. In 1874, the British explorer Samuel Baker stated:

> In that savage country [of Central Africa] . . . we find no vestiges of the past—no ancient architecture, neither sculpture, nor even a chiselled stone to prove that the Negro savage of this day is inferior to a remote ancestor. . . . We must therefore conclude that the races of man which now inhabit [this region] are unchanged from the prehistoric tribes who were the original inhabitants.

This mind-set would last deep into the twentieth century. In 1923, the leading British historian A. P. Newton would write that "Africa has practically no history before the coming of Europeans . . . since history only begins when men take to writing," ignoring totally the growing body of evidence to the contrary. Five years later, Reginald Coupland, the Beit Professor of Colonial History at Oxford University, would endorse Newton, asserting that until the nineteenth century, the main body of the Africans "had stayed, for untold centuries, sunk in barbarism. . . . They remained stagnant, neither going forward nor going back. Nowhere in the world, save perhaps in some miasmic swamps of South America or in some derelict Pacific Islands, was human life so stagnant. The heart of Africa was scarcely beating."

Robbed of its past and its culture, Africa was a blank slate, an emptiness on which Christianity and civilization could be imposed. With the intellectual groundwork complete, the "Scramble for Africa," as a columnist for the London *Times* dubbed it, could begin. Leopold was one of the instigators of this land grab. Only the second monarch of a country that had been founded in 1830, he appears now as a sort of colonialist pervert. He had been shopping for an overseas territory for decades.

In 1861, four years before his accession to the throne, he had given Belgium's anti-imperialist finance minister a fragment of marble from the Acropolis inscribed with the words *"Il faut à la Belgique une colonie"*— Belgium must have a colony. He had a penchant for Borneo and New Guinea. He tried to lease Formosa. He invested in the Suez Canal Company and examined Brazilian railways. Finally he enlisted Henry Morton Stanley, the explorer of whom Richard Francis Burton once said, "He shoots negroes as if they were monkeys," to secretly scope out the Congo basin, a giant patch of land more than thirty times the size of his own country. Stanley built roads and collected treaties, while Leopold tried to persuade the great powers to back the proposal that his International African Association take over the territory. In November 1884, Otto von Bismarck convened a diplomatic conference in Berlin, in part to resolve the Leopold question, in part to set out the ground rules for annexations that were already under way.

The delegates talked for three months, without a single African at the table. When they parted on February 26, 1885, Leopold's International African Association had been recognized as the government of the new Congo Free State, creating the legal framework for his ransacking of the territory, and the broad lines of the partition of Africa had been established. To fully own their territories, the conference stipulated, the European powers would have to show "effective occupation"; in other words, they should have forces on the ground.

Timbuktu had been aware of European encroachment for decades. In 1830, an army of thirty-four thousand French soldiers had seized Algiers from the Ottomans, and by the 1850s, after a series of campaigns against local resistance movements, they had conquered most of the surrounding territory. Hundreds of thousands of *"colons"* had crossed the Mediterranean to settle in northern Africa, and the coast was now dotted with vineyards, farms, and French architecture. In West Africa, meanwhile, they had pushed inland from their centuries-old bases in Senegal and the Gulf of Guinea. The French advance here was a more patchwork affair, often led by private traders or military officers who would use any fracas to call up gunboats or military detachments, whereupon local chiefs were forced to sign treaties ceding land. Bit by bit, Paris had taken control of Guinea, Dahomey, Ivory Coast, Upper Volta, and parts of the Niger valley.

Even knowing all this, the leaders of Timbuktu would have been surprised to learn that they were about to become part of France.

FOR A HUNDRED YEARS, European investigation into Timbuktu and the Niger had been driven by the exploration societies, geographers, and a handful of Orientalists. The study of Africa now ceased to be a discipline worthy of academic thought. No European university created chairs in the history of the continent or its languages: if Africa had had no civilization, what was the point? The study of the past depended on written source material, and since Africa had none, there was nothing to be researched. In the decades to come, the role of exploring Africa's culture would fall in the main to soldiers, colonial officers, and journalists.

Few places on the continent excited the new breed of French imperialist more than Timbuktu. Caillié's disappointment had not much dampened European curiosity about the city, or belief in the region's essential wealth. Several failed attempts to reach it were made in the latter part of the nineteenth century. In 1884 a ship was specially constructed to work its way down the Niger: it sank in Jenne in 1885, was salvaged, and set out again for Timbuktu in 1886, when it was finally forced to retreat after coming under attack from a group of Tuareg.

Even when their superiors in the colonial department in Paris tried to restrain them, expansionist senior officers looking for promotion would take it upon themselves to push deeper into West Africa. The most aggressive of these soldiers was Colonel Louis Archinard, commander of French forces in the Sudan from 1888 to 1893. The Middle Niger at this time was controlled by the Islamic Tukulor empire. French attitudes to the Tukulor sultan, Ahmadu Seku, were summed up by Archinard's predecessor, Joseph Gallieni, who noted that "we must look on all these chiefs as people to be ruined and made to disappear before very long." In April 1890, Archinard launched an unprovoked attack on the Tukulor capital at Segu, which fell without resistance. As his men rifled through Ahmadu's possessions, searching for his famed wealth (which was not as advertised), they found a large number of manuscripts. Archinard's account of the day reveals no interest in these documents, but they were seized nevertheless and shipped out in four chests. They remained in a colonial supply depot until the end of 1892, when they were given to the Bibliothèque Nationale de France in Paris. They would remain there, untouched, for several years.

After crushing the Tukulor, Archinard continued to push toward Timbuktu, acting against direct orders from his superiors in Paris. In April 1893 he took Jenne after heavy fighting, and Mopti fell later that month without a struggle, but a political shift against military expansionism finally cost Archinard his position. Two rival French officers—Lieutenant Colonel Eugène Bonnier and the naval lieutenant Henri Boiteux—now took up the baton in this new race to Timbuktu, against express orders from Archinard's replacement, who was making his way from France. Boiteux was first out of the blocks: taking two gunboats and a contingent of soldiers downriver, he entered Timbuktu on December 16, 1893. The furious Bonnier, who had nurtured a lifelong ambition to conquer the city, reached the area with a column of colonial troops a month later. Near Goundam, the party was attacked in the night by Tuareg, and Bonnier, ten of his officers, an interpreter, two European noncommissioned officers, and sixty-eight Senegalese soldiers were massacred. The city now had to be recaptured and the Tuareg punished, tasks which were efficiently done by Major Joseph Joffre, who advanced along the left bank of the Niger from Segu, killed one hundred Tuareg, and took fifteen hundred head of their cattle. Joffre was promoted for his action, and not for the last time: in 1914 he would be commander in chief of the French forces on the western front.

The capture of Timbuktu and the unwillingness of French officers in the Western Sudan to obey orders provoked fury in Paris, where the administration was split between pro-military and pro-civilian factions. Nevertheless, the occupation was a fait accompli. It was approved by the colonial office on two conditions: one, that it could be maintained without risk; two, that it would incur no additional cost to the government.

FÉLIX DUBOIS was the son of a noted chef who spent twenty years cooking for the Kaiser. His father's contacts in the upper echelons of nineteenth-century European society proved useful to Félix as he embarked on a career as a journalist, but his forays into literature were even more valuable: Dubois *père* wrote an encyclopedic range of best-selling cookbooks, and the royalties from recipes for such dishes as sheep brains in warm remoulade and veal's feet *à la genevoise* kept Félix afloat whenever his other income threatened to run dry. By 1894, at the age of thirty-two, he was an established foreign correspondent, having reported colorfully for the Paris papers from Vienna and Berlin, and from Henri Brosselard-Faidherbe's expedition to Futa Jallon. It was only natural, when news of the conquest of Timbuktu reached Europe, that the editor of the Paris newspaper *Le Figaro* should turn to him for an account from this exotic new jewel in France's crown.

The reporter landed at Dakar in August 1894 and, after exploring the coast, began to make his way east. The road to Timbuktu no longer held the perils Park and Caillié had faced: Dubois traveled into the interior under the protection of the French administration, on supply roads constructed for the military and even on the new railway that had been built between Dakar and Saint-Louis. He stopped at Jenne, where he was excited to find manuscripts, including a complete *Tarikh al-sudan*, which he had copied, and extraordinary Sudanese architecture. These two discoveries persuaded him that the Songhay civilization, which demonstrated such "intelligence and science," must have come from ancient Egypt. From Jenne he pushed north on the river, determined, he wrote later, to "raise completely the veil which has hidden the Sudan from us for so long." He traveled the last few miles from Kabara with an armed escort, and as the sandy track rose to the top of a dune, he saw for the first time his goal, which appeared to him as "an immense and brilliant sky, and an immense and brilliant stretch of land, with the grand outlines of a town uniting the two. A dark silhouette, large and long, an image of grandeur in immensity—thus appeared the Queen of the Sudan."

Entering the town, he was rapidly brought back to reality. Timbuktu in January 1895 was "tragic," in near ruin. Even the house of the Shaykh al-Bakkai, a man "known all over Europe, all over the world, and the Queen of England corresponded with him," was a wreck, with little trace of the brilliant mind that had once occupied it. The buildings of the city were in such poor condition that Dubois considered camping out, before his guide found a house to his liking. The following day he sent out letters of introduction he had acquired in Jenne, inviting the city's scholars to visit. As he conversed with these men, probing them for historical information, and as he was shown more manuscripts, his opinion again performed a volte-face. Timbuktu's glories were not a fantasy after all: they merely lay over the horizon of the distant past. The wretched spectacle that had greeted him on his arrival dissipated bit by bit, and, without his yet having set foot in the street, a new Timbuktu was built up before him:

> A secret had clearly hovered over Timbuctoo the Mysterious. I had the eyes that saw; and at last the image of the great city, the wealthy Timbuctoo of the legends, was restored to me.

The journalist had found his scoop.

Caillié had not been wrong: the Queen of the Sudan was outwardly drab. But by digging deep through its manuscripts, which were merely what remained of the marvelous libraries that had been plundered already by the Fulani and Tukulor empires of the Niger bend, Dubois uncovered "Timbuctoo the holy, the learned, the light of the Niger." Such had been the town's splendor during her golden past that "our imaginations are still dazzled by its reflections, three centuries after the setting of her star." He rushed to make parallels with Europe: Sankore, the center of the city's learned activity, had been much like the Latin Quarter in Paris, and its schools constituted a "university of Sankore"—a term coined by Dubois—whose professors "astounded the most learned men of Islam by their erudition."

Timbuktu was not merely the great intellectual nucleus of the Sudan . . . she was also one of the great scientific centres of Islam itself, her university being the younger sister of those of Cairo, Cordova, Fez and Damascus. Her collection of ancient manuscripts leaves us in no doubt upon the point, and permits us to reconstruct this side of her past in its smallest detail.

In contrast to the miserly European book-collectors of the day, he wrote, the learned doctors of Timbuktu had experienced real joy in sharing their most precious manuscripts; they were bibliophiles "in the best sense." Dubois envisaged these scholars searching passionately for volumes they did not possess and making copies when they were too poor to buy what they wanted. In this manner they swelled their book collections to between seven hundred and two thousand volumes. Among them were works of poetry and imagination, and compositions "of a kind peculiar to Arabian literature," including those of the famous scholars al-Hariri and al-Hamadhani. He found a copy of the *Book of Wonders*, a collection of travels and legends composed at Mosul by Abu Hamid of Granada in the twelfth century. "The historical and geographical works of Morocco, Tunis and Egypt were well known in Timbuktu," wrote Dubois, "and the pure sciences were represented by books on astronomy and medicine." In short, the libraries of Timbuktu might be said to have included almost the whole of Arabian literature.

The greater part of the Timbuktu collections were "entirely without interest to us," he noted, since they comprised serious scholastic and judicial treatises and Islamic texts, but a fraction of Timbuktu's literary collections were of the "highest importance," containing "those historical works which shed so much light upon the obscure past of these vast regions." Chief among these was the *Tarikh al-sudan*, but he found other chronicles as well: the anonymous *Diwan al-muluk fi salatin al-sudan*, which described the history of the city from 1591 onward, and the *Tadkhirat al-nisyan fi akhbar muluk al-sudan*, a rearrangement of the *Diwan* into a biographical dictionary. All the city's books were so highly valued, however, that Dubois was unable to purchase a single one.

Dubois's greatest literary discovery was not a manuscript at all, but a mere rumor. He was told of a work he called the *Fatassi*, a "history of the kingdoms of Ganata, Songhoi, and Timbuctoo, from their origins to the year 1554," written by the scholar Mahmud Kati. Finding this document would be of inestimable value, but no matter how many people he asked in Timbuktu, he was shown only fragments. Everyone in the city knew about it, but no one admitted having it. It was, he concluded, "the phantom book of the Sudan."

The Timbuktu *qadi* Ahmadu Sansarif, who claimed descent from Kati, told Dubois there was a reason why no copies could be found:

> The Fatassi has never been so well known as the other histories of the Sudan because it dealt with the concerns of many peoples and many men. Families, since grown rich and powerful, and the chiefs of various countries, were shown with very humble origins, sometimes being the offspring of slaves. The book caused great annoyance to many people on this account, and those interested bought all the copies they could procure and destroyed them.

Among those said to be annoyed by the book was Shaykh Ahmad Lobbo, the founder of the Fulani empire of Masina, who had ordered Laing's death in 1828. Lobbo had declared himself the twelfth caliph, the last of the successors of Muhammad, whose coming the Prophet himself had foretold. But the *Fatassi*, which was written centuries before the founding of Lobbo's empire, neglected to mention him in its list of prophecies. Was it not likely, Dubois mused, that the Fulani had destroyed copies of the *Fatassi* in order to stop the work from exposing Lobbo's trick?

The original manuscript of the *Fatassi* had been lost in unusual circumstances, Sansarif told Dubois. It had been inherited by one of his great-aunts, who lived in Kati's home village of Tindirma, sixty miles southwest of Timbuktu. To keep the controversial work safe, she had placed it in a wooden box and buried it under a small mound close to her house. She was a popular and witty woman with a gift for conversation, and people often came to visit her, sometimes asking what was under the mound. She always replied in the same way. "It is [Mahmud Kati], my venerable ancestor who is buried there," she would say, whereupon her friends never failed to murmur a short prayer over the mound, for Kati had a great reputation for piety and wisdom.

Eventually she became friendly with a Fulani man and told him the secret of what lay beneath the earth. The man immediately hurried to Lobbo to tell him about the complete *Fatassi*, and shortly afterward the sultan sent his men to dig up the precious document. As they were returning on the river to the capital, "the bearer of the priceless volume capsized his canoe." The manuscript disappeared under the waters of the Niger and was lost to the world forever.

DUBOIS'S DESCRIPTIONS of Timbuktu's Golden Age were soon enlivening the pages of *Le Figaro* and *L'illustration*, accompanied by pictures of the country he had traveled through. The full account of his journey was published in book form in France in 1897. *Tombouctou la mystérieuse* was expertly crafted to meet the popular appetite for colonial literature, conjuring a fabulous vision of a newly European land. In Dubois's hands, the city was rescued from the debunking of Caillié and the grinding observations of Barth and restored to the poetical high ground. Reprising the metaphor once used by Warrington's rival in Tripoli, Baron Rousseau, Dubois turned Timbuktu into an exotic female waiting to be "unveiled." The author would boldly undress the dusky "Queen of the Sudan" before his audience's eyes, and the glimpses of the wonders beneath would take the reader's breath away. The book was a tremendous hit.

Dubois gave the *Tarikh al-sudan* he had brought from Jenne to the Bibliothèque Nationale de France, where it joined the 518 volumes Archinard had looted from Segu, including a further copy of the *tarikh*. Both of these were now sent to the eminent Orientalist Octave Houdas at the School of Living Oriental Languages in Paris. Working from the two manuscripts, Houdas and his collaborator Edmond Benoist began to compile a complete Arabic version of the chronicle, which they published in 1898. A French translation, bolstered by the arrival of a third manuscript discovered by the explorer Louis Tautain, was produced in 1900. Together with Dubois's own book, this work would breathe new life into the myth of gilded Timbuktu.

It was ironic that the promoter of the new Timbuktu legend believed unabashedly in the superiority of his own kind. Dubois had written of Joffre's punitive expedition against the Tuareg, for instance, that it would "still be necessary from time to time to show them that their nefarious dominion is at an end, and that they have found their master." For the colonialist historians, however, it was possible simultaneously to applaud the empire and marvel at the achievements of its recently subjugated people. To legitimize the occupation of the continent, African culture had been reduced to a nothing; now that it was in European hands, it seemed its wonders could be safely proclaimed. Indeed, in Dubois's view, it was only under French occupation that Timbuktu would be able to flourish again. "I picture the city become a center of European civilisation and science, as it was formerly of Mussulman culture," he wrote in one of his many grandiloquent passages. "The reputation of her scholars will again spread from Lake Chad to the mountains of Kong and the shores of the Atlantic, and Timbuctoo will once more be the wealthy and cultured Queen of the Sudan which her distant view now so deceitfully promises her to be."

Other colonialist writers, keen to demonstrate the achievements of the newly conquered lands, would follow Dubois's lead. Among these was the intriguing figure of Flora Shaw, also known as Lady Lugard. Shaw was born into an army family in Woolwich, southeast London, and had no formal schooling, though she spent much of her childhood reading in the library of the Royal Military Academy. When she was seventeen the critic John Ruskin made her his protégé, encouraging her to write, and she became a moderately successful author. Yet it was in journalism that she would excel: she became the first woman to join the permanent staff of *The Times* and in 1893 was named its colonial editor. She was a friend and promoter of Cecil Rhodes and even coined the term "Nigeria" in a *Times* article in 1897. According to one of her contemporaries, she was "a fine, handsome, bright, upstanding young woman, as clever as they make them, capable of an immense amount of work, as hard as nails and talking like a *Times* leader." In 1902 she married the British high commissioner for Northern Nigeria, Frederick Lugard, and three years later published a history of West Africa, *A Tropical Dependency*, which pulled together an immense range of source material, including what she described as the "treasure house" of the *tarikh*.

Shaw's self-appointed task in *A Tropical Dependency* was to explain the region to a Western audience and expound on its delights. In doing so she drew often questionable parallels between Songhay history and experiences her readers might comprehend. The state prison of the as-kiyas thus served "a similar purpose to that of the Tower of London," while under Askiya the Great's successors, "orchestras, provided with singers of both sexes, were much frequented." In many respects the Songhay empire had been far ahead of contemporary Europe: there were celebrated eye surgeons who could perform cataract operations, she wrote, and enough was known about astronomy that "the appear-ance of comets, so amazing to Europe of the Middle Ages, is also noted calmly, as a matter of scientific interest, at Timbuctoo." But the Son-ghay people's greatest achievement was "Timbuktu University," the institution Dubois had conjured from his researches into the Islamic schools around the Sankore mosque. According to Shaw, the university had made Timbuktu a "very active centre of civilisation" during the Sudanese Middle Ages.

Many of these assertions would later be regarded as overblown, but they were tame compared with a theory that had first been aired in 1880, and to which Shaw now gave credence: that Malians had sailed to the Americas long before Columbus, and their descendants had helped found the Aztec empire. The source of this story is said to be an anec-dote Mansa Musa related during his pilgrimage. Asked how he had come to be king of Mali, Musa responded that his predecessor had launched an extraordinary voyage of exploration, equipping two hun-dred ships with men and a further two hundred with enough gold, water, and provisions to last them for years, and telling their commander not to return until he reached the other side of the Atlantic. Only one of these ships returned, Musa said, with the story that the others had reached a river estuary with a powerful current. Thereupon, according to Musa's alleged anecdote, the sultan prepared a new expedition:

> [He] got ready 2,000 ships, 1,000 for himself and the men whom he took with him and 1,000 for the water and provisions. He left me to deputize for him and embarked on the Atlantic Ocean with his men. That was the last we saw of him and all those who were with him, and so I became king in my own right.

Was it possible that the mighty estuary reached by the Malian armada was the Amazon? Or that the Malians had continued from there to Mexico, where they and their descendants had helped establish the Aztec empire? Shaw cited several pieces of evidence for this unlikely scenario. One was the fact that in Ibn Battuta's account of visiting the Malian court, he recorded that "poets wearing masks and dressed like birds were allowed to speak their opinion to the monarch":

> The description [Ibn Battuta] gives in some detail can hardly fail to recall similar practices inherited from the Tezcucans by the Aztecs, who in nearly the same latitude on the American continent were at this very moment, in the middle of the 14th century, making good their position upon the Mexican plateau.

Further coincidences included traditions in both countries in which people summoned to court were expected to change into shabby garments, while the Sudanese custom of putting dust on one's head before speaking to the emperor echoed the Aztecs' bowing down to touch the earth with the right hand. Chief among Shaw's exhibits, though, was the color of the two races' skins: "The Aztecs were, it will be remembered, though not negroes, a dusky or copper-coloured race, apparently of the tint which Barth describes as that of the 'red races' of the Soudan." This skin tone, according to Shaw, had been produced by a mixing of "the virility of the Arab" with "the gentle nature of the Soudanese black," which had produced a genetically superior race. "In the shock and amalgamation of these two forces, black civilization attained the greatest height which it has ever reached in modern Africa."

Despite the absence of concrete evidence, the tale of a fourteenth-century Malian naval expedition to America would still be stated as fact in some quarters a century later.

By the early twentieth century, the myth of a wealthy Timbuktu with golden roofs had long been jettisoned, but it had been replaced with the idea of the city as an enlightened university town where orchestras entertained emperors and astronomers plotted the tracks of comets even as Europe struggled out of the Dark Ages. There was more substance to this myth than the old one, but it was still a gross exaggeration, a story written to fit the new requirement for exoticism. Timbuktu, it seemed, reflected to each of the travelers who reached it something of what they wanted to find. The romantic Laing had discovered his vainglorious end. Caillié, the humble adventurer, had found a humble town. Barth, the scientist, had unearthed a world of new information. Dubois, the journalist, had landed his world exclusive, uncovering the region's secret past.

La Mystérieuse was nothing if not obliging.

15.

AUTO-DA-FÉ

JANUARY 2013

On Sunday, January 20, the video journalist Cheikh Diouara slipped through a Malian army checkpoint south of Douentza and paid a young man with a motorbike to take him across the front line. He had been traveling and filming all day. It was now dusk and he needed to eat, so when he reached the town he went into a café and ordered some food. He should be careful, the owner warned him: the jihadists who still occupied the town were twitchy and angry and had recently shot at a civilian.

A few seconds later, Diouara recalled, the neighborhood was turned upside down by an immense explosion. "I have seen earthquakes and landslides," he said, "but that has nothing on this." Anyone who was standing was blown to the ground by the force of the shock wave, and for five minutes there was nothing in Diouara's ears but white noise. Douentza itself appeared "all muddled up." As people struggled to get back to their feet, he could see jihadist vehicles racing out of town at speeds that didn't seem possible, their lights extinguished. When one of their precious vehicles didn't start, they simply abandoned it.

Still in a daze, Diouara watched a man pick up a packet of dried milk that had fallen from one of the trucks as it sped off. It struck a group of citizens then that it would be a good idea to go to the school the jihadists had used as a base to see what they had left. They climbed on their motorbikes and rode toward the building, but as they approached it a second bomb struck. "Boom! I swear it was louder than the first," said Diouara. The people fled, leaving their motorbikes. They refused to go back for them, even the following day.

These days of the French air campaign were remembered in Timbuktu as the most frightening of the entire occupation. "It was terrible," Air Mali remembered. Even when the bombs fell some distance away, people could feel the ground shake, and sometimes sections of the city's fragile rammed-earth homes would collapse. It was little better when the planes weren't bombing, since they could be heard screaming overhead every night. Targets included the gendarmerie and the ten-bedroom, fourteen-bathroom Gaddafi mansion outside the city that Abou Zeid had used as a headquarters. The building was reduced to rubble, and personal effects and correspondence were strewn across the lawn, including an electricity bill addressed to a "Mr. Khadafi."

While the planes terrified the townspeople, they had a similar effect on the occupiers. In the daytime the jihadists parked their vehicles beneath the sparse trees to try to hide them from the sky, and when they heard the sound of a jet they would open their Kurans and begin to read. They also began to take their families out of the city, evacuating them at night in convoys. They told the Arab population to leave too,

Air Mali recalled: "They said, 'If you do not leave they will kill you all. In three or four days you will all be dead in Timbuktu.'"

In these days, relations between the jihadists and the population became more strained than ever. The occupiers tried to organize marches against the airstrikes to use in propaganda videos, but no one except their own fighters and a few people from the Arab community showed up. More irritating still, some civilians couldn't contain their glee at the French advance and had openly begun to mock the jihadists. At dawn, they would awake to find that the flag of Mali had been hoisted above civic buildings in the night, and after Konna was recaptured on January 18, street children could be heard conducting loud, imaginary phone conversations with government soldiers.

"Hello, Konna?" they would say. "Konna! What's the news? Is everything going well there? Ah, very good, very good!"

A few brave opportunists even took to looting the occupiers' houses. One jihadist leader, who had commandeered the home of the director of waterworks and forestry, found that while he was away someone had stolen several guns he had left in the house. He was furious. "The jihadists searched everywhere," Abdoulaye Cissé said. "Finally they arrested one young man, saying he was one of those involved. At that moment they were really angry with the town, because they knew the people thought they were going to be driven out and they were taking advantage." The jihadists tortured the suspect for days, Cissé said, but they never found the weapons.

On Tuesday, January 22, the Islamic Police commissioner, at this time a man named Hassan, called Diadié and told him to bring the Crisis Committee to the governorate right after the dusk prayer for an urgent meeting. The other committee members were skeptical. What if it was a trap? What if Hassan intended to hold them hostage? Diadié and six others felt honor-bound to go: "I said we had been doing this for ten months, we had made commitments and the two parties had respected those commitments up until today."

From the governorate they were sent on to the mairie, where Diadié was surprised to find a group of Arabs was also present. The atmosphere was tense from the start. Hassan began by delivering a warning. People had broken into the jihadists' homes and stolen their property. They were making fun of them in the streets. The Crisis Committee must warn people that the Islamic Police no longer had time to make arrests, and if they broke the law from now on, if they came close to the jihadists' houses or stole from them, they would simply be shot. It was the committee's job to make people aware of this. He had hardly finished speaking when an Arab merchant took the floor and said he had heard that the town's youth were preparing to loot their shops, and that the committee should warn people that the Arab shopkeepers were armed, and if anyone went near them they would also be shot. The people of Timbuktu were racist toward them, he added. They had not stood side by side with them, and had even refused to march against the airstrikes.

Diadié was incensed. He told Hassan he had not come to make threats, and did not expect threats to be made against him. "If you want people to be calm, do not allow these people to lecture us, or say that we cannot walk past their shops. Who are they to tell us to march? Should we just follow like sheep? We are not Islamists and we do not march with Islamists. And if that is why you have called us here, we will leave."

Hassan tried to calm him, but Diadié and the other committee members left shortly afterward. It was their last meeting with the occupiers. The next day, the jihadists shot a young man dead. He was called Mustapha, and according to one account, his crime was to have shouted *"Vive la France!"*

"They killed a child," recalled Diadié. "A child who had jumped. They shot him dead."

The jihadist leadership tried to make amends. They presented their excuses to the family, saying it was a mistake, and gave Mustapha's father a sum of money. But relations continued to sour.

"Those were the days when we saw their terrorist face," said the tour guide Bastos. "We were all kaffirs [unbelievers] because they asked that we go out to march against the airstrikes and everyone was afraid to go. They told us, 'You guys deserve to go to hell.'"

As Haidara's contacts had predicted, the occupiers started to destroy things after that. They burned trucks and agricultural machinery. They burned the city's electricity plant. "Everything that they could do to hurt the town, they did it before leaving," recalled Abdoulaye Cissé. Timbuktu now entered the most desolate phase of the occupation. "The last days were the hardest," recalled the grand imam. "The reality was very heavy. The people were traumatized by shooting, thieves were in all corners of the town from nightfall to sunrise. The people were not able to go out. Everyone stayed at home. They were so frightened they were not able to eat."

There was no light and the electric water pumps on which Timbuktu depended no longer worked, so people had to pull water from the old wells by hand. But it was the destruction of the cellphone network that hurt the most. Bastos saw it happen: "I was there at the exchange one evening," he said. "There was a man who came with a Kalashnikov. He stopped in front of a group of us and started shooting: *bop, bop, bop, bop, bop!* The exchange exploded." The jihadists distributed walkie-talkies among themselves, but everyone else was now cut off.

"There were no phones, no communication," said the grand imam. "We did not hear anyone speak of Timbuktu. That was what traumatized people even more, because we were abandoned. No one knew how we survived."

The only positive news was that under the weight of the airstrikes, the last jihadists were leaving. On Wednesday, January 23, Bastos saw Abou Zeid paying off a group of his fighters in the street. They took what they could with them, including motorbikes, which they strapped onto the backs of their 4x4s.

"They began to withdraw because they understood that the cause was lost," said Diadié.

At dawn on Thursday, january 24—the day of the banned Mawlid festival—the caretaker of the new Ahmad Baba building in Sankore hurried to Abdoulaye Cissé to tell him the jihadists had left. This news was followed by a second report: there seemed to be a fire burning inside. Cissé hurried to look and saw wisps of white smoke emanating from the open roof. It could have been anything burning: electrical wires, furniture, a wood fire built to make tea. Or it could be coming from burning manuscripts.

Cissé was aware of the jihadists' warning that anyone who entered one of their buildings would be shot, but the caretaker felt sure the militants had gone, and as the senior man responsible for the Ahmad Baba institute in Timbuktu, he felt a duty to investigate. The two men entered by the small door on the west side and walked cautiously down one of the internal alleyways designed in the Sahelian vernacular by the South African architect. The building was quiet and cool, sheltered from the desert sun that filtered through screens of hand-chiseled stone. The smoke led them to a spot just outside the conference room. As Cissé and the caretaker approached, they saw a pile of ash that had been pushed up against a square pillar. Heaps of discarded manuscript boxes, carefully labeled with their catalogue numbers, lay to one side. The pyre was still smoldering. It appeared that the jihadists had emptied the boxes, Cissé said, then set the contents on fire.

Years later, Cissé still had difficulty comprehending this act. "To believe that these people who said they were Muslims could take something that is Islamic and set fire to it—we never thought that would happen. It was the worst thing they could do to us. Anything but that." Why had they done it? "They had no other motivation than to do bad," he said. If the manuscripts had somehow been against their ideology, they would have destroyed them when they arrived. Instead they had occupied the building for ten months and waited till the eve of their departure to burn them. "Because they were defeated, they had to leave," Cissé said. "They knew the international and scientific value of the manuscripts, and what they are worth, so they had to burn them."

He and the caretaker did not stay long, which was fortunate because the jihadists returned soon afterward. "If they had found us there, we would have been finished," said Cissé.

When Maiga learned what had happened, he took it as a personal failure. "God made it my responsibility, and now the manuscripts had burned. Manuscripts that date back centuries and centuries. So for me it was a failure. The night I learned that, I could not sleep."

Haidara was also devastated. "The day that they burned them I felt very, very ill," he said. "It was as if we had saved nothing. That was how bad I felt."

16.

CHRONICLE OF
THE RESEARCHER

1911–1913

For almost two decades after Dubois's return, the *Fatassi*, "the phantom book of the Sudan," played on the minds of the Paris Orientalists. Dubois had described this work with typical hyperbole as the "fundamental basis of all historic documentation of the Niger region," but all anyone had been able to find of it were a few remarkably similar scraps. When they were asked, the people of Timbuktu shrugged and said that as far as they knew, all copies of the manuscript had been destroyed.

In 1911, the French governor of Upper Senegal and Niger sent the explorer Albert Bonnel de Mézières to Timbuktu. There, Bonnel de Mézières befriended the scholar Sidi Muhammad al-Imam Ben Essayouti, and gained enough of his trust for the Timbuktien to show him a precious document from his personal library. It was incomplete, its paper crumbling and its ink faded, but it was believed to be the only surviving copy of an ancient history of the Sudan. Bonnel de Mézières asked if he could have a duplicate, and Ben Essayouti supervised the creation of a new manuscript, which was sent to Octave Houdas in Paris with an accompanying note explaining that it was a "collection of biographies of the kings of Songhay and a fragment of the history of the kings of the Sudan prior to the kingdom of Songhay," and was believed to have been written in the fifteenth century.

Houdas could tell from the first glimpse that it was "a document of highest importance for the history of the French Sudan," and added information to that contained in the *Tarikh al-sudan*. Since its opening pages had been lost, the manuscript was missing the title and the name of its author, but it was soon clear to Houdas that it was the work Dubois had heard about, the *Fatassi*.

To fill the gaps in the text, Houdas and his assistant Maurice Delafosse pressed Bonnel de Mézières to find another copy. The explorer wrote to Ben Essayouti asking again for his help, and the Timbuktien replied with good faith that though he knew of no more copies, he would send them his original. The translators received this document in May 1912, naming it Manuscript A, while the copy was named Manuscript B. Later that year, another document was found and copied on the instruction of a French colonial administrator in Kayes. Manuscript C, as it became known, included a preface and a chapter missing from Ben Essayouti's copy, and clearly named the work as the *Tarikh al-fattash*, or, to give it its full title in English, *The Chronicle of the Researcher into the History of the Countries, the Armies, and the Principal Personalities*. Its author was named as Mahmud Kati. According to the *Tarikh al-sudan*, Kati had been born in 1468 and was a close friend of Askiya al-hajj Muhammad.

Houdas and Delafosse now had three versions of what they thought was the same chronicle, the *Tarikh al-fattash*, each of which had its own problems: Manuscript A was the oldest and therefore most authentic, but whole sections were truncated or missing. Manuscript B was merely a copy of A. Manuscript C, meanwhile, was complete and contained many passages that were absent from the others, but was full of major errors, partly because the modern copyist had not been entirely proficient in Arabic, and partly because the manuscript from which it was derived was so damaged that sections of it had been rendered illegible.

On close reading of the documents, the Orientalists were presented with two intriguing puzzles. The first appeared to be evidence of what Dubois had been told in Timbuktu, the suppression of the chronicle by Ahmad Lobbo, the sultan of Masina. While Manuscript A's damaged opening pages recorded various prophecies that heralded the coming to the Sudan of the twelfth caliph, the start of Manuscript C specified that the caliph Ahmad would come to Masina at the beginning of the nineteenth century. This was highly suspicious: how likely was it that a chronicle begun in the sixteenth century would so clearly identify as caliph the very nineteenth-century sultan who was alleged to have suppressed it? Houdas and Delafosse took this as conclusive evidence that this passage of C had been forged, and that Lobbo had indeed ordered all copies of the *Fattash* to be doctored or destroyed to serve his political interests.

The second puzzle was one of authorship. Manuscript C named the chronicler as Kati, but the narrative of the *Fattash* concludes in 1599, when he would have been more than 130 years old. How could he have written about events that took place after his death? The chronicle must have been finished by his descendants, collated from papers he and his children had left behind, the Orientalists surmised. The *Tarikh al-*

fattash was thus the result of a collaboration among three generations: "The actual editor of the work was the grandson of Mahmud Kati, while the grandfather was the one who inspired it." It was this anonymous grandson, later identified as "Ibn al-Mukhtar," or the "son of Mukhtar," who would have completed the work around 1665.

The *Fattash*'s mysteries were at best partially resolved, but the authors nevertheless felt able to synthesize a full version. They published their collated *tarikh*—in Arabic and translated into French—in 1913. The *Fattash* would soon be regarded as the most important discovery for the history of the region since the *Tarikh al-sudan*, a major piece in the jigsaw of understanding life during Timbuktu's golden age.

After an opening doxology, Houdas and Delafosse's *Fattash* sets out its admiration for Askiya al-hajj Muhammad. The chronicle's hatred of his predecessor, Sunni Ali, knew few bounds: the "accursed one" was a poor Muslim who perpetrated "scandalous innovations" and "bloody cruelties" on the people and persecuted the scholars of Timbuktu. The contrast with Askiya al-hajj Muhammad could not be more marked. "It is difficult to enumerate [the first askiya's] many virtues and qualities," gushes the *Fattash*, "such as his excellent political skills, his benevolence towards his subjects and his concern for the poor. We cannot find his equal in any ruler who came before or after him."

There seemed to be a transparent reason both chronicles heaped praise on this usurper to the Songhay throne: under his rule, Timbuktu flourished as never before. According to the *Fattash*, this was the result of an accommodation reached between the emperor and Timbuktu. In 1498/1499, Muhammad Aqit's grandson Mahmud was appointed to the role of *qadi* for the city. He was just thirty-five, the first of Aqit's descendants to reach this most powerful position in the town's hierarchy, and he would remain in the role for fifty-five years.

One day, the *Fattash* relates, Askiya al-hajj Muhammad came to Timbuktu to remonstrate with Mahmud for not obeying his instructions. He stopped outside the city, and the *qadi* rode bravely out to the emperor's camp. The askiya began the meeting with a series of pointed questions: Was Qadi Mahmud somehow better or more holy than all his great predecessors, who had obeyed previous Songhay kings? No, Qadi Mahmud replied each time. Why, then, asked the askiya, had he repeatedly driven the emperor's messengers away without doing as he was told? The holy man responded with a rebuke:

> Have you forgotten or do you merely pretend to forget the day when you came to find me at my house, the day when you grabbed at my feet and garments and said to me: "I have come to place myself under your protection and to entrust myself to you, so that you might save me from the fires of Hell. Help me and hold me by the hand so that I do not fall into Hell. I entrust myself to you." This is the reason why I chase away your messengers and reject your orders.

Sunni Ali would doubtless have killed the *qadi* on the spot for his impudence, but Askiya al-hajj Muhammad was a religious man and instead he cried out: "I forgot, by God!" Since Qadi Mahmud had reminded him of his religious duty, he deserved a rich reward:

> You are like a barrier set up by God to keep me from the fires of Hell! I have irritated the Almighty, but I ask pardon of Him, and I return to Him. From today, I will entrust myself to you and cling to you. Stay as you are, for God is on your side, and protect me always!

The emperor then climbed on his horse and rode away, "joyous and satisfied," according to the *Fattash*.

For the next hundred years the rulers of Songhay would live under the spiritual protection of the Timbuktu holy men, while the city in turn was afforded the worldly protection of the Gao emperors. This was boom time, the period when Timbuktu would gain the reputation for being a supreme city of scholars. Under Qadi Mahmud, the city's major buildings, including the Jingere Ber mosque, were reorganized and expanded. It was a peaceful place—so calm, according to the *Fattash*, that one might come across a hundred of its citizens who carried neither spear nor sword nor knife—and a large one: there were enough inhabitants to support twenty-six tailors' workshops, each of which was supervised by a chief who had around fifty apprentices. Great numbers of scholars and students moved to Timbuktu, swelling the academic community to unprecedented size and filling between 150 and 180 Kuranic schools, each of which had tens and sometimes hundreds of students. One such school, belonging to a certain Ali Takariya, had between 173 and 345 students, according to the *Fattash*, which noted that there were 123 paddles on which students practiced writing in the courtyard, enough to carry the whole of the Kuran. These numbers would be used to produce estimates of around 25,000 students in Timbuktu at this time, but more levelheaded calculation put the number of elementary pupils at 4,000 to 5,000, and the town's population no higher than 50,000. Still, this would have made it a significant world city at the start of the sixteenth century.

Literature had an unusual grip on this society, which suffered from "acute bibliophilism," in the words of one academic. In an ascetic culture where worldly goods were frowned on, importing and copying manuscripts became one of the predominant obsessions of the elite: visitors would be courted in the hope that they might possess a new work to buy or borrow, while demand pushed up the price of books to extreme heights. The *Fattash* relates that Askiya Muhammad's successor, Askiya Dawud, helped Mahmud Kati purchase a rare dictionary for eighty mithqals, or roughly 340 grams of gold, which would be worth $16,000 in today's prices. There were cheaper books sold in Timbuktu—a single, used volume of a work titled *Sharh al-ahkam* sold for a little over four mithqals—and the eighty-mithqal dictionary may have been particularly well ornamented and would have consisted of multiple volumes. The *Fattash* tells of another Timbuktu-owned dictionary that came in twenty-eight volumes. The demand for books drove a large professional copying industry in the city and in the wider empire. Askiya Dawud employed his own scribes to copy manuscripts and often offered these to scholars as a way of buying favor and influence in Timbuktu.

Detailed information about how books were produced can be found in colophons, the short descriptions of a manuscript's origins that were often included at the end. The colophons of six volumes of a sixteenth-century copy of Ibn Sida's dictionary *al-Muhkam* describe a schedule of payments and deadlines, which show that a full-time copyist required twenty-three days to copy two volumes of the work, a total of 179 folios. There were nineteen lines of text per page, so the scribe was averaging 285 lines of text per day. Another scribe took nineteen further days to add vowels for proper pronunciation to these volumes, at a rate of around 300 lines of text per day. A copyist was usually paid one mithqal a month, on top of which half a mithqal would be paid to a proofreader acquainted with the subject matter, who would correct any errors. The cost of labor alone for a complete set of a large work such as *al-Muhkam* was around twenty-one mithqals, or ninety grams of gold, and there was also the cost of the paper to consider: it was expensive, since most was imported from North Africa and Egypt. The paper for any large volume was likely to cost five mithqals or more.

The result of Timbuktu's bibliophilism was that large numbers of manuscripts accumulated in the city. These were not gathered in public libraries of the sort that existed in other Islamic learning centers such as Baghdad or Cairo, whose al-Azhar mosque boasted tens of thousands of manuscripts as well as an extraordinary range of reader services. In Timbuktu, the collections belonged to the scholastic families, who would loan them liberally to colleagues and students. The lack of public collections may have reflected the fact that scholars in Timbuktu came from the wealthy elite—with the notable exception of the *alfas*—so there was little need for common readers to have regular access to more difficult works that they would not understand. Even so, the private collections grew to enormous sizes. Ahmad Baba's personal library, which he stated was "the smallest of any of my kin," consisted of at least 1,600 volumes, while that of Ahmad Umar ran to almost 700 volumes at his death. The breadth of reading available in Timbuktu is also clear from citations in other works written in the city. The Timbuktu scholar Ahmad ibn And-Agh-Muhammad wrote a treatise on grammar that drew on forty other works, while Baba's biographical dictionary cited twenty-three Maliki biographical sources.

By the second half of the sixteenth century, the marvels and splendors of Timbuktu had reached such heights that they were impossible to enumerate, according to the *Fattash*. It had no parallel in the Sudan:

> From the province of Mali to the extreme limits of the lands of the Maghreb, no other town was better known for the solidity of its institutions, for its political liberties, for its unblemished morals, for the security of its citizens and their goods, for its clemency and

compassion toward the poor and toward strangers, for its courtesy toward students and men of science, for its assistance to students and scholars.

The end, when it came, was therefore an enormous shock.

ASKIYA AL-HAJJ MUHAMMAD ruled for thirty-six years before he was deposed by his son, Musa, on August 15, 1529. After him came a succession of other askiyas: Muhammad Bonkana, Ismail, Ishaq I, Dawud, al-Hajj, Muhammad Bani, Ishaq II, Muhammad Gao, and Nuh. Though Timbuktu continued to flourish under their rule, only Dawud came close to earning the plaudits the city's chroniclers heaped on the first askiya, and with time the empire became degenerate. The *Tarikh al-sudan* records that the people "exchanged God's bounties for infidelity, and left no sin against God Most High that they did not commit openly, such as drinking fermented liquors, sodomy and fornication." They were so given over to this last vice that one would have thought it was not forbidden, the chronicle records, and even the sons of the sultans committed incest with their sisters.

More dangerous still, the empire was falling behind its northern neighbor, Morocco. The Sadian dynasty that ruled that country had been fighting Portuguese, Spanish, and Ottoman invaders for decades, and had even made an alliance with England against Spain. The result was a militaristic society whose troops were well drilled and equipped with English cannon, and who had adopted muskets and harquebuses, employing mercenaries and "renegades"—bands of Christian prisoners and deserters who converted to Islam—to use them.

The Sadian sultan was Ahmad al-Mansur, a quiet man of immense ambition and a tendency to explode in fits of rage. He also claimed to be the twelfth caliph, and since it was the caliph's role to restore unity to the Islamic world, the Muslim rulers of the Sudanese kingdoms would have to submit and hand over their wealth. He had already spent a fortune on the lavish "Incomparable Palace" in Marrakesh, with its gilt ceilings and marble floors, and had to fund large numbers of soldiers, spies, and agents. He began by demanding that the askiyas pay a tax on every load of salt the Songhay took out of the mines in the desert at Taghaza, which lay roughly halfway between Timbuktu and Marrakesh: it was his armies, after all, that kept sub-Saharan Africa safe from the Christians. Askiya Ishaq II responded with an insult, sending Mansur a spear and two iron shoes. Until the sultan had worn out the shoes by running, the gift implied, he would never be safe from Songhay spears. The sultan now had his casus belli, and he chose a short, blue-eyed eunuch named Jawdar to execute his plan.

Jawdar was given the most powerful force ever sent across the Sahara: it consisted of an elite and technologically advanced army of more than 4,000 soldiers, including 2,000 renegade harquebusiers, 500 mounted gunmen, seventy Christian mercenaries armed with blunderbusses, and 1,500 Moroccan cavalry. They also had mortars and cannon and carried 150 tons of gunpowder in a baggage train that was 10,000 camels long. The conquest of the Sudan would be "easy," the sultan boasted, since the Sudanese had only spears and swords to fight with.

The Moroccans reached the Niger bend midway between Gao and Timbuktu on February 28, 1591, catching Ishaq II off guard. The askiya hurriedly assembled a large force that met the Moroccans at Tondibi, thirty miles north of Gao, a fortnight later. The Songhay drove a thousand head of cattle at the enemy, but when the animals heard gunfire, they stampeded into the Songhay lines, after which the askiya's army broke "in the twinkling of an eye," according to the *Tarikh al-sudan*. Ishaq fled, and Jawdar marched on Gao. The askiya offered peace terms: he would pledge allegiance to Mansur, hand over the rights to the salt trade, and give him 100,000 mithqals of gold and a thousand slaves. Jawdar replied that he would send the terms to the sultan for approval.

Jawdar then advanced to Timbuktu, entering the city on May 30. He went straight to the *qadi*, who at this time was the elderly Umar, a son of Qadi Mahmud, and told him he needed "a large place where we can build a fort where we can stay until the Sultan orders us to return to him," according to the *Fattash*. Jawdar's men then drove the residents out of the wealthy merchants' quarter, "heaping injuries, threats and blows upon them," before they set to work joining houses together to form the fort. The soldiers press-ganged everyone they found in the streets into the construction work, while the city's merchants were ordered to produce a large quantity of grain.

The forced labor and requisition of food came as a shock to the holy city, which had been an object of veneration for a century. "No crueler or greater trial had ever befallen the people of Timbuktu," wrote the authors of the *Fattash*:

> We are unable fully to describe all the misery and losses that Timbuktu suffered when the Moroccans occupied this town. We are unable to tell the tale of all the violence and excesses that were committed within these walls.

This, however, was just the beginning.

When the sultan received Jawdar's letter outlining the peace deal, he flew into a rage and replaced him with a man who would finish the

Songhay for good. This was a volatile ex-commander of the renegades named Mahmud ibn Zargun. Pasha Mahmud reached Timbuktu on August 17, 1591, took command of the sultan's force, and immediately set off east with Jawdar in tow, in pursuit of the remaining Songhay. During his two-year absence, Timbuktu revolted against Moroccan rule, and in the autumn of 1593, Mahmud returned with a well-worked plan to punish the men he believed had been secretly backing the insurgency all along: the city's scholars and holy men. He ordered the arrest and execution of two leading Timbuktu sharifs, and announced that the people must come to the Sankore mosque in groups to renew their oaths of fidelity to the sultan. On the first day it would be the turn of the merchants from the oasis towns in the Sahara, and on the second day the turn of the people from the caravan towns in the west. On the third day, October 20, a date Ahmad Baba described as the Day of Desolation, it would be the turn of the scholars.

When the moment arrived, the Kuran and hadiths were brought out in the Sankore mosque and the cream of Timbuktu's intellectual life filed inside. Armed men were placed at the exits and on the building's roof, the doors were closed, and the scholars were bound before being dragged outside, one by one. Mahmud ordered that the prisoners be taken across town to his fort in two parties. Qadi Umar, too old and frail to walk, was put on a small donkey that was led through the center of the town, while a second group took an easterly route around the city. Near the Sidi Yahya mosque, one of the prisoners in this second party snatched a musketeer's sword and attacked him with it, whereupon the sultan's men launched into a frenzy of butchery, hacking down the prisoners all around them. Fourteen Timbuktiens were killed on the spot, including nine scholars of Sankore.

Qadi Umar was with a domestic servant when he was told about the massacre, the *Fattash* relates. The servant began to cry, so a Moroccan soldier slashed at him with his sword, killing him instantly. At this point, the *qadi* began to laugh. When he was asked why, he replied: "I had thought until now that I was more worthy than this servant, but I see now he had more merit than I, since he has preceded me to paradise." The remaining scholars were placed under guard in the fort, while Pasha Mahmud's soldiers went through their houses, taking everything of value. "His followers plundered whatever they could lay their hands on," al-Sadi recorded in the *Tarikh al-sudan*, "and brought dishonour upon the scholars, stripping their womenfolk and committing acts of indecency." Included in the loot was Ahmad Baba's substantial library.

After being held in the fort for five months, the scholars judged to be dangerous—mostly members of the Aqit family—were ordered to be taken across the desert to Marrakesh with their families. Seventy prisoners in all were packed off in chains. The journey was hard on the unworldly scholars: at one point, encumbered by his manacles, Ahmad Baba fell from his camel and broke his leg. They reached Marrakesh on May 21, 1594, and were put in prison. The elderly Qadi Umar would die there.

The surviving captives were released into a form of house arrest two years later, and Ahmad Baba was granted an interview with the sultan. He found the great ruler shielded from the gaze of ordinary mortals by a curtain, and refused to speak with him until this was drawn aside: by speaking from behind a veil, Baba argued, Mansur was imitating God. When the sultan obliged, Baba asked the question that must have been burning inside him for years: "What need had you to loot my belongings and sack my library and, above all, to have me brought here in chains?" Mansur responded that it was part of his attempt to unite the Muslim world and that, since he, Baba, was one of the most distinguished men of Islam in his country, the submission of the rest of the Songhay kingdom would surely follow his own.

The decade Baba spent in the Moroccan capital was the most productive period of his career. He became famous as a scholar and an advocate, with a reputation that spread throughout the Maghreb. He taught grammar, rhetoric, theology, and Maliki law, and wrote extensively: thirty of his fifty-six known works were written in this period. But he was homesick, as a poem he wrote in Morocco relates:

> O traveller to Gao, turn off to my city, murmur my name there
>   and greet all my dear ones,
> With scented salaams from an exile who longs for his homeland
>   and neighbours, companions and friends.

In 1607, when the sultan had died, Baba was allowed to leave Marrakesh. He reached Timbuktu the following year and was the only one of the deported scholars to see his home city again. He lived there for another nineteen years, teaching and writing, and died on April 22, 1627.

Timbuktu scholarship survived him: the chronicles, after all, were written after his death. But the destruction wrought by Pasha Mahmud had ruined the city, in the words of the *Fattash*:

> Timbuktu became a body without a soul. Its life was turned upside down, its conditions of existence changed, as did its customs. The lowest elements of the population became the most elevated, and the most elevated became the lowest. The worst scoundrel lorded over the most noble. People traded religious objects for the goods

of this world, and faith was swapped for error. The rules of justice were suppressed, tradition became mere dead letter. New doctrines carried the day, and, with the exception of Muhammad Bagha-yogho, there was no one left in the town who observed the law or who walked in fear of God.

Almost two hundred years before the African Association sent its first explorers south, Timbuktu had begun its long decline.

17.

AN INDIANA JONES
MOMENT IN REAL LIFE!

L arge drops of desert rain threatened to turn the alluvial earth to greasy red mud on the morning of January 27, 2013, when a group of French officers met at the disused airfield at Goundam, fifty miles southwest of Timbuktu. The airfield's only building was a broken-down hut with no door, and shutters that hung off their hinges, but it would have to do. This was the base from which they would plan their final advance. General Bernard Barrera, commander of Operation Serval, and Colonel Frédéric Gout, commander of the helicopter regiment, were welcomed to the hut by Colonel Paul Gèze, the leader of the armored French GTIA1 battle group that had struggled for the past four days up the desert track along the left bank of the river from Bamako. Gèze, a muscular marine, greeted his superior with a big smile and two options. "Beer," he said, "or whiskey?"

Operation Serval had been running to a tight time frame. When Gout had received orders from officials in Paris to capture Timbuktu less than a month after the start of the intervention, he had told them they were "crazy." Since then the schedule had only accelerated: he and his men were now set to attack the city the following morning, just seventeen days after the first French shots had been fired. Defeated at Konna, the jihadists had continued to withdraw, but French intelligence reports suggested they would now make a stand. "At our last briefing they told us that we would meet some jihadists," said Gout, a tall man with even white teeth, "so for us it was certain."

To the French the jihadists were *jusqu'au-boutistes*: they would fight till the last man and were probably pumped with narcotics. "When they fought us they didn't seem to suffer," remembered Gout. "In our first days in the north, they never, ever abandoned their positions. Even when they were up against tanks and helicopters with just Kalashnikovs, they stayed there." Gout was told machine guns had been mounted on the roofs of Timbuktu's houses to set up an anti-aircraft barrage, which convinced him that "we would absolutely lose" some aircraft and crew. "They were organized, they were able to use their armaments, there was no morale problem, and they were utterly convinced of their mission," he said.

At five o'clock on Sunday afternoon, General Barrera gave the order to advance. He would travel with Gèze's armored column of French and Malian soldiers, which was to seize Timbuktu airport. Gout's helicopters were meanwhile told to reconnoiter the roads and destroy anything that might oppose the battle group. The armored column moved much more slowly than was hoped, since it was soon dark and there was the constant threat of IED attack: it was eleven p.m. before they reached the outskirts of the airport.

The helicopters took no time to cover the ground, and as dusk fell, Gout saw the city for the first time. It looked frail, he recalled, almost swallowed by the sand seas that surrounded it. There was no way more than ten aircraft would go unnoticed here, and his men were tense, ready to be fired upon. The first reports from his pilots were "very detailed and crazy," with one telling him he could see a couple of motorbikes, and perhaps five or six people, which he judged to be "a real threat." The colonel told him to hold his fire.

After some time it became clear that there were no jihadists in the town. Gout sent word to the airborne brigade of French Foreign Legionnaires, GTIA4, who were awaiting his signal. As midnight approached, and as Gèze's men cut their way through the wire fence that surrounded the runway south of Timbuktu, transport planes dropped two hundred of the world's most famous desert troops into the sand to the north. It was the largest parachute drop the French military had undertaken in more than thirty years.

At dawn Gout shuttled the commander of the Foreign Legion unit to Timbuktu airport for a briefing on the final assault. Even though they now believed Timbuktu to be empty of enemy fighters, this was not going to be straightforward: General Barrera knew that the legionnaires might start shooting if they saw armed Malian soldiers. He decided to separate the town into zones, and said the Malian contingent would enter their city first.

Like everyone in Timbuktu, Air Mali knew exactly what was happening. Since the electricity plant had been destroyed, at nighttime the city was almost perfectly dark, and he had spent the previous evening watching the lights moving out in the desert as the French maneuvered. He had seen the paratroops land to the north, and the column arrive at the back of the airport where the wire fence was. At any moment, he thought he would be able to see French armored vehicles driving up the road. He kept waiting, but still nobody came.

Shortly before dawn, people gave up their vigil and went to the mosques to pray. It was only when they came out, and the sun was spreading a pale light, that they could discern distant figures walking toward the city. As the figures came closer, the people could see that they were Malian soldiers. These were the first government troops Timbuktu had seen for ten long months.

The city's youths climbed on their motorbikes and took to the Kabara road to welcome the soldiers and escort them in. At ten a.m. the French arrived and were mobbed. The women of the town had been secretly making flags for days, and that morning as the troops entered, hundreds of cheering people lined the roads, shouting, "Mali! Mali! Mali!" and "Thank you, François Hollande!" and waving the tricolors of both countries.

In that moment, everything was forgotten, Air Mali said. "Everything was over in a single day. The fact of being free . . . for us it was enough. The people were very happy."

"A free Timbuktu represents for us something indescribable," said Diadié. "No one could know the cost of ten months of privation, ten months of intolerance, ten months of humiliation."

The senior Malian army officer, Colonel Kéba Sangaré, was brought with his soldiers to the mairie, and from there they went to pay a courtesy visit to the Crisis Committee in Diadié's house. "They came into our house, they came to our chamber, Colonel Kéba and his staff," recalled Diadié. "We received them, we gave them our trust, we offered them refreshments. When we gathered the people and told them what was happening, they brought tons of rice and beef, which they offered to wish them welcome." Then the Malian army organized itself to secure the city.

Gout intended to retire to Sevare that afternoon: Timbuktu was only the second of the three major cities in the north that had to be liberated, and he needed to plan the next phase of the operation, but Barrera stopped him and suggested that they enter the city together. The general had to see that it was secure, yet he had another motive too. He had become intrigued by the myth of Timbuktu and had been reading Caillié. He wanted to see for himself the house where the French explorer had stayed.

They drove into town from the airport in a small convoy. "The population was so generous," Gout recalled. "They were applauding. There was a lot of happiness, we could see it." People came up to thank them, particularly women and children. They drove as far as they could, but soon the alleys became too narrow for the vehicles, and the officers climbed out and continued on foot. It was dusk, and light from the houses was almost imperceptible. As they approached the building where Caillié had stayed for two short weeks in 1828, an old man came out to greet them. "Ah, you are our liberator!" he said to the general, before offering him a tour. He opened the wooden door, studded with polished metal in the traditional style, and showed the soldiers inside.

The general was very proud.

FOR THE WATCHING WORLD, the liberation of Timbuktu was a significant milestone in the Malian conflict, but it was quickly overtaken by news of another event.

Early that morning, Mayor Cissé, who was in Bamako, began briefing journalists about the burning of the manuscripts at the Ahmad Baba institute. Before nine a.m., the mayor told the BBC's Thomas Fessy he had "very credible accounts of Islamist militants burning ancient manuscripts in the last few days," according to Fessy. Minutes later, the Arabic TV journalist Jenan Moussa tweeted that she had been told the same thing. By mid-morning the news had been picked up by agencies and was being sent out as snaps on newswires and repeated on social media accounts.

More interviews with the mayor followed. "It's truly alarming that this has happened," he told the Associated Press. "They torched all the important ancient manuscripts, the ancient books of geography and science. It is the history of Timbuktu, of its people." To *The Guardian*, he said: "It's true, they have burned the manuscripts. . . . They also burned down several buildings. There was one guy who was celebrating in the street and they killed him." The documents, according to the mayor, "were a part not only of Mali's heritage but the world's heritage. By destroying them they threaten the world. We have to kill all of the rebels in the north." Mayor Cissé's words seemed to be confirmed when Sky News correspondent Alex Crawford, who was with the advancing French troops, visited the Ahmad Baba building and showed pictures of burnt boxes.

The secrecy surrounding Haidara's operation had been so effective almost no one in the international media knew any different, and Cissé's pronouncement that "all the important ancient manuscripts" had been torched led to catastrophic estimates of the amount destroyed. "Everyone was talking about it, even the radio," recalled Maiga. "But they put forward imaginary numbers. Some said 200,000 manuscripts burned, something like that."

At midday, just a few hours after Cissé's first announcement, Haidara fired off an e-mail in shaky English to his friend at the Ford Foundation. Things had become "more worrisome," he began. The jihadists had begun to burn the manuscripts. He was afraid that the city's heritage could be damaged in fighting. "It is time," he concluded, "it is necessary that the means are provided for conveying estates to the south of the country." Whether this e-mail was motivated by genuine fear or by opportunism—it was a moment, after all, when the jihadist threat was surely neutralized—the Ford Foundation moved quickly, spurred on no doubt by catastrophist reports in the media. A Savama funding application was rushed through the foundation's head office in New York that day with the help of the executive who would go on to lead the organization, Darren Walker. A grant of $326,000 was agreed on, which would pay for the movement of a further 922 lockers. The running total Savama had raised for the evacuation of its manuscripts was now approaching a million dollars.

In Timbuktu, meanwhile, Abdoulaye Cissé was still thinking about the heap of ashes he had seen on Thursday morning. The jihadists had left for good on Friday, but he had not been back inside since he had realized the building might be mined. Still, he knew something didn't quite add up. There had been around 15,000 manuscripts in the building, but there hadn't been nearly enough ash outside the conference room to account for them all. "That was not the whole 15,000 that they burned," he said. He thought the jihadists must have stolen the rest. "I thought they had taken some. That was the first idea I had."

When the French soldiers reached Sankore, they asked to speak to the *responsable* for the Ahmad Baba institute, and Cissé was called. They questioned him at length about the jihadists—Who were they? Who was the chief? What nationalities were they?—then inspected the building. As elsewhere in the city, they found ammunition and grenades in the jihadists' sleeping quarters. The French soldiers "took a lot of munitions [away], and they took a lot of documents so that they could understand the rebels," recalled Cissé.

As the soldiers worked their way through the building looking for booby traps, they tagged the rooms they had cleared with red spray paint. Reaching the basement, they moved through the exhibition space and began working their way down the long corridor where the storerooms were. There were seven of these rooms in all. Six stood empty, their doors open, while the seventh was locked. A glass inspection window allowed people to look inside, but with the lights not working, all anyone could see was darkness. Opening the door, they found a plain room full of shelving units, each of which was filled with conservation boxes, row after row. Here, the great bulk of the building's manuscripts, around 10,000, lay untouched.

When the state employees tallied the collection later, they found 4,203 were missing. The lost documents were new acquisitions, they said, which had been left out in the restoration room on the upper level of the Sankore building and were an obvious target for opportunist thieves. As to why the other 10,000 had been left, Cissé said he thought the thieves must have assumed the locked storeroom was as empty as the other six, and hadn't bothered to force the door. It was clear evidence of the spiritual power of the city.

"It is truly the mystery of Timbuktu," he said.

THAT EVENING, Haidara took To Tjoelker to see more lockers coming into Bamako. Once again she was shocked by his appearance. "He was completely dirty and exhausted," she said. "I don't think he had time to wash anymore." He was also extremely tired, but "very proud of getting them out." She believed that at heart he was a shy man who had been reluctantly forced to assume a leadership role. "I think he is quite a silent guy normally . . . not a very big leader," she recalled. "But because of the circumstances he had to transform himself into the head of the association of families."

Haidara took Tjoelker to his second wife's house, a large and luxurious building with a garden on the south bank of the river, where she was shown into a room that was filled with lockers from floor to ceiling; inside each locker were collections of manuscripts. The documents themselves —the priceless artifacts at the core of the evacuation— worked their magic on the Dutch diplomat. "The contents were so beautiful. They were amazing. The manuscripts were all types of quality, you know? Some were painted, others just simple—a love letter . . . so beautiful."

Strieder, the German chargé d'affaires, was similarly impressed by what he was shown of the shipments that arrived in Bamako. It was "a really good action," he felt. "I saw many of the books—I had the opportunity to look into them at Bamako—and it was incredible, the feeling that you have some manuscripts that are thirteenth or even twelfth century, and many, many different ones . . . all done in the early centuries. It was a great feeling that we had made a contribution."

The evacuation was not yet complete, however. On January 30, two days after the liberation, Haidara informed his contact at the Ford Foundation, Joseph Gitari, that twenty boats were now leaving the Timbuktu region with three hundred boxes of manuscripts. They would do four days of sailing to reach Jenne, he wrote, before signing off with his usual: "Regards!" Gitari forwarded these e-mails to Darren Walker, adding a note of his own: "The operation continues. An Indiana Jones moment in real life!"

That Friday, February 1, ten more boats arrived in Jenne with a further 150 boxes; 157 more were landed the following day.

On Thursday, February 7, at 8:13 a.m., Haidara e-mailed Gitari with news of the final shipment. "I just want to inform you that the last canoes just arrived in Jenne. This trip terminates the transport of 922 boxes to Jenne by river. Images of first arrivals [of] boxes of manuscripts in Bamako will reach you soon. Regards!"

Haidara's Herculean task of saving the manuscripts of Timbuktu seemed finally to be complete.

18

MANUSCRIPT FEVER

1967–2003

A fter the discovery and translation of the Timbuktu chronicles, the story of the mythologized city began to settle in the latter half of the twentieth century. Though it was still easy to find academics writing of Malian expeditions to America, or of the twenty-five thousand students who attended Timbuktu University during the Sudanese Middle Ages, a small but growing band of professional Africanists chipped away at the myths in the hope of producing an objective truth. The history was remarkable enough, after all, not to require further elaboration. What was left—the "vulgate," orthodox account of Timbuktu and the Songhay—was based on the chronicles and the Songhay king lists they related, from the Zuwa dynasty to the askiyas via Sunni Ali Kulun and his successors. These details, historians could broadly agree, were facts.

Toward the end of 1967, UNESCO organized a meeting of experts on the manuscripts of West Africa in Timbuktu, in the newly independent state of Mali. Among the guests was the man who would be known as the doyen of Timbuktu manuscripts experts, John Hunwick. The meeting recommended—and in Hunwick's view it was "little more than a pious hope"—that a research institute be established at Timbuktu to collect and preserve the Islamic heritage of the region. A name was even suggested for it: the Ahmad Baba center. Within ten years, rather to Hunwick's surprise, such an institution had been founded. Mali now had its own internationally recognized program devoted to researching the region's past through its documents.

By 1992, when Hunwick returned to hunt for copies of the *Tarikh al-sudan* for a new English translation he was preparing, the institute had made further advances: it now boasted a manuscript restoration department and a section where the works could be transferred to microfiche. It also had a growing number of documents—more than 6,300—as well as a small library of printed works. Hunwick found it "difficult to do justice to the richness of the collection," he wrote. Most of the items were of local authorship and fell into two broad categories: items of "literary" character, including religious treatises, chronicles, and poems; and items of "documentary" character—letters, legal documents, manuscripts relating to the renting of houses, inheritance schedules, land ownership, and so on.

Among the literary works, Hunwick listed two copies each of the *Tarikh al-sudan* and the *Tarikh al-fattash*. There were also histories of Azawad and the Barabish people, and of the ancient trading town of Tadmakkat. There were biographical dictionaries, as well as a history of the wars between the Tuareg and the French; and a copy of the anonymous *Diwan al-muluk* chronicle Dubois had found. The prominent religious treatises included works by the family of Kunta scholars who had done so much to help Laing and Barth, including Sidi al-Mukhtar, Sidi Muhammad, and Sidi Ahmad al-Bakkai. There were works by

Ahmad Baba himself and by other members of the illustrious Aqit family. Then there was a whole host of manuscripts in Hunwick's second category, items of "documentary" character.

At this time, the staff of the Ahmad Baba center included the young Abdel Kader Haidara, who Hunwick noted had "good connections with many families in the city." The most important element in the embryonic center's development, however, was its director, Mahmoud Zouber. Zouber was a rare thing, even in the late twentieth century: a Malian scholar who was acknowledged by the world of international academia. He was fluent in Fulfulde, Songhay, Tamasheq, Arabic, and French, and had a deep knowledge of the history and culture of the Middle Niger region, and his research into the life of Ahmad Baba had earned him a doctorate from the Sorbonne.

Under Zouber's leadership, the reputation of the Ahmad Baba center grew through the 1990s, along with its collection. Haidara, meanwhile, made his first attempts to promote the private libraries. Toward the end of the decade, Timbuktu's fortunes received a major boost with the visit of a very special guest: Henry Louis Gates, Jr. The eminent head of the Department of African and African American Studies at Harvard University, Gates had come to Mali to make a film for a PBS series titled *Wonders of the African World*. Unlike the white men who had explored Timbuktu in the past, Gates approached the subject from the very different standpoint of a descendant of slaves. His visit was inevitably politically charged: in the film, first broadcast in 1999, he would declare that "as a black American, I know what it's like to have your history stolen from you."

Gates was given a tour of the Sankore mosque by the English-speaking guide Sidi Ali Ould, and taken to see Haidara and his books. In these days before the Mamma Haidara Memorial Library was built, the collection was kept in a storage room crowded with old metal trunks, and the volumes were covered with a fine layer of dust and sand. Gates was transfixed: here were thousands of manuscripts, a few bound in leather, others merely piles of loose folios carefully tied together, some with gold etchings and illustrations that he estimated would be worth thousands of dollars in the world's leading auction houses. If they were translated, he believed, they might completely rewrite the history of black Africa.

He described this moment in a diary that was published online:

Standing in Haidara's "library," . . . I imagined how that shepherd felt holding the Dead Sea Scrolls, perhaps sensing the majesty of his discovery, yet helpless to unlock its secrets. Here, at the "Gateway to the Desert," at the edge of the Sahara's grand sandy superhighway for camels, where two distinct universes have been meeting for a millennium, I held in my own hands perhaps the only remains of the black African world's intellectual achievement.

Later, speaking to camera in the courtyard of the Sankore mosque with tears in his eyes, Gates imagined himself "surrounded by black men with long gowns and turbans, which they received as their sign of their degree when they graduated, and each of them carrying books, this whole place surrounded by books":

Precisely when Europeans said that black Africans lacked the intellectual ability to read or write, this place, founded just about the time of the University of Paris or the University of Bologna . . . and fully 311 years before my own beloved Harvard . . . was brimming with 25,000 students and scholars gathered from all over black Africa and North Africa who had come here because this was Africa's great center of learning.

It was, Gates said, "enough to make you cry."

Though Gates's account of Timbuktu repeated several of the mistakes made by colonial historians, it would radically change the dynamics of the manuscript trade. Here was a black man, a black *American*, an eminent professor with a chair at Harvard, shedding tears at his personal discovery of written proof of Africa's intellectual past, the evidence of the travesty of centuries of European racism. Why had he not known about it—why hadn't the world? On his return to the United States, Gates began to drum up financial support for Haidara, which came in the form of a grant from the Andrew W. Mellon Foundation. After years of trying to scrape funding together for his private libraries project, money for the Timbuktien was at last beginning to flow. The impoverished city was soon at the heart of a manuscript boom: increasing amounts of funding—donated by UNESCO, the Ford Foundation, Norway, Luxembourg, the United States—spurred people to bring forward more documents from the villages around Timbuktu, while other Malian towns, such as Jenne and Segu, started their own manuscript projects. Manuscript owners welcomed the money, but the boom had a darker side: libraries came to be judged not only on the quality of their books but also on their quantity; the numbers claimed spiraled higher and higher, and collections were inflated through indiscriminate buying. Public and private libraries found themselves pitted against one another in the scramble for funding. A Savama grant application written in the 2000s spelled it out: the Ahmad Baba center had managed to collect twenty thousand or so manuscripts, but this was "extremely small compared to the hundreds of thousands (possibly even millions) in private hands."

Gates was not the only man with political ambitions for the manuscripts. In November 2001, South African president Thabo Mbeki came to Timbuktu in company with his Malian counterpart, President Alpha Oumar Konaré, a historian by training. Mbeki was shown the cramped exhibition space in the Ahmad Baba building on the Rue de Chemnitz, which had just two small glass display cabinets, before being led into a conservation studio full of rusty, outmoded equipment. As he was told the history of the contents of the manuscripts, the South African president recognized an opportunity.

It was only eleven years since Nelson Mandela had made his "walk to freedom," just seven years since he had been elected president and the evil of apartheid declared to be at an end. Mbeki, as Mandela's successor, was pushing hard to free the continent from the racist thinking of the past. The evidence in the Ahmad Baba center could be used to reorient the continent's intellectual life away from its bias favoring the old colonial capitals of London and Paris, he realized, and could help forge a homegrown identity for the continent.

On his return to South Africa, Mbeki initiated a giant project tasked with exploiting the manuscripts. Over the next decade, millions of dollars of South African money would be poured into construction, conservation, and research programs in Mali and South Africa to develop what Shamil Jeppie, the head of the Tombouctou Manuscripts Project at the University of Cape Town, called "a vastly underestimated literary heritage that is potentially a symbol of a much wider continental heritage of creativity and a written tradition in particular." In 2009, the new $8.36 million South African–designed building for the Ahmad Baba center was opened next to the Sankore mosque, with facilities to restore, catalogue, and digitize the manuscripts.

As money poured in, and their numbers reached fantastic heights, it was surely only a matter of time before the documents offered up discoveries of historical significance. On this front, though, progress was slow. In 1999, Hunwick seemed to be on the brink of a major revelation when he was shown a trove of documents in the Fondo Kati library that appeared to contain original source material for the *Tarikh al-fattash*, written in the margins of other texts. It was these documents that, a *Chicago Tribune* reporter was told in 2001, represented the African equivalent of an Anglo-Saxon Chronicle, which would profoundly alter long-accepted views of African history. Hunwick had a stroke in 2000, however, and research on the documents stopped. In fact, when the apple cart of Sudanese history was upset once again, it was not because of new finds in the manuscripts at all. In the 2000s, the most significant revelations about the Songhay period came from an entirely different source: the medieval Arabic inscriptions written on tombstones in the region.

The man who decoded this epigraphic evidence was a Brazilian medical doctor turned historical sleuth named Paulo Fernando de Moraes Farias. He had lived and worked for many years in West Africa and had developed an interest in these centuries-old writings. What did they mean? Which cultures had produced them? He spent thirty years finding out. His magnum opus, *Arabic Medieval Inscriptions from the Republic of Mali*, appeared in 2003, four years after Hunwick published his landmark new English translation of the *Tarikh al-sudan*. The results would challenge the very foundations of the vulgate, accepted history of Timbuktu and the Songhay empire that had begun with Barth's discovery of the *Tarikh al-sudan* in 1853.

Since the epigraphs, which had been rediscovered early in the twentieth century, were contemporaneous, they were the oldest and most reliable sources of writing in the region, predating the chronicles by hundreds of years. Yet they had been more or less ignored because they didn't agree with the history in the *tarikh*s. Academics had reacted to them with "bursts of enthusiasm" followed by "paralyzing uncertainty," Farias wrote, as they had no idea how to relate them to the established documentary sources: dates didn't match up, nor did names of dynasties or individual rulers. Only someone with the knowledge and dedication of Farias could make sense of them and work out how they and the chronicles fit together.

What the Brazilian began to realize was that although they were an invaluable source, large parts of the chronicles were not historically accurate at all: in fact, their authors had confected a narrative of Songhay history for the political task of reunifying the people who lived on the Niger bend after the invasion. The Moroccan conquest had turned the askiyas into puppet kings and reduced the privilege that literate urbanites had enjoyed under their rule, while the new power brokers in the Songhay region still struggled for legitimacy. The chronicles were therefore designed as a form of "catastrophe management," Farias argued, a new form of literature aimed at reconciling the elites and enabling them to move forward together. They had been constructed in a way that made the story of the Songhay appear as "a single and taut narrative," but this was synthetic: periods of influence of foreign powers such as Mali were shortened and the rule of the Songhay kings extended both forward and backward in time. This nationalist Songhay version of events squeezed entire dynasties out of the king lists, such as a dynasty bearing the title *malik*, some of whom preceded the Zuwa, and at least six female rulers who took the title *malika* and constituted a royal series in their own right.

To help fill the inconvenient gaps in Songhay history, the authors of the *tarikh*s had borrowed from other cultures' preexisting myths. The story of Ali Kulun, for instance, was lifted from Tuareg traditions, and he was probably no more real than Zuwa Alayaman, the mythical king who slew the fish-god.

There were two reasons why earlier historians hadn't noticed these errors, Farias wrote. One was the accident of fate that meant Barth happened upon the *Tarikh al-sudan* and not the epigraphic evidence. After historians had been presented with the chronicles and all their colorful detail, they were reluctant to take on board evidence that contradicted them. The second reason, according to Farias, was an offshoot of the racist culture of the late nineteenth century. The French Orientalists had held up Ahmad Baba as the paragon of the Timbuktu scholar because of his beautiful Arabic prose, while the authors of the *tarikh*s, writing later and in inferior Arabic, were credited only with being able to faithfully transmit the findings of their more brilliant forebears.

To Farias, these discoveries did not make the Timbuktu chronicles irrelevant. Far from it. They were much more sophisticated than anyone had allowed. In embellishing history in this way, they had composed the most innovative writing ever to have emerged from the city. "We must rely less on the chronicles' reconstructions of the early past," he concluded, "while learning to respect the chroniclers' skills as text craftsmen and ideological agents."

Even at the start of the twenty-first century, then, when many of the building blocks of world history might be said to be settled, West Africa's past was the subject of serious revision. Farias had shown that, once again, what had long been believed about Timbuktu was wrong.

19.

THE MYTH FACTORY

2013–2015

In the days after Mayor Cissé's dramatic announcement, news of the evacuation was slow to filter out. No one seemed to want to reveal the truth, that almost all the manuscripts were safe, too soon. At the University of Cape Town, the Tombouctou Manuscripts Project team took calls from journalists looking for an expert analysis of what had happened. The academics urged caution. As soon as they had seen the TV pictures from the Ahmad Baba building, they knew that not all the documents had been burned: there simply wasn't enough damage, not enough ashes. When they called their colleagues in Mali they were surprised that none of them would explain exactly what had happened. "They wouldn't tell us about it," remembered Susana Molins Lliteras, then a doctoral student with the project. "They told us it was for security reasons, that it was too unsafe." By that time, it seemed to her, such caution was unnecessary.

For those who knew Haidara well, however, selected information was starting to drip out. Jean-Michel Djian, a French writer who specialized in West African culture, told *The New Yorker* on the day of liberation that the majority of the Timbuktu manuscripts—"about fifty thousand"—were safe and that Haidara had transported more than 15,000 to the capital two months previously to protect them. Later that week, the veteran Africa correspondent Tristan McConnell wrote articles for GlobalPost and *Harper's* in which Haidara revealed details of the evacuation. Working with "a handful of volunteers," the librarian had set about hiding Timbuktu's manuscripts, he wrote. With "15 colleagues," he had worked every night for a month to pack them into lockers, starting with the Mamma Haidara collection and then moving on to others. "Well over 1,000" boxes of manuscripts had been buried beneath mud floors, hidden in cupboards and rooms in private houses, or sent upriver. Haidara had refused offers of further help, he told McConnell, because he didn't want anyone else to know where the manuscripts were hidden.

As the world's media came to realize that what was thought destroyed had really been saved, a new round of coverage began, and the number of manuscripts evacuated began to mount. By February 25, according to *Der Spiegel*, the 15,000 Djian reported had become "more than 200,000 documents, or about 80 percent of [the manuscripts in Timbuktu]," citing the German foreign ministry as a source. A German briefing document later put the number at 285,000, while in April, in *The New Republic*, Haidara was cited as claiming that "roughly 95 percent of the city's 300,000 manuscripts made it safely to Bamako." By 2015 this 95 percent would be 377,491 manuscripts, shipped in almost 2,500 lockers. This was not counting the 24,000 or so evacuated from the old Ahmad Baba building, which would put the total over 400,000.

On March 13, 2013, six weeks after the liberation, Diakité launched a new fund-raising drive, T160K: Timbuktu Libraries in Exile, with a talk at the University of Oregon. ("T160K" refers to "the first 160,000" manuscripts that had been evacuated from Timbuktu, she said.) In her lecture, Diakité recollected how the people of Timbuktu and the villages surrounding it, afraid for their lives and futures, not receiving any kind of income because their businesses or jobs had disappeared with the crisis, had come forward to help save the heritage. She was moved to tears by the power of the story. "I'm going to start crying any second here again," she said. "Here I go."

She spoke for fifty minutes—"a pretty short amount of time for an adventure of this magnitude," as she put it—but enough for her to reveal intriguing new findings about the manuscripts. During the evacuation, the workers had made a rough inventory, she said, and discovered for the first time that religious texts were far outnumbered in the collections by secular works, which included poetry, novellas, essays, cookbooks, works of medieval science, medicine, music, and "much, much more." What she still found most exciting, however, was a theme she had mined a decade earlier under the aegis of the Special Conflict Resolution Research Group in Mali: the manuscripts contained texts that had once been used by a corps of Islamic diplomats called the "ambassadors of peace," she said, and in her opinion these texts should now be deployed to spearhead the Malian reconciliation process. They could even contain the template to resolve conflicts all over the continent.

> The way the manuscripts alone brought people together during the evacuation leads us to believe that they, and this material, could drive the process of enduring peace in Mali, and this may be the destiny of the manuscripts, at least in this iteration of their existence.

Before the manuscripts could fulfill this destiny, though, more funds were needed. Far from being secure, the manuscripts in Bamako were threatened by the city's humid climate, and this new crisis required even larger amounts of cash than the evacuation. T160K's target—promoted in old and new media alike—was $7 million. Two months later, on May 15, Haidara published an "Action Plan for the Rescue, Preservation and Valorization of the Timbuktu Manuscripts Evacuated in Bamako," which detailed the costs of conserving, digitizing, cataloguing, and researching the Savama documents. The price tag for this three-year program was set far higher, at a little over $22 million: an enormous sum in a country where the average annual income was just $1,500.

Several donors answered the new shout-outs. The German foreign ministry and the Gerda Henkel Foundation contributed around $1 million a year, while a University of Hamburg team led the effort to preserve the manuscripts and examine their contents. Dehumidifiers were bought, and a large building in southern Bamako was restored to serve as Savama's base. There, the slow process of making new acid-free boxes for the manuscripts and photographing them began in earnest, with Haidara recruiting a growing army of employees. Savama was now well on its way to eclipsing the state-run archive as the principal authority for Malian manuscripts.

Offers of help for the famous little city meanwhile began to flood in from all over the world. UNESCO pledged to rebuild all the demolished mausoleums; it would complete the job in the summer of 2015. An American-led initiative, the Timbuktu Renaissance Action Group, was founded with the intention of reviving Mali through its cultural heritage. Timbuktu Renaissance's project included a deal with Google to let the company film the city for a Street View version, in which, for a fee, distant users would be able to take a virtual tour and watch footage of locals telling stories about the city. "It's going to be a tourist tool for us," said the Malian culture minister, N'Diaye Ramatoulaye Diallo. "They wanted to make it in a way that you can visit Timbuktu completely, you can see the manuscripts, you can visit the mosques, the monuments, everything that is in Timbuktu." There were even plans afoot to construct the city's first real university, at an estimated cost of $80 million, with courses in everything from literature to farming to renewable energy.

In autumn 2014, Haidara traveled to Europe to receive the prestigious German Africa Prize, in recognition of his efforts to save the manuscripts and avert an "unimaginable loss" to world heritage, and for his tireless commitment to the development and preservation of African history. Presenting the award, the German foreign minister said, "It could have had quite a different outcome, but today we are pleased that 95 percent of the manuscripts were saved."

NOT EVERYONE CAUGHT the new outbreak of Timbuktu fever. In autumn 2015, a multinational group of Africanists gathered at the leafy campus of the University of Birmingham for a symposium in honor of the institution's honorary senior research fellow, Paulo Fernando de Moraes Farias. Academics from all over the world gathered in white-walled conference rooms to deliver presentations on subjects as diverse as Catholic missionary education in the kingdom of Kongo and the role of the West African griot. Among the delegates were leading experts on the Islamic heritage of West Africa, including Farias, Shamil Jeppie, Charles Stewart and Mauro Nobili of the University of Illinois, and Bruce Hall.

Hall, a tall, soft-spoken assistant professor from Duke University, had known Diakité, Haidara, and Hunwick since 1999, when, as a young Ph.D. student, he had spent several years in Timbuktu working with the manuscripts. He was one of the few Westerners who could read and understand the texts that filled West Africa's Islamic libraries. Since 2013 he had become the most outspoken critic of Savama. Watching a video of Diakité's lecture at Oregon and reading her shout-out for funding, he had felt a growing sense of frustration. He had experienced firsthand the commercialization of the private collections and the restrictions on access for researchers that often ensued. The sums Savama was trying to raise, the secrecy, and the mystic terms in which the manuscripts were being described had been red flags to Hall, who sent out a highly skeptical response to Diakité on the Mansa-1 mailing list, which went out to African studies departments around the world.

According to Hall, Diakité had mischaracterized the nature of the documents. Contrary to her claims that they were polyglot, encyclopedic, and secular in nature, 98 percent were written in literary Arabic and, apart from the many single-page letters and contracts, the vast majority were Islamic religious texts. This was not to underestimate them: "They provide a wonderfully important resource for scholars, both Malian and non-Malian, but they are best understood as the product of a wider tradition of Islamic scholarship across West Africa and the broader Muslim World," Hall wrote. They did not need to be made into objects of veneration.

Hall continued to mine this theme in Birmingham. He was now using the F-word—"fraud"—openly. Since the founding of the Ahmad Baba center, millions of dollars had been given to people in the manuscript business, and the number of manuscripts had been inflated to attract further funding. But any group that tried to work with the documents in Timbuktu had become frustrated, he said: "The money [for Timbuktu] depends on a certain fraud, a misrepresentation of materials and amount of materials." For Hall, 300,000 was a best guess of the "total number of Arabic manuscripts that are extant in Northern Mali altogether." Even Haidara himself in 2011 had put the number in the whole Timbuktu region at 101,820, Hall said. Unless they were being imported on a huge scale, the number in the city itself must therefore be far lower. The state-owned Ahmad Baba institute was by far the most significant collection: if all the single-page letters, contracts, poems, and other material were counted, it might reach 30,000 items. Haidara's was the largest private collection. Most others were small, Hall said, with the majority numbering only in the several hundreds.

At the heart of the issue of numbers lay a problem of definition. In 2000, London's Al-Furqan Islamic Heritage Foundation had catalogued the Mamma Haidara collection and found just four thousand documents, but this did not include the large numbers of single-page bills of sale, legal judgments, and so on, each of which was now commonly defined in Timbuktu as a manuscript in itself. In my first meeting with Haidara in 2013, he had plumped for an even broader definition by scribbling on a Post-it note and declaring that, in his father's view, even this would have been called a manuscript. For Hall, such a definition was meaningless.

Hall did not doubt that the evacuations of the old Ahmad Baba building, the Fondo Kati, or the Mamma Haidara library had taken place. "Well-placed officials in the Malian government insisted early on that the manuscripts from [the old Ahmad Baba building] were mostly safe, and that they had been hidden or smuggled out of Timbuktu during the Salafist occupation," he wrote in a footnote to his paper. But contacts in Timbuktu had told him that many other manuscript collections had remained in the town during the occupation, and that some had been moved to Bamako only *after* liberation, in order to support the claims that such vast numbers had been evacuated. The story had then been grossly inflated for the international media, and the result was a huge injection of Western money into Savama.

"The narrative of rescued manuscripts is at best misleading," he noted, "and, at worst, completely dishonest and fraudulent."

None of the experts in the room disagreed with the substantive points of his deeply critical assessment. How, asked Tom McCaskie, a professor at the School of Oriental and African Studies at the University of London, had it come about that Timbuktu's manuscripts had been inflated into something they were not? "Are we talking about an entire structure built on . . . I was going to say 'lies,' but I now say 'nothing'?"

If Hall was right, the hero of Timbuktu had greatly exaggerated the scale of the rescue operation, and Savama had received money to evacuate manuscripts that had either never moved or didn't even exist.

Reexamining the narrative of the private library evacuation with Hall's skeptical eye turned up many unanswered questions. Putting the significant issue of the numbers aside for the moment, why had Haidara provided no eyewitnesses to corroborate the more dramatic parts of the operation, though he had repeatedly been asked for them? At first he had said that it was a matter of security; later, that people had been angry with him for giving their names to reporters. Why did some of his associates initially agree to talk, then become mysteriously unavailable? Even the most willing interviewees from the state library would clam up when asked about the evacuation of the privately owned manuscripts: "Ah, no, no, no!" one Ahmad Baba employee said, laughing. "I cannot talk about the private libraries!"

When other accounts were finally obtained, they often disagreed with Haidara's or Diakité's version of events, and the terrible twosome even disagreed with each other. Why, for instance, would Diakité have told Deborah Stolk that the Lere route was used just as much as the Douentza route—and that "supervisory and security personnel" were "camped out all along it"—when Haidara said it had been tried only once, and that had resulted in a hijacking? Why would Haidara initially deny the great kidnapping of twenty Niger boats, since he supposedly ransomed it "like he was using his credit card"? Why had other Niger captains who plied the river at that time not heard about this major incident, which would have had a direct bearing on their trade? Why would Diakité say that French helicopters saluted the couriers while they held up manuscripts, when Haidara said, "That's false. That's just commentary"?

While certain details appeared unreliable, the academics raised more fundamental questions with the Savama story. How great, really, was the jihadist threat, when all the private collections were hidden? Thomas Strieder, the German chargé d'affaires, came away from his meeting with Savama believing that documents were being destroyed "again and again," but Haidara himself recalled only vaguely hearing of two early instances of destroyed manuscripts, which he said were "little, little things." To Tjoelker, meanwhile, was led to believe the jihadists had promised a ceremonial book-burning, an auto-da-fé, on the day of Mawlid, and Haidara made this part of his grant request to the Dutch embassy. They needed money urgently, he wrote in his application letter, since they had to evacuate "before . . . 24 January next, the date at which the jihadists threaten to take action and to proceed to destroy this cultural heritage." The correspondent of *The New Republic* was even told that librarians had been instructed to gather their manuscripts together for just such an occasion. Yet none of the Timbuktiens I interviewed recalled any such threat. Asked specifically if the jihadists had spoken of burning the manuscripts at Mawlid, the head of Timbuktu's cultural mission, El-Boukhari Ben Essayouti, responded: "No, I have not heard that." The grand imam, the man who led negotiations over Mawlid with the jihadists, and a most unimpeachable source, denied it outright: "They did not threaten to burn the manuscripts of Timbuktu," he told me.

While the destruction of the mausoleums was evidence of the clash between the Salafists' beliefs and those of most Timbuktiens, the jihadists' attitude toward the manuscripts was different. Certain documents would no doubt have been viewed as *haram*, forbidden, but given that it could take an expert hours to decipher a single page, how likely was it that these often illiterate fighters would find time to weed out the works they disapproved of, or else burn the manuscripts wholesale, including many copies of their holiest texts? On several occasions, the jihadists had promised to protect them, and if Diadié and Sane Chirfi Alpha were correct, the Islamic Police had not even objected to their being shipped south for conservation.

And what of that widely reported act of destruction on the day of liberation itself? If Mayor Cissé really believed they had "torched all the important ancient manuscripts," as he told the world's media, why did it take so long to correct this mistake? Later, the Ahmad Baba institute estimated that 4,203 documents had been lost, but few seemed to believe even this many had been burned. They had probably been stolen, most said, and the fire was set to cover the theft. This seemed plausible, and could perhaps explain how 10,000 manuscripts had been left in the basement. Still, it was odd that no one seemed to care what the missing manuscripts actually were, or know which families had given them to the institute.

(Later, when I asked Haidara if he had exaggerated the threat, he responded: "If you believe that there was no threat, that's your opinion and it does not concern us. The threat existed before Mawlid, during, and after this event. To understand this . . . it is sufficient to look to the case of the manuscript burnings that the world media broadcast.")

The academics' skepticism extended even to the biggest question of all: the manuscripts' vaunted contents. Many of these experts thought the documents' historical value was as overrevved as the numbers: great claims were made for the private collections, but access was so tightly controlled that few of these claims could be verified. Most damning in this regard was a new study by a South African academic of the documents Hunwick had become so excited about in the Fondo Kati, which were said to have contained the original notes for the *Tarikh al-fattash*. According to the study, at least some of this material had been forged.

With almost everything about the private evacuation now in doubt, I turned to the Dutch diplomats, at least three of whom—To Tjoelker, the ambassador Maarten Brouwer, and his press attaché, Mirjam Tassing—had witnessed lockers of manuscripts arriving in Bamako in early 2013. They were astonished by the accusations. Tjoelker, who had done so much to find money for Savama, produced photographs of stacks of lockers in Bamako, some of which were open and filled with manuscripts. "There were hundreds of boxes of metal lockers of the kind you would transport when you are going on a long journey. It was really very, very impressive," she recalled. "They kept coming in and we made a very rapid count—I can't remember how—and there were something like 150,000 manuscripts there." Every locker was numbered, so they could tell who paid for it and which family the manuscripts came from, so they had "a registration of all those big lockers."

Brouwer was similarly incredulous. "Whatever people are saying, I can tell you the story is for real," he said. He was alarmed enough by Hall's accusations, however, to make inquiries of his own. He met with Haidara and was shown the contents of his Bamako safe houses, where many of the manuscripts were still being stored. The result was conclusive, he wrote in an e-mail:

> We observed a large quantity of manuscripts that were already inventoried and/or registered, in total 110,000. This number would equal an estimated 800–1000 containers. We have seen ourselves roughly 1300 full containers with manuscripts not yet unpacked, making a total of 2100–2300 containers. Of course these are rough calculations, but we feel comfortable to say that the total of 2400 mentioned by Haidara is most certainly correct. We visited all seven locations within a timespan of three hours and no containers have been moved in the meantime. . . . At all locations we opened some containers and boxes, and manuscripts were inside. We lifted containers to check if they were full or not and all were fully loaded.

On the evidence Brouwer had seen, Hall's objections were misplaced. Why, he wondered, were such accusations being made? "Apparently there is a lot of competition and envy around these manuscripts," he wrote. "And Savama has bypassed all academia with this rescue operation."

In Brouwer's view, then, there was no doubt.

. . .

BAMAKO IN LATE 2015 was reeling from a new terrorist attack. On Friday, November 20, two jihadists walked into the Radisson Hotel, took 170 people hostage, and shot twenty dead. In the years since the French intervention, the armed groups in the north had reasserted themselves: tens of UN peacekeepers had been killed, terrorist violence had crept into southern and central Mali, and foreign journalists had left after receiving personalized death threats. In the wake of the latest attack, international organizations were pulling their people out, and the country was in a formal state of emergency. Giant Hesco sandbags blocked the entrance to the government village, and soldiers in flak jackets inspected the undersides of vehicles looking for bombs. Police stopped cars in the streets, and guards waved metal-detecting wands over hotel guests before allowing them entry. Asked to sum up the security situation, one diplomat said simply, "Not very good."

Haidara was unwell that week, but agreed nevertheless to meet several times. The first of these encounters was in the early evening, the *petit soir*, the time he most liked to talk, in his apartment in Baco Djicoroni. We sat, as we had so many times before, on the floor between the sofas, and he set out confidently across the now familiar foothills of the occupation's early days, as usual brushing aside disagreements over the details. We worked through the narrative, past the Ahmad Baba evacuation toward the heights of the private libraries. There, confronted with the greatest discrepancies in the story, his assertiveness seemed to slip.

The fleet of forty-seven boats and the vast numbers of taxis, the calls to each of the three hundred couriers several times a day, the schedule on the wall with people to phone every few minutes, was all that true?

Not exactly a "Yes" this time. More of a "Hmmm."

What about the October "window of opportunity," which culminated in the October 17 contract with the Prince Claus Fund and the start of the evacuation of the private manuscripts the following day? Could he confirm that had happened?

"I don't know. We had begun in August."

He'd begun with the private libraries in August?

"Hmmm," he said. "We did a lot of operations."

What of the idea—which Diakité had spelled out in an e-mail to the Prince Claus Fund—that they had used the track that followed the left bank of the river and passed through Lere as much as the main route via Mopti? What did he make of that?

"Hmmmm."

What about the incident at the edge of Lake Debo, where bandits had ambushed the boats and held the manuscripts ransom, and Haidara had to pay for their release. Had that really happened?

He coughed spectacularly. *"Il faut le laisser comme ça,"* he said. "Leave that as it is."

What did he mean, leave it as it is?

"It's good."

The conversation turned to numbers. It wasn't just Hall and his fellow academics who questioned them. Few of Haidara's colleagues in the business—including Ismael and Maiga—believed such vast quantities of manuscripts existed. "If you do the sums of the different libraries," Ismael had said, "how are you going to get 200,000? Is it possible?" Maiga, who had worked with the Luxembourg-funded project MLI/015, said that they had done a catalogue of all the manuscripts in Timbuktu and had not even reached 100,000. How could Haidara possibly claim to have evacuated 377,491?

These people were not specialists, Haidara said. Bruce Hall had worked mainly with the Ahmad Baba institute and had not even been to Mali for years. Even Maiga, in his view, was not a specialist. Previous, lower estimates had been made before they had been able to do a proper count.

If the 377,491 private manuscripts figure was real, how could he explain that it had taken almost 2,500 lockers to move them, while the Ahmad Baba institute's 24,000 manuscripts were shipped in just thirty-six lockers?

"Ah, that is easy to respond to," he said, sitting up and taking a long drink from a water bottle. The manuscripts were different sizes. Some of them consisted of a single page. You could fit a lot of these single-folio manuscripts into a locker, but very few large manuscripts.

That didn't explain why, on average, Savama shipped 157 manuscripts per locker, whereas more than six hundred fit into each Ahmad Baba box. At that density, he could have moved almost two million manuscripts in 2,500 lockers.

"I don't know," he said. "Perhaps the [Savama] manuscripts are bigger."

The following day we met in the Savama building. There, I asked him to go through the list of private libraries on the organization's website to check which he had moved and which he hadn't. The results were surprising. Of the thirty-five libraries in the town listed on savamadci.net, he claimed to have evacuated only seventeen. These included two private libraries whose owners had told me their manuscripts had not been moved by Savama: Ismael's Fondo Kati and Sane Chirfi Alpha's Bibliothèque Alimam Alpha Salum. There were further discrepancies: Abdoul Hamid Kounta, the owner of the Zawiyat al-Kunti library, told me in two separate interviews that Savama had moved his books in June—four months before the "window of opportunity." Worse, another manuscript owner in Timbuktu, Abdoul Wahid Haidara, said that three major private libraries had been moved long after the liberation, in what he believed was an effort to prop up Savama's exaggerated claims.

How, I wondered, could this much-reduced number of libraries, which excluded such notable repositories as those of the grand imam and the al-Wangari family, amount to the 95 percent evacuation he claimed?

The more famous libraries were not always the biggest ones, was Haidara's response.

"There is not only one account of the evacuation," he had told me in his apartment. "Each person will have his own take on it. Bruce [Hall] will have one account, Ismael another, Maiga yet another, while I have my own version. All these accounts will be different, but they will all be true. If everyone agreed what the story was, then it would certainly not be true."

ON MY LAST EVENING in Bamako, Haidara played his trump card, taking me on a tour of the safe houses. Once again it was dusk, and as we drove across Bamako's Bridge of Martyrs the sun was dropping, pink and heavy, into the Niger. It was the time of the harmattan, and the dust churned up by this strong, warm wind hung heavy over the city. Dressed in a bronze-colored gown of shining waxed cotton with a matching kufi cap, Haidara led a wild ride around southern Bamako, through the gathering darkness and the rampant crosstown traffic.

Following him along the back roads of this unknowable city, in pedantic pursuit, was a surprising endgame in a story that had once seemed straightforward.

The car would pull in suddenly, and he would step out, heading cheerfully into the slow-streaming traffic and hurrying up a gloomy alley. He would shout a greeting to the watchmen talking or praying on a mat outside without breaking stride, flick on his phone to light a stairwell and scatter a rat. Up flight after flight, I followed the big man, both of us breathing hard. A blank-walled corridor, a steel security gate, a trusty with a key, and a room filled with tens or hundreds of lockers, some in plain colors, some in brushed steel, some decorated with pictures of rockets and abstract stencil shapes. They were stacked in piles, some closed with a single padlock, some with two, some not clasped at all. A dehumidifier hummed.

The lids of the unlocked chests could be opened, and inside there were always manuscripts, some still in the acid-free boxes in which they had been brought south, some in colored folders, others bound in animal hide. Here were a hundred in one sheaf; there a single volume eight inches thick. Rooting through to the back, to the middle of a stack of lockers, I found documents in there too. Prying open the lid of a chest closed with a single lock, peering inside: more documents.

Sometimes the drive between stops was five minutes; sometimes it was half an hour across the suburbs of the Malian capital, headlights picking out the trucks, the policemen, the army 4x4s, the clouds of buzzing scooters. Another destination. More lockers, more shelves of manuscripts. Here a printed card announcing the library of Aboubacrine Ben Said, which possessed 7,610 manuscripts; there it was Alpha Mahamane of Diré, who had 6,450. Another room, another tally to add to the spiraling total.

So many boxes. So many manuscripts. Could it really all add up? Skepticism, in the face of this confident, charming man, was oddly hard to maintain. Maybe he had exaggerated a little; was that so bad? The donors didn't seem to care. It was now more than three years since the evacuation, and even the team from the University of Hamburg who were studying the manuscripts and whose government had put in millions of euros of funding hadn't done a full count, even a rough one. Did it really matter?

The double-locked boxes were heavy, no doubt. Could Haidara open one of those? He'd left the keys at the apartment, he said. It was too far away to go back now. Anyway, there was one at the top of a stack there, with a key already in its padlock. The caretakers must have left it by mistake. Look in there. What do you see? Manuscripts!

The last location was a grand house with a pleasant garden in a walled compound. There was a broad entrance gate, a drive covered with flagstones. In a room here were 140 more lockers—the running total was now above 1,000, and more would be produced the following day. These were all still full, he said. They were also all still double-locked.

A final request, as we left the storeroom. Could we go back to the apartment together, pick up the keys, and return to open a handful of the double-padlocked boxes? This would be the final, crucial proof; then we would be finished.

"No," he said.

It was the first point-blank refusal in two days of difficult questions.

"You have to have trust," he said, his voice rising. "You are accusing me of being a thief! I have my dignity. I have been ill, and tonight I have driven all over Bamako and I have opened everything up. I have shown you everything. I have my dignity. I am not a child."

No one is calling you a thief, I said, but there are people who don't believe this is quite real. They need evidence that it is.

"Those people will never believe it, even with all the proof in the world," he said, strident now. "People put words in people's mouths— they even put words in the mouth of the Prophet! These are our manuscripts, not yours. These are the manuscripts of Mali. They belong to us! They are not for you!"

You will not open the locked chests?

"No."

There were no more questions. There was nothing else to see. Haidara did something surprising after that. He reached over suddenly and pulled me in, taking my arm under his own large biceps, holding my hand in his in an unexpected embrace, smiling. Was he asking for forgiveness? Clemency?

We marched in this clasp down the dimly lit corridor, toward the front door, and out into the garden, with its tropical flowers and chiming crickets, to where his assistants and his chauffeur were waiting.

EPILOGUE

———

This book is as much historiography as history. That is to say, it is an account of the interpretations of Timbuktu's past at least as much as it is the story of what actually happened there. The reasons for this will, I hope, have become clear: Timbuktu's story is in perpetual motion, swinging back and forth between competing poles of myth and reality. Spectacular arguments are made and then dismissed before another claim is built up, in an apparently continuous cycle of proposition and correction.

From its earliest days, the legend of the New Jerusalem across the desert—called Timbuktu or Tombouctou, Tenbuch or Tombut—was fed from a mix of misinformation, credulity, and the European greed for gold. Why this place? Why was it this city that became the focus of the world's misconceptions about Africa, and not, say, Jenne or Gao or Kano? It was partly a matter of geography: since Timbuktu lay at the southern end of the caravan routes to Morocco and Libya, exaggerated reports of its wealth that were carried across the desert were easily passed to Europe. It helped that the place had such a resonant name, an unforgettable slogan that "catches the ear and conveys images of wonder," as the historian Eugenia Herbert put it. Crucial, too, was the city's elusiveness: you could say what you liked about Timbuktu and no one was going to correct you. Robert Adams, an American sailor who improbably claimed to have reached the city in 1812, told the world it was governed by King Woollo and Queen Fatima, who never washed but greased their bodies daily with goat's-milk butter. In a later era, Bruce Chatwin learned that Timbuktiens ate mouse soup, which was served complete with little pink feet. Even as momentous geographical discoveries were being made in the Arctic and South America, explorers failed time after time to penetrate La Mystérieuse. When Alexander Gordon Laing finally struggled, half dead, into its precincts in 1826, Europeans had been fantasizing about it for at least five centuries.

The "Timbuktu of the mind" overpowered the little-known reality of the place, and deflating it was not an inviting task. Having at last attained his prize, the normally verbose Laing seems to have wrestled with what to say. He stayed five weeks without sending a word home, and when, finally, he was forced to put pen to paper, he revealed almost nothing. We can imagine why: his discovery was that the great city that had dwelled so long in the European imagination was a small town of humble, earth-built dwellings. In those circumstances, who would not have written, as he did, that "the great Capital of central Africa" had "completely met my expectations"—and, well, gotta run?

René Caillié's description of Timbuktu as "nothing but a mass of ill-looking houses" did more to correct the misconception, but it was widely disbelieved, and those who followed him only mined deeper for myth. The journalist Félix Dubois's excitement seventy years later at discovering the fantastical backstory of a culture founded by ancient

Egyptians that "still dazzled . . . three centuries after the setting of her star" is palpable. Not satisfied with the city's genuine tradition of scholarship, he inflated it, repackaging Timbuktu as Carthage and Alexandria combined, and elements of his "Timbuktu University" legend were still being repeated a century later. Even Heinrich Barth, a genius of African exploration, mistakenly introduced the tradition of reading the *Tarikh al-sudan* as history, when in fact its narrative proved to be synthetic, an imaginative reworking of past events to suit the politics of the time. This confusion was compounded by the Orientalists Houdas, Benoist, and Delafosse, who understood the chroniclers' pedestrian Arabic to mean their authors were capable only of relaying the information accurately laid down by their forebears, rather than inventing history anew. For a century, the supposed facts in the chronicles edged out the contradictory but more reliable epigraphic evidence.

Europe was not the sole author of the Timbuktu myths: the citizens of the town played a splendid part in its aggrandizement. Neither *tarikh* passed up the opportunity to elaborate on what al-Sadi called a "virtuous, pure, undefiled and proud city, blessed with divine favour," which, the *Fattash* said, "had no parallel in the land of the Blacks." Ahmad Baba, writing in an earlier generation, talked up the Timbuktu scholars' miraculous deeds: these holy men could walk on water and make people impervious to enemy arrows and fire. The exaggeration of the city's divinity may have grown up as a way to protect it, a sort of mystic defense, much as saints in medieval Europe were invoked to intimidate would-be invaders.

The great twenty-first-century story of Timbuktu, the account of the manuscript evacuation, fits neatly into this tradition. As Joseph Gitari pointed out, it appeared as an Indiana Jones story in real life, one in which the people of the sainted city, led by librarians, rescued their semi-magical patrimony from the hands of the book-burning jihadists. With such resonant, universal themes of good versus evil, books versus guns, fanatics versus moderates, this modern-day folktale proved irresistible. It was all the more powerful for being built around a kernel of truth, just as the more glorious legends of the city's past were: only the most skeptical academic would deny that Timbuktu was once an important center of Islamic scholarship in the Western Sudan. The manuscript owners, I believe, worked to protect their literary heritage from the threat of looting, mostly by hiding the documents, some by evacuating them in operations overseen by Savama. The Ahmad Baba manuscripts in particular were saved in the manner that was described to me. These operations undoubtedly took chutzpah and courage, from the directors of libraries as well as more junior colleagues who braved the jihadists' sharia punishments. From these fundamentals, the operation was spun into something larger and more dangerous than it really was.

Legend, by its nature, is oversimplification. E. P. Thompson described the tendency to simplify the lives of people who have gone before as "the enormous condescension of posterity." We might add the condescension of distance, the impulse of one culture to imagine the people of another to be less sophisticated, more two-dimensional than they really are. This was what led the West to mistake the Timbuktu chronicles for first-rate history but second-rate literature, when the reverse was true: the chroniclers had embroidered heavily on the past, producing the most innovative writing ever to come out of the city. As Farias pointed out in that context, we outsiders underestimate the intellectual originality of Timbuktiens at our peril. Narratives of the place and its history are still distorted by this failing: our inability to imagine the city's full complexity. Yet the misreadings of it have been the making of Timbuktu. What else would draw the world to this remote town but legends, rumors, its "far fame," in Laing's description? How much reduced would the city be without them?

I imagine Timbuktu's story as a series of myths and corrections laid down one on top of the other. In the future, perhaps, some psycho-geographer will drill down through all these tight-packed layers that reach into the Sudanese past. At the bottom they will find the story of Zuwa Alayaman slaying the fish-god at Kukiya. They will watch Ali Kulun riding past on his way to liberate the Songhay, his horse strengthened with special food. They will look on as the powerful slave woman Tinbuktu, with her sticking-out navel, sets up her desert camp, and see Malian armadas preparing to depart for the Americas, and craftsmen sheathing Musa's palace with gold. And at the top, closest to the present, they will watch combat helicopters circle a great convoy of Niger *pinasses* that forges its way upstream, carrying its cargo of invaluable books. Hundreds and hundreds of thousands of books.

NOTES

My account of Timbuktu in 2012–2013 is drawn from hundreds of hours of interviews conducted in Mali, the United States, the United Kingdom, Germany, Belgium, the Netherlands, France, Spain, and South Africa between 2013 and 2016. Supporting material, including correspondence, reports, and grant applications, was provided by foreign ministries and donor organizations, often willingly, and occasionally under Freedom of Information legislation. The narrative of exploration, meanwhile, is drawn from the rich range of works written by explorers and their sponsors. The African Association was diligent in documenting its purpose and activities, issuing *Proceedings of the Association for Promoting the Discovery of the Interior Parts of Africa* periodically to members. These were made publicly available in a two-volume edition in 1810, and in 1964 were collected by Robin Hallett, along with other papers from the association, and published as *Records of the African Association 1788–1831*, with an insightful introductory history of the organization. Papers relating to other West African explorers, Alexander Gordon Laing in particular, were definitively compiled by the amateur historian E. W. Bovill in his series *Missions to the Niger*. In addition to these works, I returned again and again to a handful of more recent sources. Chief among them were translations of the Timbuktu scholars, including John Hunwick's *Timbuktu and the Songhay Empire*, which provides the most authoritative translation of the *Tarikh al-sudan*, and Octave Houdas and Maurice Delafosse's earlier translations into French of the *Tarikh al-sudan* (Houdas) and the *Tarikh al-fattash* (Houdas and Delafosse). Pekka Masonen's *The Negroland Revisited* provides one of the few detailed narrative accounts of Europe's relationship with the region, while Paulo Fernando de Moraes Farias's *Arabic Medieval Inscriptions from the Republic of Mali* is a salutory warning that the history of Timbuktu is in a state of perpetual flux.

A NOTE ON LANGUAGE AND NAMES

As readers of early drafts of this book pointed out, there are few greater obstacles to cross-cultural understanding than a profusion of unfamiliar names or foreign words with unrecognized diacritical marks. So although I have opted to follow the style used by the journal

Sudanic Africa for Arabic transliteration, I have removed some of these marks, including in quoted passages, in an attempt to simplify the experience of the general reader.

Names of people and places have provided a particular challenge, since they have often been romanized differently in different languages. This has created some inconsistencies: I have used the English spelling "Timbuktu," for instance, as opposed to the Francophone "Tombouctou," but have spelled the name of modern Malians who share their name with that of the Prophet as "Mohamed," the way they would spell it, and not as the standard English "Muhammad," which is the spelling used for historical figures. The relatively small pool of surnames in Mali, meanwhile, has made a mockery of the Western style of using the last name on second mention. (In this story, there are at least five Haidaras, four Maigas, and five Tourés.) Malians get around this by using a variety of names or name combinations. The country's current leader, President Keita, for example, is known universally as Ibrahim Boubacar Keita, or IBK, and his predecessor Amadou Toumani Touré as ATT. Nicknames—such as "Jansky," "Air Mali," and even "John Travolta"—are also widely adopted, and are sometimes printed on people's business cards.

My guiding principle has been to try to make everything as straightforward as possible for the reader, without intending any disrespect.

PROLOGUE: A MAN OF ENTERPRISE AND GENIUS

For E. W. Bovill, Alexander Gordon Laing was "the most neglected of the African explorers," partly because he did not survive to tell his tale, and partly because his journal was not recovered. My account of his expedition to Timbuktu is drawn largely from his papers, which I found in the British National Archives ("Major Laing's Mission to Timbuctoo: Papers Relating to His Death") and in *Missions to the Niger*, volume 1, edited by Bovill. Details of Laing's early life have been drawn from Robert Chambers, *A Biographical Dictionary of Eminent Scotsmen*, volume 3, and from Christopher Fyfe's entry on him in the *Oxford Dictionary of National Biography*. An entertaining modern retelling of his story can be found in Frank T. Kryza's *The Race for Timbuktu*.

Bruce Chatwin's reflections on "Timbuctoo, Tumbuto, Tombouctou, Tumbyktu, Tumbuktu or Tembuch?" were published as "Gone to Timbuctoo" in *Vogue* in 1970 and later included in his *Anatomy of Restlessness*.

PART ONE. OCCUPATION

The excerpt from *The Thousand and One Nights* is drawn from Edward William Lane's 1841 translation.

1. A SEEKER OF MANUSCRIPTS

The accounts of Abdel Kader Haidara's childhood and early life, and his actions on March 30, 2012, are derived largely from many interviews with him. He included a brief portrait of his father's career and the history of the Mamma Haidara library in his essay "An Overview of the Major Manuscript Libraries in Timbuktu." His childhood friend Sane Chirfi Alpha picked out the visit to Timbuktu by Amadou Hampâté Bâ as the moment Haidara identified his purpose in life. Anyone seeking a detailed exploration of the country's culture and West African Islam could do no better than read Hampâté Bâ's *A Spirit of Tolerance: The Inspiring Life of Tierno Bokar.*

The group of which Haidara is executive president is the Organisation Non Gouvernementale pour la Sauvegarde et la Valorisation des Manuscrits pour la Défense de la Culture Islamique (SAVAMA-DCI), referred to generally as Savama. The manuscript research institute founded in Timbuktu was called the Centre de Documentation et de Recherches Ahmad Baba, or CEDRAB, but was later renamed the Institut des Hautes Études et de Recherche Islamique Ahmad Baba, or IHERIAB. For simplicity, I have used neither of these official names but have referred to it as the Ahmad Baba center or institute. Minutes of the founding meeting were published in "Report of the UNESCO Meeting of Experts on the Utilisation of Written Sources for the History of Africa Held at Timbuktu" in 1968, and its early history was recounted by John Hunwick in "CEDRAB: The Centre de Documentation et de Recherches Ahmad Baba at Timbuktu," and in Louis Brenner and David Robinson, "Project for the Conservation of Malian Arabic Manuscripts." Hunwick noted the presence on the center's staff of "a young sharif," Haidara, who had inherited a considerable library from his father and carried out "prospection campaigns" in the city to establish lists of manuscripts that were available for purchase. Details of Haidara's work as a manuscript prospector, including the figure of 16,000 manuscripts collected in twelve years, come from interviews with him and from the Tombouctou Manuscripts Project at the University of Cape Town (tombouctoumanuscripts.org).

Hugh Trevor-Roper's 1963 comments on African history are in cited in M. E. Chamberlain, *The Scramble for Africa*, among other sources. Henry Louis Gates, Jr.'s visit to Timbuktu was documented in the PBS film *Wonders of the African World.* The PBS microsite www.pbs.org/wonders has further information about Gates's journeys, including extracts from his diaries. Thabo Mbeki's pronouncement that the manuscripts opened up possibilities for thinking in new ways about the world was delivered on August 7, 2008, at the Castle of Good Hope, Cape Town. I found the full text on the website of the Presidency of South Africa, at http://www.thepresidency.gov.za/pebble.asp?relid=3336. John Hunwick, Sean O'Fahey, and David Robinson were quoted in Ron Grossman's article "African Manuscripts Rewriting History: Northwestern Professor Uncovers 16th Century Writings by a Black African That Contradict Many Western Preconceptions."

The 2011 claim of more than 100,000 manuscripts in Timbuktu's collections is from Haidara's "An Overview of the Major Manuscript Libraries in Timbuktu." He writes that "the most recent surveys suggest the existence of about one million manuscripts preserved in several private and public libraries [in Timbuktu and surrounding areas]. The most important of them in Timbuktu hold a total of no less than 101,820 manuscripts." Haidara later told me that this represented only the number that had been tallied by that time.

An authoritative take on the causes of the 2012 Malian conflict can be found in the International Crisis Group report *Mali, Avoiding Escalation*. Judith Scheele describes the scale of the desert's black economy in *Smugglers and Saints of the Sahara*, in detail worth recounting: "Flour, pasta and petrol come down from Algeria on small jeeps, on antique trucks, or even on the backs of camels and donkeys. Livestock and cigarettes come up from Mali. . . . Veils, perfumes, jewellery, incense and furniture arrive from southern Morocco and Mauritania, places at the forefront of feminine fashion with harbours wide open to Chinese imports; these commodities are often traded by women. . . . Narcotics arrive from Mauritania, via the Western Sahara, or from the Gulf of Guinea, and travel themselves around the southern tip of Algeria through Niger and Chad to Egypt, and thence to Israel and Europe. Arms come up from long-standing crisis zones, such as Chad, or are unloaded in the large ports of the Gulf of Guinea and are sold throughout the area."

2. A WIDE EXTENDED BLANK

Details of the establishment of the African Association and its early exploits are drawn from *Proceedings of the Association for Promoting the Discovery of the Interior Parts of Africa*, and from Robin Hallett, *Records of the African Association 1788–1831*, which gives a clear picture of what was known in Europe about the continent and why Joseph Banks and his associates wanted to explore it. A colorful modern retelling of the association's activities can be found in Anthony Sattin's *The Gates of Africa*.

Banks has been the subject of several biographies, among them Harold B. Carter's *Sir Joseph Banks 1743–1820* and *Joseph Banks: A Life* by Patrick O'Brian, a writer best known for his Aubrey–Maturin seafaring novels. Some 20,000 pieces of Banks's correspondence are said to survive; many of these have been collected by Neil Chambers in *The Letters of Sir Joseph Banks: A Selection 1768–1820*.

The scientist's own observations on visiting the African continent in 1771 can be read in *The Endeavour Journal of Sir Joseph Banks*. Jonathan Swift's thoughts on

African maps are part of his 1733 poem "On Poetry: A Rhapsody." Horace Walpole's remarks about James Bruce's exploits in Ethiopia can be found in *Letters of Horace Walpole, Earl of Orford, to Sir Horace Mann: His Britannic Majesty's Resident at the Court of Florence, from 1760 to 1785*, volume 2. The English merchant's comments on the significance of the African trade are drawn from John Peter Demarin's anonymously published *A Treatise upon the Trade from Great-Britain to Africa, Humbly Recommended to the Attention of Government, by an African Merchant*.

The various theories of the origins of Timbuktu's name have been explored by Riccardo Pelizzo in his article "Timbuktu: A Lesson in Underdevelopment" and by Sékéné Mody Cissoko in *Toumbouctou et l'empire Songhay*. Sources on the geography of the Niger bend include John Hunwick's *Timbuktu and the Songhay Empire* and Sanche de Gramont's *The Strong Brown God*. The climate history of the Sahara is explored in Susan Keech McIntosh and Roderick McIntosh, "West African Prehistory," which presents evidence that between 8000 and 5500 BCE the Sahara was a mosaic of shallow lakes and marshes, roamed by elephant, giraffe, rhinoceros, and crocodile. Evidence for this Saharan "green period" was found by Heinrich Barth in June 1850, in the form of prehistoric rock carvings of hunters and oxen in the arid central desert.

My summary of classical geographers' knowledge of sub-Saharan Africa is drawn from Hallett's *Records* and from C. K. Meek, "The Niger and the Classics: The History of a Name." Further information about the trans-Saharan gold trade can be found in Ward Barrett, "World Bullion Flows, 1450–1800," and Ian Blanchard's *Mining, Metallurgy and Minting in the Middle Ages*, volume 3. The marvel that is Abraham Cresques's 1375 map, the Catalan Atlas, which contains the first representation of Timbuktu in Europe, is in the Bibliothèque Nationale de France in Paris, and can be viewed online at gallica.bnf.fr.

Quotations from Leo Africanus's *Description of Africa* are from John Hunwick's translation, found in *Timbuktu and the Songhay Empire*. The "architect of Béticos" who built the Jingere Ber mosque is often said to have been the Andalusian man of letters Abu Ishaq al-Sahili, one of several educated Muslims who returned from Mecca with Mansa Musa (for more on al-Sahili, see page 135). There was no "king of Timbuktu," as such, and Leo was probably referring to Askiya al-hajj Muhammad, who reigned at Gao.

Richard Jobson's exploits were recorded in *The Golden Trade; Or, A Discovery of the River Gambra, and the Golden Trade of the Aethiopians*, first published in 1623. The growth of Timbuktu's allure in the European imagination is drawn in part from Pekka Masonen, *The Negroland Revisited*, as well as Eugenia Herbert's "Timbuktu: A Case Study of the Role of Legend in History." The metaphor of Timbuktu as the magnet that drew Europeans to West Africa was coined by A. S. Kanya-Forstner in *The Conquest of the Western Sudan*. The wonderfully pithy put-down of African exploration—"There was nothing to discover, we were here all the time"—has been attributed to a former president of Malawi, Hastings Banda.

The naive explorer's kit—little more than a pistol and an umbrella—is drawn from Mungo Park's *Travels in the Interior Districts of Africa*, although Park also carried "a small assortment of beads, amber and tobacco . . . a few changes of linen, and other necessary apparel . . . [a] pocket sextant, a magnetic compass, and a thermometer; together with two fowling pieces, two pairs of pistols, and some other small articles." Later explorers would set out with more extensive resources, though few returned with them.

For data on European death rates in West Africa, see Philip D. Curtin's *Disease and Empire* and "The End of the 'White Man's Grave'? Nineteenth-Century Mortality in West Africa." In the lecture "Rivers of Death in Africa," Michael Gelfand stated that "there is no other illness I know that humbles a clinician as greatly as [malaria]," and estimated that 80 percent of the Europeans in Mungo Park's second expedition died from it.

John Ledyard's life story was compiled by Jared Sparks in 1828, in *Memoirs of the Life and Travels of John Ledyard from His Journals and Correspondence*. Ledyard's canoe journey down the Connecticut River inspired the creation of the Ledyard Canoe Club at Dartmouth College in 1920; it still runs paddling trips in New England. Ledyard's last mission is documented in *Proceedings* and in Hallett, *Records*. Thomas Jefferson's thoughts on meeting John Ledyard can be found in the third U.S. president's *Autobiography*.

3. HELL IS NOT FAR AWAY

The dunetop negotiation of Friday, March 30, 2012, was related to me by Kader Kalil and Boubacar "Jansky" Mahamane, who was also present, and by Mayor Halle Ousmane Cissé, Diadié Hamadoun Maiga, and Governor Mamadou Mangara, who were told what had happened. According to Kalil, the idea for a meeting was floated by leaders of the Arab militia; without exception among my interviewees in Timbuktu it was seen as a trick to ensure that the southerners, and the military, left without a fight. Jansky believed the strange circumstances of the meeting were a deliberate tactic to mystify the delegates: it was "a joke, a great production," he said. It seems that the junta had already ordered a withdrawal anyway; according to a soldier in the reinforcement column from Niafounke, as soon as the troops reached Timbuktu they were told to retreat toward Sevare. Governor Mangara said of the decision to abandon the city: "After the coup d'état there was no immediate force that could defend it in a way that was suitable, despite the desire that was there." Gaston Damango declined to be interviewed.

In addition to the interviewees mentioned in the text, I have used a few published sources for the events of April 1, including Houday Ag Mohamed's *Tombouctou 2012: La ville sainte dans les ténèbres du jihadisme*. The resident who recalled grenades falling from a pickup like mangoes from a tree was speaking to researchers from Human Rights Watch, who included it in the organization's 2012 report *Mali: War Crimes by Northern Rebels*. The MNLA's statements from the period can be read in large part in the archives of the Toumast Press website. There are two aspects of the day's events worth noting here: First, several theories exist about why the ammunition store in the army camp exploded; without being able to find an eyewitness, I have gone with the theories of Jansky and Ag Mohamed, who agree that someone was trying to shoot the lock off. Second, there were differing accounts of how the young man was killed; some say he was hit by a shell fragment. Fatouma Harber's account, however, seems reliable, as she was with him minutes before he died.

Jenny Blincoe and the community of the NaturePlus program at London's Natural History Museum helped identify the Madagascar periwinkle, *Catharanthus roseus*, in the garden of the Hôtel Bouctou, from photographs.

4. THE FOURTH TRAVELLER

More detailed accounts of the extraordinary lives and travels of Simon Lucas and Daniel Houghton can be found in *Proceedings of the Association for Promoting the Discovery of the Interior Parts of Africa* and in Robin Hallett, *Records of the African Association 1788–1831*. The account of Mungo Park's first journey, drawn from interviews by the African Association's Bryan Edwards and published in Park's *Travels in the Interior Districts of Africa*, is still an easy and unpretentious read. Christopher Fyfe's entry on Park in the *Oxford Dictionary of National Biography* notes that some readers of his *Travels* were disconcerted that he failed to condemn slavery explicitly, and indeed he lived for some time with two slavers, Dr. John Laidley and Karfa Taura. Nevertheless, as Pekka Masonen has pointed out, on this first journey he seems to have encountered African people without many of the prejudices of earlier or later generations. The Duchess of Devonshire's rewriting of the hospitable Bambara girls' song can be found in Lindley Murray's *Introduction to the English Reader; or, A Selection of Pieces, in Prose and Poetry . . . with Rules and Observations for Assisting Children to Read with Propriety* (first published 1816). Two likenesses of Park are in the collection of the National Portrait Gallery in London. The first, painted around the time of his first voyage, shows a bold, blue-eyed young adventurer; the second, painted around 1805 by the satirist Thomas Rowlandson, shows an aging, balding individual who appears to have a broken nose. Joseph Banks's remarks at the Star and Garter in 1799 are recorded in *Proceedings*. The account of Park's second journey and death is from "Isaaco's Journal of a Voyage After Mr. Mungo Park, to Ascertain His Life or Death" and Park, *The Life and Travels of Mungo Park*.

Park's voyages played a key part in building the Timbuktu myth, according to E. W. Bovill, and in driving other explorers toward it. Banks in particular was quite carried away by Park's account of "gold in abundance in all the torrents that flow into the Joliba."

5. AL-QAEDA TO THE RESCUE

Reliable information about jihadist groups in the Sahara is hard to come by, but I found interviews and the following sources useful: Wolfram Lacher, "Organized Crime and Conflict in the Sahel-Sahara Region"; Andrew Lebovich, "The Local Face of Jihadism in Northern Mali"; Stephen Harmon, *Terror and Insurgency in the Sahara-Sahel Region*; and Mohammed Mahmoud Abu al-Ma'ali's report "Al-Qaeda and Its Allies in the Sahel and the Sahara." The biographies of several of the most wanted jihadists can be found in the American Foreign Policy Council's *World Almanac of Islamism*. The U.S. diplomat's cable describing Iyad Ag Ghaly as a "bad penny" can be found on the WikiLeaks website. For a hostage's firsthand view of living with jihadist brigades in the desert, see *A Season in Hell* by Robert Fowler, a Canadian diplomat who was kidnapped in 2008.

Sanda Ould Bouamama's complaints about the conditions in the looted city were published by the Al-Akhbar news agency: "You know that we came here late, and found the city partly destroyed. . . . Many of the institutions were plundered, and its headquarters were smashed, and its cars stolen." Iyad Ag Ghaly's declaration of sharia was published in Arabic by the Nouakchott News Agency; I have used an English translation by Aaron Y. Zelin, a fellow at the Washington Institute. The Bamako paper *La nouvelle république* reported Kalil's interview with Ag Ghaly on April 4 and summarized it as blaming "all the misfortune of the people [on] their lack of faith in God and [on the fact they had] abandoned the practice of sharia, which has been transformed under the guidance of white Westerners. . . . Because of that there is misery, debauchery, and other scourges [on] our society." Kalil and Mayor Cissé both spoke to the Associated Press for a piece titled "Islamists Impose Sharia in Mali's Timbuktu." Kalil said that under sharia, women would be forced to wear the Salafist veil, thieves would be punished by having their hands cut off, and adulterers would be stoned to death. "Things are going to heat up here," said Mayor Cissé. "Our women are not going to wear the veil just like that."

6. IT SHALL BE MINE

The 1823 British expedition to Africa that inspired a response from the Société de Géographie included Dixon Denham, Hugh Clapperton, and Walter Oudney. In *The Bornu Mission*, volume 2 of *Missions to the Niger*, E. W. Bovill observed that "it remains difficult to recall in all the checkered history of geographic discovery . . . a more odious man than Dixon Denham." Clapperton, by contrast, was a successful and respected explorer whom Alexander Gordon Laing would regard as his closest rival in the race for Timbuktu.

Details of the Société de Géographie's snowballing Timbuktu prize are found in the relevant issues of the society's *Bulletin*.

For the principal sources for Alexander Gordon Laing's journey, see the notes to the prologue. It is worth clarifying here the identities of the Kunta Arab shaykhs, who sometimes confused Laing. The "Cheif Maraboot Mouckta" to whom Babani was supposed to deliver the explorer was probably the scholar Shaykh Sidi al-Mukhtar, who had died in 1811, leaving more than eight children. His son Shaykh Sidi Muhammad, who received the injured Laing in 1826, died of a fever later that year. Next in line was al-Mukhtar al-Saghir, who enabled Laing to continue to Timbuktu and eventually wrote to the pasha about the explorer's death. Al-Mukhtar al-Saghir died in 1846 or 1847 and was succeeded by his younger brother Ahmad al-Bakkai, who lived until 1865. This family represented something of a mini-renaissance in the scholarly activities of the region. More details of their lives and works can be found in Shamil Jeppie and Souleymane Bachir Diagne, *The Meanings of Timbuktu*.

Baron Rousseau's letter announcing the death of Laing, first published in *L'étoile* on May 2, 1827, and datelined Sukkara-Ley-Tripoli, begins: "Major Laing, whose tragic end has been announced, perished as a result of his courageous perseverance after having nevertheless been able to visit the famous town of Timbuktu." It can be found in E. W. Bovill's *Missions to the Niger*, volume 1. The baron's mention of a "detailed history of the town," probably a reference to the *Tarikh al-sudan*, is in a letter published in the *Bulletin de la Société de Géographie*, volume 7, while excerpts from letters on the history of "Sidi Ali Baba of Arawan," dated March 3 and June 12, 1828, can be found in volume 9. Baron Rousseau described Timbuktu as having become for Europeans what the enchanted pleasure city of Irem-Zatilemad was to the ancient Arabs, or the fountain of youth to Eastern mythology. It was Rousseau who appears to have first used the adjective "mysterious" to describe the city.

Réné Caillié's account of his successful visit to Timbuktu—and his critique that "the city presented, at first view, nothing but a mass of ill-looking houses, built of earth"—is told in English in *Travels Through Central Africa to Timbuctoo*. The 1830 edition is prefaced by a survey of the awful toll of African explorers: "In vain, however, have Houghton, Browne, Hornemann, and Park—in vain have their successors, our countrymen, Tuckey, Peddie, Campbell, Gray, Ritchie, Bowdich, Oudney, Clapperton, Denham and Laing—in vain have other European travellers, Burkhardt, Beaufort, Mollien, Belzoni, started from different points of the coast of Africa, animated with the hope of removing the veil which enveloped the mysterious city:—all have either perished or been baffled in the attempt."

The critical reception of the French edition of Caillié's book was published in *The Quarterly Review* in 1830. In "Timbuktu: A Case Study of the Role of Legend in History," Eugenia Herbert summarizes the British response to Caillié: "There is no need to repeat the arrogant incredulity with which the news was received in Britain, the bitter charges made against [Edme-François] Jomard, his champion and the president of the Société de Géographie, or the insinuations in some quarters that the entire story was a fabrication drawn from the papers of the murdered Laing. The sad truth was that Laing had been cast in a heroic mold befitting the conqueror of Timbuktu and Caillié was uneducated, a provincial, a man obsessed, acting entirely on his own. Not until [Heinrich] Barth verified the essentials twenty years later was Caillié grudgingly given his due in England."

According to estimates at measuringworth.com, Caillié's 10,000 franc prize would be worth roughly $60,000 today, while the Peddie expedition's 1816 budget of £750,000 is the equivalent of around $72 million currently.

The mystery of what had become of Laing's papers rumbled on for another century. In 1910, a further account of Laing's death was given to the French explorer Albert Bonnel de Mézières. He found an eighty-two-year-old Barabish Arab who had been brought up by his uncle Ahmadu Labeida. The old man told Bonnel de Mézières that Labeida had often told him how and where he had killed Laing. In this account, Labeida and three other men on horseback caught up with Laing while he was resting in the shade of a tree and asked him to renounce his faith and become a Muslim. Laing refused, and Labeida ordered the other men to kill him. They hesitated, so Labeida had to stab him himself while the other three held Laing's arms. They also killed the Arab boy who accompanied Laing, and cut off the explorer's head before burning all his papers in case they contained magic.

Bonnel de Mézières found two buried skeletons at the spot he had been shown. Medical officers in Timbuktu examined the remains and confirmed that they had belonged to a European adult and an Arab youth. They were buried in the local Christian cemetery.

Joshua Hammer's recent book *The Bad-Ass Librarians of Timbuktu and Their Race to Save the World's Most Precious Manuscripts* contains a claim that Laing's journals are in the Mamma Haidara collection. "One of his father's most prized works was the original travel diary of Major Alexander Gordon Laing. . . . A few years after Laing's murder, a scribe had written a primer of Arabic grammar over the explorer's papers—an early example of recycling." This would be remarkable if true: Dmitry Bondarev of the University of Hamburg, who is working closely with Haidara, told me it was a "shaky claim."

7. ISMAEL'S LIST

Ismael Diadié Haidara's comment "We do not know really what is happening" was made to Valérie Marin La Meslée and published in "Tombouctou, patrimoine mondial aux mains des islamistes?" Warnings about the manuscripts' future are culled from various news sources: UNESCO chief Irina Bokova sent out her warning on April 2, 2012; the petition to preserve the manuscripts circulated by the West African Research Association can be found at http://www.bu.edu/wara/timbuktu/; Shamil Jeppie was quoted as saying, "I have no faith in the rebels," in Pascal Fletcher, "Timbuktu Librarians Protect Manuscripts from Rebels"; Hamady Bocoum's words about the secular order were published in Serge Daniel, "Timbuktu's History at Risk As Rebellion Moves In."

Evidence of a long-standing threat against secular education in Mali can be found in Amnesty International's report *Mali: Five Months of Crisis: Armed Rebellion and Military Coup*. A resident of Timbuktu told Amnesty's researchers that AQIM had sent several warnings to teachers forbidding them to instruct pupils in French, starting in 2008. Other educators told me in interviews that girls and boys had to be separated, and that early on, certain subjects were removed from the curriculum.

The figure of approximately half a million refugees or internally displaced from northern Mali in 2012 is taken from the International Organization for Migration report *The Mali Migration Crisis at a Glance*. According to the IOM, by March 2013, a total of 175,412 people had been forced to flee to other countries, and 260,665 were internally displaced. The pre-crisis population of the north as a whole was estimated at 1.3 million.

The account of Ismael Diadié Haidara's departure from Timbuktu is his own. It corresponds with what he told Susana Molins Lliteras of Cape Town University, who has worked closely on the Fondo Kati collection and who verified his smuggling of four manuscripts south. According to her article "The Making of the Fondo Ka'ti Archive: A Family Collection in Timbuktu," these included a Kuran dating from 1482 and three manuscripts with marginal notes written, Ismael said, by famous ancestors.

There is some discrepancy in the timing of the hiding of other libraries. Mohamed Touré of the Mamma Haidara library said he had begun to take manuscripts off the shelves on the night of Saturday, March 30, 2012, after discussing the matter on the phone with Abdel Kader Haidara, who was in Bamako that morning. Haidara denied this, and said no manuscripts were moved until at least a week later. Haidara also disputed Mohamed Cissé's timing on the move of the al-Wangari library, saying it was moved on the eve of the occupation rather than afterward. Since it was Cissé who evacuated the al-Wangari manuscripts, I have gone with his version of events.

The jihadist Adama was colorfully profiled by *La dépêche* in "Révélations sur les hommes qui sèment la terreur au nord Mali": "Known by the name Commissioner Adama, for having protected the people of the town at a certain time against the looters of the MNLA . . . Of Chadian nationality, he was always noticeable in the town for his particular style of dress: cartridge belt, explosive vest, and Kalashnikov on his shoulder."

The Ford Foundation confirmed it had indeed awarded a grant to Haidara to learn English at Oxford.

The footage shot by the Al Jazeera crew on Saturday, April 14, showing the Mamma Haidara library empty, was available online. The Manuscrits de Tombouctou Facebook account, run by Haidara's assistant, Banzoumana Traoré, referred to Al Jazeera's visit in a posting on April 18, and said the manuscripts had been moved by this time: "At the level of private libraries . . . particularly Mamma Haidara and Imam Ben Essayouti, which contain a large amount of manuscripts . . . the manuscripts were transferred to other premises away from the usual depositories."

Several days after he was barred from the building, Abdoulaye Cissé was told that Abou Zeid was staying inside "with his people." The AQIM emir had his hostages there too, Cissé was told, including for a time a Swiss national, Beatrice Stockly. According to the tourist guide Bastos, Stockly was also briefly held in the bank opposite his house. She was released, after a ransom was reportedly paid, on Tuesday, April 24. She returned to Timbuktu and was abducted again by AQIM in January 2016.

PART TWO. DESTRUCTION

The quotation from Omar Khayyám, a favorite of the late Christopher Hitchens, is with Richard Le Gallienne's paraphrasing.

8. THE ARMCHAIR EXPLORER

I owe William Desborough Cooley's presence in the narrative to Pekka Masonen, who gives him "the real honour of establishing [the] modern historiography of Sudanic Africa" and describes his book *The Negroland of the Arabs Examined and Ex-*

plained as "epoch-making." Aside from Masonen, and Cooley's own work, I have drawn from R. C. Bridges, "W. D. Cooley, the RGS and African Geography in the Nineteenth Century," and Bridges's entry on Cooley in the *Oxford Dictionary of National Biography*. Cooley's review of Jean-Baptiste Douville's three-volume *Voyage au Congo et dans l'intérieur de l'Afrique équinoxiale* was published in *The Foreign Quarterly Review* in 1832. The Arab sources Cooley used, including al-Bakri and Ibn Khaldun, are in N. Levtzion and J. F. P. Hopkins, *Corpus of Early Arabic Sources for West African History*. John Ralph Willis was writing in the introduction to the 1966 edition of Cooley's *Negroland of the Arabs*.

9. A HEADLESS HORSEMAN

The description of life for the librarians in Bamako in May 2012 is drawn from interviews with all three. Their accounts largely correlated. According to UNESCO's press office, the high-level meeting in Bamako from May 18 to 20 was attended by UNESCO's assistant director-general for Africa, Lalla Aicha Ben Barka, and the director of its World Heritage Centre, Kishore Rao, who met senior government officials, among them the interim prime minister, Cheick Modibo Diarra, and the culture minister, Diallo Fadima Touré. The account of what happened at the meeting is Abdel Kader Haidara's.

Acts of brutality by the rebels in the occupied north were documented by Human Rights Watch in its April 2012 report *Mali: War Crimes by Northern Rebels*. These acts included the alleged gang rape of a twelve-year-old girl in Timbuktu by three Arab militiamen, though I have not independently verified this.

My description of the creeping radicalization of Timbuktu is based chiefly on interviews, in particular with Mohamed "Hamou" Dédéou, a respected Timbuktu scholar who works with manuscripts, who told me the visits of Salafist preachers began in the 1990s. Many Timbuktiens like to emphasize the foreignness of the jihadists, though there were many influential Malians and Timbuktiens among them, including Oumar Ould Hamaha, Mohamed Ag Mossa, Ag Alfousseyni Houka ("Houka Houka"), and Ahmad al-Faqi al-Mahdi, known also by the jihadist name Abou Turab. Al-Mahdi, who is described in some reports as Houka Houka's son-in-law, was indicted in 2015 by the International Criminal Court for the war crime of attacking religious and historical buildings in Timbuktu. He was sent to The Hague, where on August 22, 2016, he pleaded guilty to all charges against him and sought the forgiveness of the people of Timbuktu. "I would like them to look at me as a son who has lost his way," he said. He was subsequently sentenced to nine years in prison. Transcripts of evidence given at the trial can be found on the ICC's website, at www.icc-cpi.int (see especially https://www.icc-cpi.int/Transcripts/CR2016

_05767.PDF). A film portrait of al-Mahdi's time as a leader of Timbuktu's Islamic Police, made by the journalist Othman Agh Mohamed Othman of Sahara Media, *Mali sous le régime des islamistes*, was broadcast as a special report on France 2 on January 31, 2013. It can be found online.

There was some confusion among interviewees as to who led the Islamic Police during the occupation. It seems clear that al-Mahdi and Mossa were in charge of the Hizba, or morality brigade, at different moments. According to both Kader Kalil and transcripts of the ICC trial of al-Mahdi, the now dead Chadian Adama was initially head of the Islamic Police. The Malian reporter Baba Ahmed, in "Mali: Le fantômes de Tomboctou," meanwhile, describes a man named Khoubey as commissioner, with Hassan Dicko as "superintendent"; and according to Diadié Hamadoun Maiga of the Crisis Committee, at the end of the occupation Hassan was the commissioner. It appears the Hizba was separate or a subdivision of the Islamic Police, and that four or five different jihadists occupied these leadership roles at different times.

For the description of al-Farouk's role in Timbuktu, I am indebted to Miranda Dodd, a former Peace Corps volunteer who lived in the city for many years and married a Tuareg chief, poet, and historian. Her Explore Timbuktu website was a useful source for local traditions, while Bruce Hall told me that the legend exists in other parts of the world, and is an Islamic idea given a Timbuktu gloss. Explaining the mausoleums' "spiritual rampart," Sane Chirfi Alpha related that an army colonel told him that in 1992 rebels had fired enough grenades and rockets to blow up the city, but no damage was done: "The colonel never understood how . . . they were all thrown and not a single one exploded," Alpha said. "He said he could not scientifically explain it."

The aptly named Mohamed Kassé was interviewed on video by Cheikh Diouara, who gave me the footage, which can also be found on the Al Jazeera website. The April 21, 2012, march on the military camp was reported in Aljimite Ag Mouchallatte, "Tombouctou: Manifestation anti Ansar Adine/AQMI ce weekend." The account of the Friday, May 4, attack on the tomb of Sidi Mahmud is drawn from contemporary news reports, including "Mali Islamist Militants 'Destroy' Timbuktu Saint's Tomb" and "Mali: Un mausolée profané par Aqmi à Tombouctou," and from UNESCO's *Decisions Adopted by the World Heritage Committee at Its 36th Session*. Baba Akib Haidara and Cheikh Oumar Sissoko were interviewed for "Mali: L'indignation des artistes et intellectuels après les profanations de Tombouctou." The city's May 14 cry for help was published on tombouctoumanuscripts.org and elsewhere. Hamaha's explanation of the Salafists' belief in low-level tombs was recorded by Diouara. Abdel Kader Haidara revealed his fears about Mawlid to me in interviews, while the festival itself was explained to me by Ismael Diadié Haidara and by Fatouma Harber.

10. THE POPE OF TIMBUKTU

Students of Heinrich Barth are lucky to have a recent account of his life and expedition to Central Africa in Steve Kemper's *A Labyrinth of Kingdoms*, from which the translations of Gustav von Schubert, Barth's brother-in-law, are drawn. Other details of Barth's life come from A. H. M. Kirk-Greene's introduction to *Barth's Travels in Nigeria* and from *Heinrich Barth: Ein Forscher in Afrika*, edited by Heinrich Schiffers. The greatest source on Barth is, of course, the explorer's own monumental *Travels and Discoveries in North and Central Africa*. The Longman edition (1857–1858) contains evocative color illustrations by Johann Martin Bernatz, which are based on Barth's sketches. It can be viewed online on the British Library website, at www.bl.uk.

The italics in Barth's "to be *useful* to humanity" are mine.

The review of Barth's *Wanderings Along the Punic and Cyrenaic Shores of the Mediterranean* (*Wanderungen durch das punische und kyrenäische Küstenland*; the book was published in German only) appeared in *The Athenæum* in 1850.

James Richardson's eight volumes of journals were published posthumously as *Narrative of a Mission to Central Africa Performed in the Years 1850–51*. Richardson was deeply interested in the people who made up his expedition, and to a modern reader his account is more gossipy and somewhat more engaging than Barth's. G. W. Crowe's opinion of Richardson is cited in Kemper, *A Labyrinth of Kingdoms*.

John Nicholson's translations of two poems written by al-Bakkai to the sultan of Masina in defense of Barth were included as an appendix in the explorer's *Travels*.

The opinion that Barth's portrait of the economic life of the historic city would not be bettered is from Elias Saad's *Social History of Timbuktu*. Details of the funeral in which Barth's grieving relatives buried all the still-living explorer's possessions are found in Kemper, *A Labyrinth of Kingdoms*.

Eduard Vogel did not return alive to Europe. He was murdered in 1856 in Wara, the capital of Waday, by the sultan of that kingdom.

11. SECRET AGENTS

The connection between the cultural destruction and UNESCO was well understood by Timbuktiens. "Every time UNESCO spoke about the manuscripts, we told them, 'No, no, really, do not speak about them, because if you do, this is how [the jihadists] will react,'" said Sane Chirfi Alpha. The United Nations body was nevertheless in a difficult position, as director-general Irina Bokova explained to me in

2016: "I know there is this thinking that we don't have to tease them, we have to appease them . . . [but] we have to speak out."

There are numerous contemporary news reports of the battle of Gao, including "Nord du Mali: Gao est aux mains des islamistes." The best sources for the account of the destruction in Timbuktu, meanwhile, are the videos shot by journalists who had been told in advance what was going to happen. The smashing of the Sidi Yahya door can be seen in Othman Agh Mohamed Othman's film *Mali sous le régime des islamistes* (Sahara Media). Sanda Ould Bouamama's question "UNESCO is what?" was reported by Serge Daniel in "Mausolées détruits au Mali: Bamako dénonce une furie destructrice." Hamaha was cited by Julius Cavendish in "Destroying Timbuktu: The Jihadist Who Inspires the Demolition of the Shrines." Transcripts from the ICC trial of Ahmad al-Faqi al-Mahdi (especially "23 August 2016 | Trial Chamber VIII | Transcript," https://www.icc-cpi.int/Transcripts/CR2016_05767.PDF; and "24 August 2016 | Trial Chamber VIII | Transcript," https://www.icc-cpi.int/Transcripts/CR2016_05772.PDF) were also useful in reconstructing those days.

Reaction to the destruction has been culled from contemporary news reports, including "Mali Separatists Ready to Act over Destruction of Tombs" and "Destruction des mausolées de Tombouctou: Un 'crime de guerre' selon la CPI." Pages from the memo penned by Abdelmalek Droukdel were authenticated by the French counterterrorism expert Mathieu Guidère. Portions appeared in Rukmini Callimachi, "In Timbuktu, al Qaida Left Behind a Manifesto," and Jean-Louis Le Touzet, "La feuille de route d'Aqmi au Mali," while the full eighty-page document was published in Nicolas Champeaux, "Le projet du chef d'Aqmi pour le Mali." Details of the fractious relationship between Droukdel and Belmokhtar are analyzed by Guidère in "The Timbuktu Letters: New Insights about AQIM."

According to Haidara, Maiga and Ismael accompanied him to the Ministry of Higher Education and Scientific Research, where they met with the ministry's secretary-general, the adviser in charge of the Ahmad Baba institute, and the national director of higher education.

Haidara did not want to give the name of the friend who paid for his ticket to Geneva, or of other contacts he met there.

The account of the Ahmad Baba rescue operation was related to me principally by Alkadi Maiga, Bouya Haidara, Hassini Traoré, Mohamed Diagayeté, and Abdel Kader Haidara. Their individual accounts agreed in most significant aspects. The "little cocktail" at which the men from the ministry were shown the evacuated manuscripts was confirmed by the civil servant responsible for the Ahmad Baba institute, Drissa Diakité. The minister in charge of the institute at this time, who berated Maiga for moving the manuscripts without permission, was Harouna Kanté.

The quotations from Juma al-Majid were remembered by Abdel Kader Haidara, although the Juma al-Majid Center confirmed its contribution to the evacuation.

PART THREE. LIBERATION

12. LIVES OF THE SCHOLARS

Heinrich Barth's letter of December 15, 1853, announcing the discovery of the *Tarikh al-sudan* was published in 1855 as "Schreiben des Dr. Barth an Prof. Rödiger" in *Zeitschrift der Deutschen Morgenländischen Gesellschaft*. Christian Ralfs's "Beiträge zur Geschichte und Geographie des Sudan, Eingesandt von Dr. Barth" appeared later in the same publication.

Abd al-Rahman al-Sadi described the first settlers of Timbuktu as both Tuareg and Massufa. According to John Hunwick in *Timbuktu and the Songhay Empire*, the chronicler conflated distinct Berber groups: the Massufa were part of the great tribal federation known as the Sanhaja, who dominated the Timbuktu region and spoke Znaga, while the Tuareg speak Tamasheq, a different Berber dialect. For Hunwick, a plausible derivation of the name Timbuktu is from the Znaga root *b-k-t*, "to be distant or hidden," combined with the feminine possessive particle *tin*. The city, he points out, is situated in a slight hollow.

Al-Sadi also describes the rule of Askiya al-hajj Muhammad and his descendants as lasting "one hundred and one years," from April 2, 1493, to April 12, 1591—a period that is of course only ninety-seven years. In fact, askiyas descended from Muhammad are listed in the *Tarikh al-sudan* to at least 1656, but after the Moroccan invasion they split into those who fought a guerrilla war from a much-reduced territory, and those who became puppets of the Moroccan administration. "One hundred and one years" nevertheless corresponds loosely to the period the askiyas ruled independently at Gao.

Ahmad Baba's best-known work, the *Kifayat al-muhtaj*, is an abbreviated and revised version of his *Nayl al-ibtihaj*, which was intended as a complement to the *Dibaj al-mudhahhab* (a biographical dictionary of the scholars of the Maliki school) by Burhan al-din ibn Farhun, a sage from Medina, who died in 1397. Auguste Cherbonneau's translation was made from two reasonably accurate manuscripts that were sent to him by students, according to his "Essai sur la littérature arabe du Soudan d'après le *Tekmilet-ed-dibadje* d'Ahmed Baba, le tombouctien."

In his *Social History of Timbuktu*, Elias Saad estimated that by 1325, when it was incorporated into the Mali empire, Timbuktu had around ten thousand inhabitants. The city's presence on the Catalan Atlas in 1375 is often cited as evidence of its status as a commercial center in the mid–fourteenth century. It continued to grow: Saad is also the source of estimates that at its sixteenth-century peak it housed as many as 150 to 180 Kuranic schools, where basic reading and recitation of the Kuran were taught, and had a maximum enrollment of four to five thousand students. Nehemia Levtzion, Pekka Masonen, and others have suggested that two to three hundred individuals were able to attain the status of fully qualified scholars in the sixteenth century. Not everyone agrees with the portrait of the city as an intellectual hub, however: Charles Stewart argues that Timbuktu's historical significance has been exaggerated at the expense of other Sudanese centers of scholarship, which lay in what is now Mauritania, in part because of the prolific Ahmad Baba. "There may have never been much of a center of learning in Timbuktu," Stewart wrote to me, "since early authors there have left almost no trace of teaching the Arabic language." This contrasts with "the lands to the west where Arabic grammar was a blockbuster of a topic—clear indication of an aspiring and expanding, literate Arabic culture. . . . This does not negate the importance of 20th century book collecting in and around Timbuktu or the current libraries there, but there certainly is dubious evidence that any of the recent fame has much of an historical foundation."

My portrait of Barth's later life is drawn from Steve Kemper, Pekka Masonen, and R. Mansell Prothero. W. D. Cooley's review of Barth's work appeared in "Barth's Discoveries in Africa." Barth's contribution to the world's knowledge of Africa was not fully recognized until a century after his death, with Heinrich Schiffers's *Heinrich Barth: Ein Forscher in Afrika*, which detailed the advances Barth had made in the fields of history, geography, botany, medicine, linguistics, archaeology, and ethnology.

13. THE TERRIBLE TWOSOME

The portrait of life in the house in ACI 2000 was provided by sources close to the operation who preferred to remain anonymous. Abdel Kader Haidara confirmed that he worked in Stephanie Diakité's house, and parts of the account of their early setup are drawn from interviews with him. Details of the communications between Savama and the Prince Claus Fund were provided by Deborah Stolk. She also confirmed that much of their correspondence was written by Diakité.

Hamed Mossa's crackdown on the women was related by numerous interviewees in Timbuktu, who remained outraged by it years later. A valuable source was Tina Traoré, a fishmonger who was persecuted by Mossa and his men; she was one of the instigators of the women's march on October 6, 2012, and was among the women who were brought before the jihadist leadership. Reports of the march appeared in Admana Diarra, Tiémoko Diallo, and Agathe Machecourt, "Manifestation de femmes contre la charia à Tombouctou," and Baba Ahmed, "Mali: À Tombouctou, près de 200 femmes marchent contre les islamistes," which estimated that up to two hundred women were involved. Asa Ag Ghaly described her persecution by Mossa, including her time inside the women's "prison," which I visited in October 2014 when it had returned to its former use as an ATM kiosk.

Deborah Stolk received the "window of opportunity" e-mail between October 10 and 17, 2012, she said. The approximate forty-dollar (25,000 West African francs) cost of traveling between Bamako and Timbuktu at this time was mentioned by the inveterate traveler Alkadi Maiga. *The New Republic*'s piece on the evacuation, "The Brazen Bibliophiles of Timbuktu: How a Team of Sneaky Librarians Duped Al Qaeda," by Yochi Dreazen, was published online with one of the verification photographs that had been sent to Stolk.

The story of the problems with the Savama office in Timbuktu and the subsequent trouble between Mohamed Touré and the jihadists was related by all four of the protagonists (Alpha, Diadié, Touré, Haidara). The timing of events was difficult to pin down: Alpha dated the threat to requisition the office to August, but this seems to be at odds with Touré's statement to the commissioner that he was moving the manuscripts before the rainy season, which in Timbuktu lasts from July to September.

Touré's account of his "worst trip" was supported by Haidara, although Touré's employer said he was not traveling alone: "There were four people traveling with the lockers," according to Haidara.

The kidnapping incident near Niafounke was recounted by Haidara. I was unable to verify it with others.

Diadié and others recalled the gathering at Essakane. The figure of three hundred pickups was reported by Xan Rice in "Day a One-Eyed Jihadist Came to Timbuktu." The eyewitness to the destruction of five more mausoleums using "picks and shovels" was Othman Agh Mohamed Othman of Sahara Media, who spoke to France 24 for "Dans Tombouctou coupée du monde, le règne de la débrouille." Iyad Ag Ghaly's demands to the Malian government and the subsequent assault on the south are drawn from media reports, including Laurent Touchard, "Mali: Retour sur la bataille décisive de Konna," and Moussa Sidibe, "Comment les populations ont vécu la bataille de Konna et l'occupation des régions du nord," as well as "Bataille de Konna" on wikipedia.fr.

Shamil Jeppie's fears about the military intervention were shared with Vivienne Walt, "For the Treasures of Timbuktu, a Moment of Grave Peril." The date of January 4 for Haidara and Diakité's visit with Thomas Strieder comes from the German embassy in Bamako; Strieder, the former chargé d'affaires, told me about it. Diakité's lecture at the University of Oregon, "The Evacuation of the Tumbuktu Manuscripts and Their Life in Exile: The Work of T160K," was posted on March 13, 2013, to the university's media channel and is available at http://media.uoregon.edu/channel/archives/5647. The accounts of Diakité's and Haidara's meetings with the Dutch, and of their donations, are based on interviews with To Tjoelker and the Dutch ambassador, Maarten Brouwer, and on internal Dutch foreign ministry documents. I am grateful to Klaas Tjoelker for sending me photographs he and To took of manuscripts in Bamako in late January 2013. Details of autos-da-fé and Nazi book burning were taken from J. M. Ritchie, "The Nazi Book-Burning."

14. KING LEOPOLD'S PAPERWEIGHT

Conrad's *Heart of Darkness* first appeared as a three-part serial in *Blackwood's Magazine* in 1899, and was included in his 1902 book *Youth: A Narrative, and Two Other Stories*. The estimate of ten million deaths under Leopold's regime is drawn from Adam Hochschild's *King Leopold's Ghost*, which cites a Belgian government commission of 1919 and other sources. Georg F. W. Hegel is quoted from John Sibree's translation in *The Philosophy of History* (1900).

There is dispute over the exact causes of the Scramble for Africa, but the drivers most frequently cited are those I have mentioned, including the Western economic slump, the technology gap, racism, and the competitive atmosphere generated by the activities of Leopold, France, and other players; for further discussion, see M. E. Chamberlain in *The Scramble for Africa*. In "European Partition and Conquest of Africa: An Overview," G. N. Uzoigwe states that although the Berlin conference did not dole out specific parts of Africa to particular countries, it did establish the legal framework for doing so. "The argument that the conference, contrary to popular opinion, did not partition Africa is correct only in the most technical sense. . . . To all intents and purposes, the appropriation of territory did take place at the conference and the question of future appropriation is clearly implied in its decisions. By 1885, in fact, the broad lines of the final partition of Africa had already been drawn."

The racist remarks of Samuel Baker were made at a banquet in his honor in Brighton in 1874, and were reported by *The Times*, while those of A. P. Newton are cited in A. Adu Boahen, *Africa Under Colonial Domination 1880–1935*.

The reasons for Barth's rejection by the Royal Academy of Sciences in Berlin are explored in Steve Kemper, *A Labyrinth of Kingdoms*; A. H. M. Kirk-Greene, introduction to *Barth's Travels in Nigeria*; and Heinrich Schiffers, *Heinrich Barth: Ein Forscher in Afrika*. My account of the French conquest of Africa is drawn chiefly from Robert Aldrich, *Greater France*, and A. S. Kanya-Forstner, *The Conquest of the Western Sudan*. The lack of European university chairs in African history was pointed out by Pekka Masonen in *The Negroland Revisited*. Details of what happened to Louis Archinard's looted manuscripts are from Noureddine Ghali and Mohamed Mahibou's *Inventaire de la Bibliothèque 'Umarienne de Segou*. It also tallies the contents of the library, which included, among other highlights, a 189-page *Tarikh al-sudan*; a 363-page copy of the *Nayl* of Ahmad Baba; a noted treatise on slavery by the same author; fragments of a *Tarikh al-fattash*; and several letters from Ahmad al-Bakkai. A biography of Archinard by Richard Roberts is in Emmanuel K. Akyeampong and Henry Louis Gates, Jr.'s *Dictionary of African Biography*, volume 6. Joseph Joffre's account of his recapture of the region is in *My March to Timbuctoo*.

The best source for Félix Dubois's journey is his own *Timbuctoo the Mysterious*. Further details of his life, and that of his famous chef father, are found in Yves-Jean Saint-Martin's *Félix Dubois 1862–1945: Grand reporter et explorateur de Panama à Tamanrasset*. The gift of Dubois's copy of the *Tarikh al-sudan* to the Bibliothèque Nationale is recorded in Octave Houdas's introduction to his 1900 French translation, which also includes details of the various manuscripts from which he and Edmond Benoist worked. For his 1999 translation in *Timbuktu and the Songhay Empire*, John Hunwick found further copies of the manuscript in the Ahmad Baba collection and in the National Library of Algeria, Algiers. Details of al-Sadi's life and the *Tarikh al-sudan* are from Houdas and Benoist and from Hunwick, and excerpts from the *Tarikh* are from Hunwick. A short biography of Houdas by Alain Messaoudi and Jean Schmitz can be found in the *Dictionnaire des orientalistes de langue française*.

Flora Shaw's *A Tropical Dependency* remains a fascinating period piece. Details of her extraordinary life are in Dorothy O. Helly's "Flora Shaw and the *Times*: Becoming a Journalist, Advocating Empire." My skeptical take on the likelihood of a Malian armada's making it to Mexico follows that of Masonen in *The Negroland Revisited*, but there are many modern proponents of the theory, including Ivan Van Sertima, *They Came Before Columbus*, and Gaoussou Diawara, *Abubakari II, explorateur mandingue*.

15. AUTO-DA-FÉ

I am grateful to Cheikh Diouara for sharing his memories of being on the receiving end of French airstrikes during Operation Serval. Details of what remained of the Gaddafi mansion after it was hit were recorded by Drew Hinshaw, in "In Gadhafi's Timbuktu Villa, an al Qaeda Retreat." Diadié remembers that the last meeting between the Crisis Committee and the jihadists took place the day before the young man was killed by the jihadists, which media reports record as January 23. It was David Blair, who interviewed the dead man's sister for "Timbuktu: The Women Singled Out for Persecution," who reported that Mustapha was shot for shouting *"Vive la France!"* on a street corner.

Like Abdoulaye Cissé, Air Mali, who lived near the Ahmad Baba building in Sankore, recalled the moment when he realized manuscripts had been destroyed. "We got up in the morning, and we found the manuscripts right away. They had taken them out into the courtyard and gathered them together. Everything they could, they had burned."

16. CHRONICLE OF THE RESEARCHER

Octave Houdas and Maurice Delafosse gave a detailed account of their difficulties with the *Tarikh al-fattash* in the introduction to their own work of synthesis, *Tarikh el-fettach ou chronique du chercheur*, in 1913. Mauro Nobili and Mohamed Shahid Mathee, in "Towards a New Study of the So-Called *Tarikh al-fattash*," have authoritatively argued that what Houdas and Delafosse thought to be a single chronicle is in fact two separate texts, one produced in the seventeenth century by a scholar known as Ibn al-Mukhtar, and the other a nineteenth-century forgery produced by a counselor of Ahmad Lobbo, the sultan of Masina, which was falsely attributed to Mahmud Kati. In 2011, Christopher Wise and Hala Abu Taleb published an English translation, *Ta'rīkh al fattāsh: The Timbuktu Chronicles 1493–1599*, but failed to take into account the problems with the text. The quoted sections here are my translations from Houdas and Delafosse's French version, and should be treated with caution. The *Tarikh*'s "full title in English" is given by Paul E. Lovejoy, "Islamic Scholarship and Understanding History in West Africa Before 1800."

Timbuktu's sixteenth-century standing as a "city of scholars" is from Elias Saad's *Social History of Timbuktu*, as is the estimate that the population was no higher than 50,000: "The data at our disposal indicate that the population of the city ranged between 30,000 and 50,000 inhabitants in the sixteenth century when Timbuktu experienced its 'golden age' of prosperity and Islamic learning." The expression "acute bibliophilism" is from Brent Singleton's "African Bibliophiles: Books and Libraries in Medieval Timbuktu." Mahmud Kati's rare dictionary, according to the *Tarikh al-fattash*, was *al-Qamus al-muhit*. The price of the *Sharh al-ahkam* is from Saad, and the dictionary that came in twenty-eight volumes was the *Muhkam fi'l-Lugha*, also mentioned by Saad. Details of the cost of copying a manuscript are from Singleton.

Sources for the Moroccan invasion of Songhay and the reign of Ahmad al-Mansur include Stephen Cory's "The Man Who Would Be Caliph," as well as the *tarikh*s. Most of the account of the Day of Desolation is from the *Tarikh al-sudan*, which has the greater detail; relevant passages in the *Tarikh al-fattash* agree with the main points. For additional details of Ahmad Baba's life, see Mahmoud Zouber's *Ahmad Baba de Tombouctou*.

The extract from Ahmad Baba's poem of longing for Timbuktu was recorded by the Moroccan scholar Muhammad al-Saghir al-Ifrani, who was born in 1669/1670. It is written in the entrance to the old Ahmad Baba building, and can also be found in John Hunwick, *Timbuktu and the Songhay Empire*.

17. AN INDIANA JONES MOMENT IN REAL LIFE!

The account of the French advance on Timbuktu was related to me by Colonel Frédéric Gout. It was he who recollected Colonel Gèze's offer of drinks to the officers at Goundam airstrip, General Barrera's interest in Caillié, and their visit to the house where the explorer had stayed in 1828.

News reports of the fire in the Ahmad Baba institute have come from numerous sources. Twitter's timeline on January 28, 2013, puts Thomas Fessy's "burning ancient manuscripts" tweet at 8:47 a.m. and Jenan Moussa's at 9:08 a.m. Luke Harding's story in *The Guardian* was headlined "Timbuktu Mayor: Mali Rebels Torched Library of Historic Manuscripts." Not everyone believed what Mayor Cissé said: in "The Secret Race to Save Timbuktu's Manuscripts," Geoffrey York hinted that many had been moved, while in Vivienne Walt, "Mali: Timbuktu Locals Saved Some of City's Ancient Manuscripts from Islamists," Mahmoud Zouber commented that "the documents which had been there [in the institute] are safe."

Innocent Chukwuma of the Ford Foundation kindly provided details of the organization's correspondence with Abdel Kader Haidara in the last days of the occupation, including Dr. Gitari's immortal line "An Indiana Jones moment in real life!" Asked why manuscripts still needed to be moved to Bamako after the city had been liberated, Haidara argued that it was better to complete the evacuation than to leave them in the villages.

18. MANUSCRIPT FEVER

John Hunwick's description of the founding of the Ahmad Baba center was published in the article "CEDRAB: The Centre de Documentation et de Recherches Ahmad Baba at Timbuktu." Concise profiles of other major libraries in Timbuktu can be found on the website of the Tombouctou Manuscripts Project, at tombouctoumanuscripts.org.

The part that Henry Louis Gates, Jr.'s documentary played in inflating the reputation of the manuscripts was emphasized by Jean-Louis Triaud in "Tombouctou ou le retour du mythe." Triaud, without wishing to diminish the interest and the value of these documents, stated that Gates's visit had led to their celebration as much more than simply the rich patrimony of knowledge that they really were. "There is something of a heroic and mythical saga in their mediatized rediscovery," he wrote. For more details of Gates's visit, see the notes to chapter 1.

More details of Thabo Mbeki's visit to Timbuktu are recounted in Shamil Jeppie's "Re/discovering Timbuktu."

19. THE MYTH FACTORY

Jean-Michel Djian was quoted by Lila Azam Zanganeh in "Has the Great Library of Timbuktu Been Lost?" According to Zanganeh, Mayor Cissé had been told by his "communications attaché," who had just escaped the city, that the Ahmad Baba center had burned and more than half of its manuscripts had been consumed in the fire. "Yet," reported Zanganeh, "he also seemed to hint that not all of the city's manuscripts had been destroyed." Tristan McConnell's pieces were "Meet the Unlikely Group That Saved Timbuktu's Manuscripts" and "How Timbuktu Saved Its Books." *Der Spiegel*'s online story, in English, was headlined "Most Timbuktu Manuscripts Saved from Attacks." The figure of 377,491 private manuscripts rescued was given to me by Haidara in December 2015.

On May 28, 2013, an e-mail from T160K signed by Stephanie Diakité was sent to the Mansa-1 mailing list, stating that "the estimated $7 million cost is an ambitious goal, but raising this money is imperative." Not all recipients of the shout-out were happy about it. One eminent anthropologist responded: "Thanks for the scam but I don't buy this. . . . It's a shame that you use academic networks to sell your bogus project." The figure of $1 million a year paid by the German foreign ministry and the Gerda Henkel Foundation was mentioned to me in interview by a source closely involved with the project. Some of this money goes to other libraries in Mali.

More details about Timbuktu Renaissance are at www.timbukturenaissance .org. The proposal for Google to film the city, and the plans for Timbuktu University, were shared with me by N'Diaye Ramatoulaye Diallo, the Malian culture minister. Details of Abdel Kader Haidara's German Africa Prize of 2014 can be found at the Deutsche Afrika Stiftung website.

The conference at the University of Birmingham, "Symposium in Honour of Paulo Fernando de Moraes Farias," was held on November 12 and 13, 2015. At the time of this writing, Bruce Hall's "Rethinking the Place of Timbuktu in the Intellectual History of Muslim West Africa" was due to be published in a collection of papers from the conference.

In April 2016, Stephanie Diakité's name surfaced in a bizarre $4.25 million legal case unrelated to the evacuation. In a motion filed in the Illinois Supreme Court, she was accused of being a "fraudster" who orchestrated a "series of illegal payoffs to government officials in Mali" in return for false documents (Frank Main, "Inmate Says Bribes Led to Contempt Case, Ordered Freed on Bond," *Chicago Sun-Times*, April 26, 2016). The documents Diakité obtained had secured the conviction of a

Malian man, Bengaly Sylla, who was sentenced to six years in prison, the court was told. Diakité, it was alleged, was also not an attorney as she had at times claimed. A lawyer for the company that was said to have hired her in the Sylla case stated that there was no proof that illegal payoffs had been made. The case is ongoing at the time of this writing.

The official figure of 4,203 lost Ahmad Baba manuscripts was given to me by Alkadi Maiga. It was impossible to determine what exactly they were. Abdoulaye Cissé said they were documents that had been acquired but not yet processed, and therefore not much was known about them.

The study of the Fondo Kati documents was made by Susana Molins Lliteras of Cape Town University for her Ph.D. thesis, "Africa Starts in the Pyrenees: The Fondo Kati, Between al-Andalus and Timbuktu." The thesis had not been made publicly available at the time of this writing, but an abstract, published online, notes that the dissertation "raises questions around the authenticity of the marginalia, in terms of their dates of production and authorship."

On the subject of the movement of libraries after liberation, the Timbuktu manuscript proprietor Abdoul Wahid Haidara told me: "There were two or three libraries that were moved just after the occupation, when Savama had already announced that they had taken all the manuscripts from Timbuktu, and they had to find other libraries to follow them." He named these collections as Bibliothèque Ahmad Baba Aboul Abbass, Bibliothèque Moulaye, and Bibliothèque Zawiyat al-Kunti, and gave timings of specific conversations about these post-liberation moves that he had had with the libraries' owners.

LAST WORDS

In September 2016, I put a number of the allegations that arose in the course of researching this book to Abdel Kader Haidara, Stephanie Diakité, and selected protagonists via e-mail. In particular, I asked them to address the question of whether the threat to the manuscripts had been exaggerated, along with their numbers and the story of their rescue.

Abdel Kader Haidara replied that he had not heard the allegations from anyone but me. "We have neither seen nor read anything about it. Would you be the only one to hold this information? What are your sources?" He and his colleagues had worked hard in this area for twenty-seven years and knew the approximate number of manuscripts from their time as professional prospectors. He had also worked hard to build trusting relationships with his partners, who all came to Mali to monitor the actions carried out in Bamako during the emergency and the evacuation. It would be foolish for him to have been "lying to the whole world," he stated.

"We remain convinced that nothing led us to undertake what we have accomplished but the love of our heritage and the conscience that drives us to protect this heritage," he wrote. "We did not invent a story. Today, our manuscripts are saved and we will continue to work for their conservation with all the financial, human, and technological resources that the moment gives us."

Stephanie Diakité declined to comment, about either this or the case in Illinois Supreme Court.

Dmitry Bondarev, who is leading research into the manuscripts for the University of Hamburg's Centre for the Studies of Manuscript Cultures, told me he believed some international specialists had recently started changing their tone to be less condemning and more realistic: "There might soon be the time when the others will feel as uncomfortable about their assertive verdicts on what happened in 2012 (whichever side of the 'truth' they take) as I feel now whenever I have to make allusions to 'the rescue operation.'" There was "so much irrational going on in the rational minds of my colleagues," he wrote, that he found his blood pressure rising. In his view, the current estimate of around 377,000 privately owned manuscripts was "realistic, inasmuch as one takes into account the different approaches to what constitutes a manuscript." As for his dealings with Savama, which had once been difficult, he said, "We are now in much better relationship—these things take huge time and need patience, especially in West Africa and especially if one wants to be more practical rather than destructively critical."

Bruce Hall, meanwhile, maintained that aspects of the Savama story were a "huge fraud."

SELECTED BIBLIOGRAPHY

Abu al-Ma'ali, Mohammed Mahmoud. "Al-Qaeda and Its Allies in the Sahel and the Sahara." Al Jazeera Centre for Studies, April 30, 2012.

Abun-Nasr, Jamil M. *A History of the Maghrib in the Islamic Period*. Cambridge, England: Cambridge University Press, 1987.

Adams, Robert. *The Narrative of Robert Adams, a Sailor, Who Was Wrecked on the Western Coast of Africa, in the Year 1810, Was Detained Three Years in Slavery by the Arabs of the Great Desert, and Resided Several Months in the City of Tombuctoo*. London: John Murray, 1816.

Ag Ghaly, Iyad. Transcript of audio message to the people of Timbuktu. Translated by Aaron Y. Zelin. Cited at jihadology.net.

Ag Mohamed, Houday. *Tombouctou 2012: La ville sainte dans les ténèbres du jihadisme*. Bamako: La Ruche à Livres, 2013.

Ag Mouchallatte, Aljimite. "Tombouctou: Manifestation anti Ansar Adine/AQMI ce weekend." Toumast Press, April 24, 2012.

Ahmed, Baba. "Mali: À Tombouctou, près de 200 femmes marchent contre les islamistes." *Jeune Afrique*, October 8, 2012.

_____. "Mali: Le fantômes de Tomboctou." *Jeune Afrique*, May 25, 2012.

Akyeampong, Emmanuel K., and Henry Louis Gates, Jr. *Dictionary of African Biography*. Oxford: Oxford University Press, 2012.

Aldrich, Robert. *Greater France: A History of French Overseas Expansion*. Basingstoke, England: Macmillan, 1996.

"Alexander Gordon Laing." In Robert Chambers, ed., *A Biographical Dictionary of Eminent Scotsmen*, vol. 3. Glasgow: Blackie and Son, 1835.

American Foreign Policy Council. *World Almanac of Islamism*. Lanham, MD: Rowman & Littlefield, 2014.

Amnesty International. *Mali: Five Months of Crisis: Armed Rebellion and Military Coup*. May 2012.

Apollonj Ghetti, Pietro M. *Étude sur les mausolées de Tombouctou*. Paris: UNESCO, 2014.

Archinard, [Louis]. *Le Soudan en 1893*. Le Havre: Société des Anciens Courtiers, 1895.

―――. *Le Soudan français en 1889–1890: Rapport militaire* . . . Paris: Imprimerie Nationale, 1891.

Banks, Joseph. *The* Endeavour *Journal of Sir Joseph Banks* (1768–1771). Teddington, England: Echo Library, 2006.

Barrett, Ward. "World Bullion Flows, 1450–1800." In *The Rise of Merchant Empires: Long Distance Trade in the Early Modern World, 1350–1750*, edited by James D. Tracy. Cambridge, England: Cambridge University Press, 1991.

Barth, Heinrich. "Schreiben des Dr. Barth an Prof. Rödiger." *Zeitschrift der Deutschen Morgenländischen Gesellschaft* 9, no. 1 (1855): 261–308.

―――. *Travels and Discoveries in North and Central Africa: Being a Journal of an Expedition Undertaken Under the Auspices of H.B.M.'s Government, in the Years 1849– 1855*. London: Longman, Brown, Green, Longmans & Roberts, 1857–1858.

―――. *Wanderungen durch das punische und kyrenäische Küstenland oder Mâg'reb, Afríkía und Barká* [Wanderings Along the Punic and Cyrenaic Shores of the Mediterranean . . .]. Volume 1 of *Wanderungen durch die Küstenländers des Mittelmeeres ausgefuhrt in den Jahren 1845, 1846 und 1847*. London: Williams & Norgate, and David Nutt; Berlin: Wilhelm Herz; Paris: Klincksieck, and A. Franck, 1849.

Blair, David. "Timbuktu: The Women Singled Out for Persecution." *The Daily Telegraph*, February 3, 2013.

Blanchard, Ian. *Mining, Metallurgy and Minting in the Middle Ages*, vol. 3: *Continuing Afro-European Supremacy, 1250–1450*. Wiesbaden: Franz Steiner Verlag, 2005.

Boahen, A. Adu, ed. *Africa Under Colonial Domination 1880–1935*. Volume 7 of *General History of Africa*. Paris: UNESCO; London: Heinemann; Berkeley: University of California Press, 1985.

Bonnel de Mézières, Albert. "Major Gordon Laing, and the Circumstances Attending His Death." *The Geographical Journal* 39, no. 1 (1912): 54–57.

Bovill, E. W., ed. *Missions to the Niger*, vol. 1: *The Journal of Friedrich Hornemann's Travels from Cairo to Murʒuk in the Years 1797–98* and *The Letters of Major Alexander Gordon Laing, 1824–26*. Cambridge, England: Published for the Hakluyt Society at the University Press, 1964.

―――. *Missions to the Niger*, vols. 2–4: *The Bornu Mission, 1822–25*. Cambridge, England: Published for the Hakluyt Society at the University Press, 1966.

Brenner, Louis, and David Robinson. "Project for the Conservation of Malian Arabic Manuscripts." *History in Africa* 7 (1980): 329–32.

Bridges, R. C. "W. D. Cooley, the RGS and African Geography in the Nineteenth Century. Part I: Cooley's Contribution to the Geography of Eastern Africa." *The Geographical Journal* 142, no. 1 (1976): 27–47.

———. "William Desborough Cooley (1795?–1883)." In *Oxford Dictionary of National Biography*.

Burton, Richard F. *Zanzibar: City, Island, and Coast*. London: Tinsley Brothers, 1872.

Caillié, René. *Journal d'un voyage à Temboctou et à Jenné, dans l'Afrique centrale . . . pendant les années 1824–1828*. Paris: Atlas, 1830.

———. *Travels Through Central Africa to Timbuctoo; and Across the Great Desert, to Morocco, Performed in the Years 1824–1828*. London: Henry Colburn and Richard Bentley, 1830.

Callimachi, Rukmini. "In Timbuktu, al Qaida Left Behind a Manifesto." Associated Press, February 14, 2013.

Carter, Harold B. *Sir Joseph Banks 1743–1820*. London: British Museum (Natural History), 1988.

Cavendish, Julius. "Destroying Timbuktu: The Jihadist Who Inspires the Demolition of the Shrines." *Time*, July 10, 2012.

Chamberlain, M. E. *The Scramble for Africa*. London: Longman, 1999.

Chambers, Neil, ed. *The Letters of Sir Joseph Banks: A Selection 1768–1820*. River Edge, NJ: Imperial College Press, 2000.

Champeaux, Nicolas. "Le projet du chef d'Aqmi pour le Mali." RFI/*Libération*, October 6, 2013.

Chatwin, Bruce. *Anatomy of Restlessness: Uncollected Writings*. Edited by Jan Borm and Matthew Graves. London: Jonathan Cape, 1996.

Cherbonneau, Auguste. "Essai sur la littérature arabe du Soudan d'après le *Tekmilet-ed-dibadje* d'Ahmed-Baba, le tombouctien." *Annuaire de la Societé Archéologique de la Province de Constantine* 2 (1854–1855).

Cissoko, Sékéné Mody. *Tombouctou et l'empire Songhay: Épanouissement du Soudan nigérien aux XVe–XVIe siècles*. Paris: L'Harmattan, 1996.

Conrad, Joseph. *Heart of Darkness*. London: Penguin, 2012.

Cooley, W. D. "Barth's Discoveries in Africa; Made During an Expedition Undertaken Under the Auspices of H.M. Government, 1849–1855." *The Edinburgh Review* 109 (1859).

———. *The Negroland of the Arabs Examined and Explained; or, An Inquiry into the Early History and Geography of Central Africa*. London: J. Arrowsmith, 1841. Reprinted London: Frank Cass, 1966.

———. Review of Jean-Baptiste Douville, *Voyage au Congo et dans l'intérieur de l'Afrique équinoxiale*. *The Foreign Quarterly Review* 10 (August 19, 1832): 163–206.

Cory, Stephen. "The Man Who Would Be Caliph: A Sixteenth-Century Sultan's Bid for an African Empire." *The International Journal of African Historical Studies* 42, no. 2 (2009): 179–200.

Crone, G. R., ed. *The Voyages of Cadamosto and Other Documents on Western Africa in the Second Half of the Fifteenth Century.* London: Hakluyt Society, 1938.

Curtin, Philip D. *Disease and Empire: The Health of European Troops in the Conquest of Africa.* Cambridge, England: Cambridge University Press, 1998.

———. "The End of the 'White Man's Grave'? Nineteenth-Century Mortality in West Africa." *The Journal of Interdisciplinary History* 21, no. 1 (1990): 63–88.

———. *The Image of Africa: British Ideas and Action, 1780–1850.* Madison: University of Wisconsin Press, 1973.

Daniel, Serge. "Mausolées détruits au Mali: Bamako denónce une furie destructrice." AFP, in *La Presse* (Canada), June 12, 2012.

———. "Timbuktu's History at Risk As Rebellion Moves In." AFP, in *National Post* (Canada), April 3, 2012.

"Dans Tombouctou coupée du monde, le règne de la débrouille." Les Observateurs, France 24, January 2, 2013.

Davidson, Basil. *Africa in History: Themes and Outlines.* London: Phoenix Press, 2001.

De Jorio, Rosa. "The Fate of Timbuktu's Sufi Heritage: Controversies Around Past Traces and Current Practices." In *Cultural Heritage in Mali in the Neoliberal Era,* 116–34. Urbana: University of Illinois Press, 2016.

[Demarin, John Peter.] *A Treatise upon the Trade from Great-Britain to Africa, Humbly Recommended to the Attention of Government, by an African Merchant.* London: R. Baldwin, 1772.

"Destruction des mausolées de Tombouctou: Un 'crime de guerre' selon la CPI." *Le monde,* July 1, 2012.

Diarra, Admana, Tiémoko Diallo, and Agathe Machecourt. "Manifestation de femmes contre la charia à Tombouctou." Reuters, October 6, 2012.

Diawara, Gaoussou. *Abubakari II, explorateur mandingue.* Paris: L'Harmattan, 2010.

Dreazen, Yochi. "The Brazen Bibliophiles of Timbuktu: How a Team of Sneaky Librarians Duped Al Qaeda." *The New Republic,* April 25, 2013.

Dubois, Félix. *Timbuctoo the Mysterious.* Translated by Diana White. London: William Heinemann, 1897.

Farias, P. F. de Moraes. *Arabic Medieval Inscriptions from the Republic of Mali: Epigraphy, Chronicles and Songhay-Tuāreg History.* Oxford: Published for the British Academy by Oxford University Press, 2003.

Fletcher, Pascal. "Timbuktu Librarians Protect Manuscripts from Rebels." Reuters, April 11, 2012.

Fowler, Robert R. *A Season in Hell: My 130 Days in the Sahara with Al Qaeda.* Toronto: HarperCollins Canada, 2011.

Fyfe, Christoper. "Alexander Gordon Laing (1794–1826)." In *Oxford Dictionary of National Biography.*

_____. "Mungo Park (1771–1806)." In *Oxford Dictionary of National Biography*.

Gates, Henry Louis, Jr. Excerpts from diary. In "Explore Gates' Diary: The Road to Timbuktu." *Wonders of the African World*, PBS, http://www.pbs.org/wonders /fr_gt.htm. (Cited as being from *The New Yorker*.)

Gelfand, Michael. "Rivers of Death in Africa, an Inaugural Lecture Given at the University College of Rhodesia and Nyasaland" (1963). London: Oxford University Press, 1964.

Ghali, Noureddine, and Mohamed Mahibou, with Louis Brenner. *Inventaire de la Bibliothèque ʿUmarienne de Segou (conservée à la Bibliothèque Nationale—Paris)*. Paris: Centre National de la Recherche Scientifique, 1985.

Gobineau, Arthur de. *The Moral and Intellectual Diversity of Races: With Particular Reference to Their Respective Influence in the Civil and Political History of Mankind*. Edited and expanded by H. Hotz and J. C. Nott. Philadelphia: J. B. Lippincott, 1856.

Gout, Frédéric. *Libérez Tombouctou! Journal de guerre au Mali*. Paris: Tallandier, 2015.

Grossman, Ron. "African Manuscripts Rewriting History: Northwestern Professor Uncovers 16th Century Writings by a Black African That Contradict Many Western Preconceptions." *Chicago Tribune*, April 9, 2001.

Guidère, Mathieu. "The Timbuktu Letters: New Insights about AQIM." *Res Militaris* 4, no. 1 (Winter–Spring 2014).

Haidara, Abdel Kader. "An Overview of the Major Manuscript Libraries in Timbuktu." In *The Trans-Saharan Book Trade: Manuscript Culture, Arabic Literacy and Intellectual History in Muslim Africa*, edited and translated by Graziano Krätli and Ghislaine Lydon, 241–64. Leiden: Brill, 2011.

Haidara, Ismael Diadié. *Une cabane au bord de l'eau*. Málaga, Spain: Fondo Kati, 2015.

Hall, Bruce S. *A History of Race in Muslim West Africa 1600–1960*. Cambridge, England: Cambridge University Press, 2001.

Hallett, Robin, ed. *Records of the African Association 1788–1831*. London: Thomas Nelson and Sons, 1964.

Hammer, Joshua. *The Bad-Ass Librarians of Timbuktu and Their Race to Save the World's Most Precious Manuscripts*. New York: Simon & Schuster, 2016.

_____. "The Race to Save Mali's Priceless Artifacts." *Smithsonian Magazine*, January 2014.

Hampâté Bâ, Amadou, and Roger Gaetani. *A Spirit of Tolerance: The Inspiring Life of Tierno Bokar*. Bloomington, IN: World Wisdom, 2008.

Harding, Luke. "Timbuktu Mayor: Mali Rebels Torched Library of Historic Manuscripts." *The Guardian*, January 28, 2013.

Harmon, Stephen A. *Terror and Insurgency in the Sahara-Sahel Region: Corruption, Contraband, Jihad and the Mali War of 2012–2013*. Burlington, VT: Ashgate, 2014.

Harris, James. *Hume: An Intellectual Biography*. New York: Cambridge University Press, 2015.

"Head of UN Cultural Agency Urges Warring Factions in Mali to Safeguard Timbuktu." UN News Centre, April 2, 2012.

Helly, Dorothy O. "Flora Shaw and the *Times*: Becoming a Journalist, Advocating Empire." In *Women in Journalism at the* Fin de Siècle: *"Making a Name for Herself,"* edited by F. Elizabeth Gray, 110–28. Basingstoke, England: Palgrave Macmillan, 2012.

Herbert, Eugenia. "Timbuktu: A Case Study of the Role of Legend in History." In *West African Culture Dynamics: Archaeological and Historical Perspectives*, edited by B. K. Swartz, Jr., and Raymond E. Dumett, 431–54. The Hague: De Gruyter Mouton, 1980.

Hinshaw, Drew. "In Gadhafi's Timbuktu Villa, an al Qaeda Retreat." *The Wall Street Journal*, February 4, 2013.

Hochschild, Adam. *King Leopold's Ghost: A Story of Greed, Terror, and Heroism in Colonial Africa*. Boston: Houghton Mifflin, 1998.

Houdas, Octave, trans. *Tarikh es-soudan par Abderrahman Ben Abdallah Ben 'Imran Ben 'Amir es-Sa'di*. Paris: Ernest Leroux, 1900. Arabic text, prepared with the collaboration of Edmond Benoist, published Paris: Ernest Leroux, 1898.

Houdas, Octave, and Maurice Delafosse, trans. *Tarikh el-fettach ou chronique du chercheur . . . par Mahmoûd Kâti Ben El-Hâdj El-Motaouakkel Kâti et l'un de ses petits-fils*. Paris: Ernest Leroux, 1913.

Human Rights Watch. *Mali: War Crimes by Northern Rebels*. April 2012.

Hunwick, John O. "Ahmad Baba and the Moroccan Invasion of the Sudan (1591)." *Journal of the Historical Society of Nigeria* 2, no. 3 (1962): 311–28.

———. *Arabic Literature of Africa*, vol. 4: *Writings of Western Sudanic Africa*. Leiden: Brill, 2003.

———. "CEDRAB: The Centre de Documentation et de Recherches Ahmad Baba at Timbuktu." *Sudanic Africa* 3 (1992): 173–81.

———. "Timbuktu: A Refuge of Scholarly and Righteous Folk." *Sudanic Africa* 14 (2003): 13–20.

———. *Timbuktu and the Songhay Empire: Al-Sa'di's Ta'rīkh al-sūdān down to 1613 and Other Contemporary Documents*. Leiden: Brill, 1999.

Hunwick, John O., Alida Jay Boye, and Joseph Hunwick. *The Hidden Treasures of Timbuktu: Historic City of Islamic Africa*. London: Thames & Hudson, 2008.

International Criminal Court. "Al Mahdi Case. *The Prosecutor v. Ahmad Al Faqi Al Mahdi*, ICC-01/12-01/15." https://www.icc-cpi.int/mali/al-mahdi.

International Crisis Group. *Mali, Avoiding Escalation*. July 18, 2012.

International Organization for Migration. *The Mali Migration Crisis at a Glance*. March 2013.

"Isaaco's Journal of a Voyage After Mr. Mungo Park, to Ascertain His Life or Death." *Annals of Philosophy* 4, no. 23 (November 1814): 369–85.

Jefferson, Thomas. *Autobiography of Thomas Jefferson: 1743–1790*. New York: G. P. Putnam's Sons, 1914.

Jeppie, Shamil. "Re/discovering Timbuktu." In Jeppie and Diagne, *The Meanings of Timbuktu*.

Jeppie, Shamil, and Souleymane Bachir Diagne, eds. *The Meanings of Timbuktu*. Cape Town: HSRC Press in association with CODESRIA, 2008.

Jobson, Richard. *The Golden Trade; Or, A Discovery of the River Gambra, and the Golden Trade of the Aethiopians* (1623). London: William Dawson & Sons, 1968.

Joffre, General [Joseph]. *My March to Timbuctoo*. London: Chatto & Windus, 1915.

Kaba, Lansiné. "Archers, Musketeers, and Mosquitoes: The Moroccan Invasion of the Sudan and the Songhay Resistance (1591–1612)." *The Journal of African History* 22, no. 4 (1981): 457–75.

Kanya-Forstner, A. S. *The Conquest of the Western Sudan: A Study in French Military Imperialism*. London: Cambridge University Press, 1969.

Katz, Marion Holmes. "Women's 'Mawlid' Performances in Sanaa and the Construction of 'Popular Islam.'" *International Journal of Middle East Studies* 40, no. 3 (2008): 467–84.

Kemper, Steve. *A Labyrinth of Kingdoms: 10,000 Miles Through Islamic Africa*. New York: W. W. Norton, 2012.

Kirk-Greene, A. H. M. Introduction to *Barth's Travels in Nigeria: Extracts from the Journal of Heinrich Barth's Travels in Nigeria, 1850–1855*. London: Oxford University Press, 1962.

Kryza, Frank T. *The Race for Timbuktu: In Search of Africa's City of Gold*. New York: Ecco, 2006.

Lacher, Wolfram. "Organized Crime and Conflict in the Sahel-Sahara Region." In *Perilous Desert: Insecurity in the Sahara*, edited by Frederic Wehrey and Anouar Boukhars, 61–85. Washington, DC: Carnegie Endowment for International Peace, 2013.

Laing, Alexander Gordon. *The Letters of Major Alexander Gordon Laing, 1824–26*. In Bovill, *Missions to the Niger*, vol. 1.

Le Touzet, Jean-Louis. "La feuille de route d'Aqmi au Mali." *Libération*, October 7, 2013.

Lebovich, Andrew. "The Local Face of Jihadism in Northern Mali." *CTC Sentinel*, June 25, 2013.

Ledyard, John. *A Journal of Captain Cook's Last Voyage to the Pacific Ocean, and in Quest of a North-West Passage . . . Faithfully Narrated from the Original MS . . .* Hartford: Nathaniel Patten, 1783.

Leo Africanus. "Description of the Middle Niger, Hausaland and Bornu." In Hunwick, *Timbuktu and the Songhay Empire.*

Levtzion, Nehemia. *Ancient Ghana and Mali.* London: Methuen, 1973.

————. "A Seventeenth-Century Chronicle by Ibn al-Mukhtār: A Critical Study of 'Ta'rīkh al-fattāsh.'" *Bulletin of the School of Oriental and African Studies* (University of London), 34, no. 3 (1971): 571–93.

Levtzion, N., and Hopkins, J. F. P., eds. *Corpus of Early Arabic Sources for West African History.* Translated by J. F. P. Hopkins. Cambridge, England: Cambridge University Press, 1981.

Lovejoy, Paul E. "Islamic Scholarship and Understanding History in West Africa Before 1800." In *The Oxford History of Historical Writing*, vol. 3: *1400–1800*. Oxford: Oxford University Press, 2012.

"Mali: L'indignation des artistes et intellectuels après les profanations de Tombouctou." RFI Afrique, May 6, 2012.

"Mali: Un mausolée profané par Aqmi à Tombouctou." *L'express* and AFP, May 6, 2012.

"Mali Islamist Militants 'Destroy' Timbuktu Saint's Tomb." BBC News, May 6, 2012.

"Mali Separatists Ready to Act over Destruction of Tombs." CNN, July 2, 2012.

Marin La Meslée, Valérie. "Tombouctou, patrimoine mondial aux mains des islamistes?" *Le point*, April 4, 2012. http://www.lepoint.fr/monde/tombouctou -patrimoine-mondial-aux-mains-des-islamistes-04-04-2012-1448503 _24.php.

Masonen, Pekka. *The Negroland Revisited: Discovery and Invention of the Sudanese Middle Ages.* Helsinki: Finnish Academy of Science and Letters, 2000.

McConnell, Tristan. "How Timbuktu Saved Its Books." *Harper's Magazine*, February 4, 2013.

————. "Meet the Unlikely Group That Saved Timbuktu's Manuscripts." GlobalPost, February 3, 2013.

McIntosh, Roderick J., and Susan Keech McIntosh. "The Inland Niger Delta Before the Empire of Mali: Evidence from Jenne-Jeno." *The Journal of African History* 22, no. 1 (1981): 1–22.

McIntosh, Susan Keech, and Roderick J. McIntosh. "West African Prehistory." *American Scientist* 69, no. 6 (1981): 602–13.

Meek, C. K. "The Niger and the Classics: The History of a Name." *The Journal of African History* 1, no. 1 (1960): 1–17.

Messaoudi, Alain, and Jean Schmitz, "Octave Houdas." In *Dictionnaire des orientalistes de langue française*, edited by François Pouillon. Paris: Institut d'Études de l'Islam et des Sociétés du Monde Musulman and Karthala, 2008.

Molins Lliteras, Susana. "Africa Starts in the Pyrenees: The Fondo Kati, Between al-Andalus and Timbuktu." Ph.D. thesis, University of Cape Town, August 2015.

————. "The Making of the Fondo Ka'ti Archive: A Family Collection in Timbuktu." *Islamic Africa* 6 (2015): 185–91.

Nobili, Mauro, and Mohamed Shahid Mathee. "Towards a New Study of the So-Called *Tarikh al-fattash*." *History in Africa* 42 (2015): 37–73.

"Nord du Mali: Gao est aux mains des islamistes." RFI Afrique, June 27, 2012.

Norris, H. T. "Ṣanhājah Scholars of Timbuctoo." *Bulletin of the School of Oriental and African Studies* (University of London), 30, no. 3 (1967): 634–40.

O'Brian, Patrick. *Joseph Banks: A Life*. London: Collins Harvill, 1989.

Oxford Dictionary of National Biography. Edited by H. C. G. Matthew and Brian Harrison. Oxford: Oxford University Press, 2004.

Park, Mungo. *The Life and Travels of Mungo Park*. Edinburgh: William and Robert Chambers, 1838.

————. *Travels in the Interior Districts of Africa, Performed Under the Direction and Patronage of the African Association, in the Years 1795, 1796, and 1797*. London: G. and W. Nicol, 1799.

Pelizzo, Riccardo. "Timbuktu: A Lesson in Underdevelopment." *Journal of World-Systems Research* 7, no. 2 (2001): 265–83.

Proceedings of the Association for Promoting the Discovery of the Interior Parts of Africa. London: C. Macrae, 1810. Reprint of issues from 1788 through 1810.

Prothero, R. Mansell. "Heinrich Barth and the Western Sudan." *The Geographical Journal* 124, no. 3 (1958): 326–37.

Pruneau de Pommegorge, Antoine E. *Description de la nigritie*. Amsterdam: Maradan, 1789.

Purchas, Samuel. *Hakluytus Posthumus or, Purchas His Pilgrimes* (1625). Cambridge, England: Cambridge University Press, 2014.

Ralfs, C[hristian]. "Beiträge zur Geschichte und Geographie des Sudan, Eingesandt von Dr. Barth." *Zeitschrift der Deutschen Morgenländischen Gesellschaft* 9, no. 2 (1855): 518–644.

"Report of the UNESCO Meeting of Experts on the Utilisation of Written Sources for the History of Africa Held at Timbuktu, 30 November–7 December 1967." *Research Bulletin* (Centre of Arabic Documentation, University of Ibadan), 4 (1968): 52–69.

"Révélations sur les hommes qui sèment la terreur au nord Mali." *La dépêche*, January 9, 2013. maliweb.net.

Review of Heinrich Barth, *Wanderings Along the Punic and Cyrenaic Shores of the Mediterranean* (*Wanderungen durch das punische und kyrenäische Küstenland*). *The Athenæum*, no. 1166 (March 2, 1850): 229–30.

Review of René Caillié, *Journal d'un voyage à Temboctoo [sic] et à Jenné, dans l'Afrique centrale, &c. The Quarterly Review* 42, no. 84 (March 1830): 450–75.

Rice, Xan. "Day a One-Eyed Jihadist Came to Timbuktu." *Financial Times*, January 25, 2013.

Richardson, James. *Narrative of a Mission to Central Africa Performed in the Years 1850–51*. Edited by Bayle St. John. London: Chapman and Hall, 1853.

Ritchie, J. M. "The Nazi Book-Burning." *Modern Language Review* 83, no. 3 (1988): 627–43.

Rousseau, Jean-Baptiste Louis Jacques. Excerpts of letters. *Bulletin de la Société de Géographie* 7, no. 54 (October 1827): 176–77; 9, no. 63 (July 1828): 41.

Saad, Elias N. *Social History of Timbuktu: The Role of Muslim Scholars and Notables, 1400–1900*. Cambridge, England: Cambridge University Press, 1983.

Saint-Exupéry, Antoine de. *Wind, Sand and Stars*. [Translated by Lewis Galantière.] London: Pan Books, 1975.

Saint-Martin, Yves-Jean. *Félix Dubois 1862–1945: Grand reporter et explorateur de Panama à Tamanrasset*. Paris: L'Harmattan, 1999.

Sanche de Gramont. *The Strong Brown God: Story of the River Niger*. New York: Mariner, 1991.

Sattin, Anthony. *The Gates of Africa: Death, Discovery, and the Search for Timbuktu*. New York: St. Martin's Press, 2005.

Scheele, Judith. *Smugglers and Saints of the Sahara: Regional Connectivity in the Twentieth Century*. Cambridge, England: Cambridge University Press, 2012.

Schiffers, Heinrich, ed. *Heinrich Barth: Ein Forscher in Afrika*. Wiesbaden: Franz Steiner Verlag, 1967.

Schubert, Gustav von. *Heinrich Barth, der Bahnbrecher der deutschen Afrikaforschung: Ein Lebens- und Charakterbild*. Berlin: Reimer, 1897.

Shaw, Flora [Dame Flora Louise Lugard]. *A Tropical Dependency: An Outline of the Ancient History of the Western Soudan with an Account of the Modern Settlement of Northern Nigeria*. London: James Nisbet, 1905.

Sidibe, Moussa. "Comment les populations ont vécu la bataille de Konna et l'occupation des régions du nord." Maliweb.net, March 8, 2013.

Singleton, Brent D. "African Bibliophiles: Books and Libraries in Medieval Timbuktu." *Libraries & Culture* 39, no. 1 (2004): 1–12.

"Smuggled Out: Most Timbuktu Manuscripts Saved from Attacks." *Der Spiegel* (English website), February 25, 2013.

Sparks, Jared. *Memoirs of the Life and Travels of John Ledyard from His Journals and Correspondence*. London: Henry Colburn, 1828.

Spurr, David. *The Rhetoric of Empire: Colonial Discourse in Journalism, Travel Writing, and Imperial Administration*. Durham, NC: Duke University Press, 1993.

Touchard, Laurent. "Mali: Retour sur la bataille décisive de Konna." *Jeune Afrique*, January 30, 2014.

Triaud, Jean-Louis. "Tombouctou ou le retour du mythe: L'exposition médiatique des manuscrits de Tombouctou." In *L'Afrique des savoirs au sud du Sahara, XVIe–XXIe siècle: Acteurs, supports, pratiques*, edited by Daouda Gary-Tounkara and Didier Nativel. Paris: Karthala, 2012.

UNESCO. *Decisions Adopted by the World Heritage Committee at Its 36th Session (Saint-Petersburg, 2012). World Heritage 36 COM*. United Nations Educational, Scientific and Cultural Organization Convention Concerning the Protection of the World Cultural and Natural Heritage, World Heritage Committee, Thirty-sixth Session. Saint Petersburg, June 24–July 6, 2012.

Uzoigwe, G. N. "European Partition and Conquest of Africa: An Overview." In Boahen, *Africa Under Colonial Domination 1880–1935*, 19–44.

Van Sertima, Ivan. *They Came Before Columbus: The African Presence in Ancient America*. New York: Random House, 2003.

Walpole, Horace. *Letters of Horace Walpole, Earl of Orford, to Sir Horace Mann: His Britannic Majesty's Resident at the Court of Florence, from 1760 to 1785*, vol. 2. London: R. Bentley, 1843.

Walt, Vivienne. "For the Treasures of Timbuktu, a Moment of Grave Peril." *Time*, January 26, 2013.

———. "Mali: Timbuktu Locals Saved Some of City's Ancient Manuscripts from Islamists." *Time*, January 28, 2013.

Wesseling, H. L. *Divide and Rule: The Partition of Africa, 1888–1914*. Translated by Arnold J. Pomerans. Westport, CT: Praeger, 1997.

Wise, Christopher, and Haba Abu Taleb, trans. *Ta'rīkh al fattāsh: The Timbuktu Chronicles 1493–1599: English Translation of the Original Works in Arabic by Al Hajj Mahmud Kati*. Edited by Christopher Wise. Trenton, NJ: Africa World Press, 2011.

York, Geoffrey. "The Secret Race to Save Timbuktu's Manuscripts." *Globe and Mail*, December 27, 2012.

Zanganeh, Lila Azam. "Has the Great Library of Timbuktu Been Lost?" *The New Yorker*, January 29, 2013.

Zouber, Mahmoud. *Ahmad Baba de Tombouctou (1556–1627): Sa vie et son oeuvre*. Paris: G.-P. Maisonneuve et Larose, 1977.

ACKNOWLEDGMENTS

A great surprise of writing contemporary nonfiction is how willing people are to give an account of the events they witnessed to a badly dressed man with a tape recorder. In this regard I am particularly grateful to those in Timbuktu and elsewhere in Mali whose memories I have mined, and who suffered my repeated visits with patience and good humor. No one was tested more in this way than Alkadi Maiga, who managed to find a smile however many times I appeared at the offices of the Ahmad Baba institute in Bamako. Other Malians I would like to single out for thanks include the grand imam Abderrahmane Ben Essayouti, Abdoulkadri Idrissa Maiga of the Ahmad Baba institute, and Ismael Diadié Haidara of the Fondo Kati, as well as Mohamed Diagayeté, Kader Kalil, Tina Traoré, Abdoul Wahid Haidara, and Cheikh Diouara. Abdel Kader Haidara also has my respect and gratitude for the many hours we spent together.

Reporting from distant and occasionally dangerous places is possible only with the help of others, and few were more crucial to this project than those who facilitated my interviews and, on a few occasions, recorded them on my behalf. In this I was fortunate to have the expertise of Ousmane Diadié Touré and Mamadou Tapily in Bamako, who worked long hours and traveled great distances in pursuit of this story, and Fatouma Harber in Timbuktu, who shared her extensive knowledge of her home city with me. The assistance of Tahar Haidara, meanwhile, was invaluable during my 2014 visit.

From the start, I have relied on a group of friends and colleagues who at various stages improved the idea, the state of the manuscript, or the mood of the author. These included Nicholas Blincoe, Toby Clements, Jon Henley, Paul Hamilos, Charlotte Higgins, Julian Borger, Sarah Holloway, Andy Beckett, Pascal Wyse, Sam Wollaston, Ingrid Karikari, and Tom Campbell. I also drew on a handful of former West Africa correspondents—Alex Duval-Smith, Sean Smith, Afua Hirsch, and Mark Tran—who shared contacts and important travel advice. I would not have visited Timbuktu at all without knowing that Jan Thompson, Judith Soal, Jamie Wilson, and Karen Plews of *The Guardian* were aware of my trip, and that if things went seriously wrong, Ian Katz would at least watch the videos. Melissa Denes, Clare Longrigg, Lucy Lamble, and Charlotte Northedge aided me by commissioning articles as I went along. Charlotte Albin greatly improved my French; Juliette Courtois did most of the transcribing; Philip Oltermann rendered my freedom-of-information requests into German; Edgar Schmitz helped translate the responses.

A number of diplomats and expats in Mali also deserve my thanks. These include To and Klaas Tjoelker, Maarten Brouwer, and Mirjam Tjassing, all of the Dutch embassy in Bamako; Thomas Strieder, Günter Overfeld, and Josef Hinterseher of the German foreign service; Deborah Stolk of the Prince Claus Fund; Innocent Chukwuma of the Ford Foundation; Michael Hanssler of the Gerda Henkel Stiftung; Bassam Adnan Daghestani of the Juma al-Majid Center for Culture and Heritage; and Sally Haydock and Krystle van Hoof of the World Food Programme. Colonel Frédéric Gout generously invited me to NATO's Brussels HQ, and shared with me a draft of his book *Libérez Tombouctou! Journal de guerre au Mali*, which I would recommend to students of the conflict. Irina Bokova, director-general of UNESCO, took time out of her exceptionally busy schedule to explain the causes and effects of cultural destruction, as did Lazare Eloundou Assomo, the organization's representative in Bamako. N'Diaye Ramatoulaye Diallo, the Malian culture minister, explained the government's plans for the city, post-crisis.

ACKNOWLEDGMENTS

A number of people who know this material far better than I do generously gave advice on the history of the region and its manuscripts. Chief among these were Mauro Nobili of the University of Illinois at Urbana-Champaign; Bruce Hall of Duke University, who alerted me to his concerns about the evacuation story; and Dmitry Bondarev of the University of Hamburg. Further academic expertise was shared by Susana Molins Lliteras (of the University of Cape Town), Charles Stewart (also at Illinois), Georges Bohas (of the University of Lyon), and Alida Jay Boye (formerly of the University of Oslo). I was also very glad to have the advice of Joseph Hunwick, whose spectacular photographs of the city and its manuscripts can be found in *The Hidden Treasures of Timbuktu*. I regret that I did not begin the task early enough to have met his father, John Hunwick.

There are at least four people without whom this book would not exist. These are my two agents, Felicity Rubinstein in London and Stuart Krichevsky in New York, who nursed both manuscript and author through the tougher stages of the research and writing processes. Without them, I would not have found Rebecca Saletan at Riverhead, whose good judgment, persistence, and superlative editing skill have made the book what it is. The quartet is completed by Arabella Pike at William Collins, whose enthusiasm and support kept me on track. I would also like to thank Anna Jardine and Michelle Koufopoulos at Riverhead, and Juliet Mahoney at Lutyens & Rubinstein, for their good work on the book's behalf.

Finally, I would like to express my gratitude to my family: to Barbara English, who read the early drafts but more important let me drive across the Sahara as a teenager; to Hugh English, for always patching up my cars; and to Harry, Arthur, and Eddie English, who will soon be having adventures of their own.

Above all, I would like to thank Lucy Blincoe, to whom this book is dedicated, for her love and her faith.

INDEX

PHOTO CREDITS